Clips & CONSEQUENCES

a memoir

Beth Myrle Rice

PURPLE STRIPE PUBLISHING

For information about permission to reproduce
selections from this book write to

PURPLE STRIPE PUBLISHING
4616 25th Avenue NE #45
Seattle, WA 98105
or to the respective authors cited in this book.

Please visit: www.purplestripepublishing.com
where you will find full size, full color versions
of most of the graphics presented in these pages
and links to informative resources.

Cover art: *Living Free* by Martha Brouwer,
www.marthabrouwer.com

Cover photo: Jamie VanBuhler of VisualLife Photography,
www.jvanbuhler.com

Cover and interior design: Beth Myrle Rice

ISBN 978-0-615-48151-7

Printed in the United States of America,
specifically, in the great state of Washington
by Gorham Printing

A portion of the proceeds of sales
will be donated to select organizations
found in the *Afterword* of this book

for my daughter for me

for humanity
that all plants should grow free

with heartfelt thanks to all
who have read, commented,
and encouraged me along the way,
leading me to believe
I can and should do this
you have been invaluable to me

In fond memory of

Jack Herer, author of The Emperor Wears No Clothes,
for his tireless decades of work
will live on in the hearts and actions of many

Brave Washingtonians and Seattle Hempfesters
Robert Lunday
James Matthiessen
Share Parker
Billy Mitchell
Meril Draper
Ralph and Judith Seeley
who each worked toward the day
all plants would be free to grow
but left us too soon to see it

Harold Hunter and Jeff Klindt
skaters to the core
and so much more
we'll meet again
dear friends
til then
rest in peace

with special gratitude

to Kara Chipoletti Jones,
for without her, "When will you quit saying,
"I'm going to write a book" and just write it?"
I might not have started this journey

to Tom Jenks and Carol Edgarian
of *Narrative Magazine*
for accepting me in their workshop

to Kyra Freestar of *Bridge Creek Editing*
for her guidance in shaping this book and
for inspiring me to tell more of my truth
so to better connect the dots

to Martha Brouwer, creator of the cover art: *Living Free;*
to Teresa Carol, Dr. Chérie Carter-Scott,
Washington Supreme Court Justice Richard Sanders,
Evelyn Edens Ringman at The Seattle Times,
and Merck & Co., Inc. —for permissions

to Maia Black for introducing me to both Sayulita and to
Doris Doyon, for "Just come . . .the universe will provide."
Indeed. I am reminded and
very thankful for the magical space
in which I completed much work

to Dan-o and The Guv for always welcoming,
giving a place to hang my hat time and again

to Kim and to Kathleen for trust and patience

and, above all, to my daughter for being herself
—full of love, light and laughter—
and for loving me still

Contents

Preface

One of the items my mother gifted to me Christmas 1985 was a book of blank pages. When all the gifts under the tree had been opened and my five year old Zoey was busy with her new toys I went to the kitchen to see what I might do to help Mom. She said everything was under control but I stayed any way. It was in our quiet moment together she suggested that, in light of the changes my life was going through, I might want to keep track of happenings and my feelings in the journal she'd given me, that it could be a good place to sort my thoughts.

The first journal entry I wrote was May 17, 1986, around the time my divorce from Zoey's father was finalized:

> I am many people. Aren't we all? It seems we often deprive ourselves of some facets of our own personality. I desire to be all of who I am.

This is my true story. Most names have been changed and identifying features altered or omitted to preserve the privacy of the characters in my life story.

Part 1: The Shit Hits the Fan

". . .There is a legal issue that will come up that could seem very devastating. It feels almost as if it has to do with. . . I almost want to say child support, child custody. . . something that involves someone who is trying to manipulate you through a third party. . . But, I don't feel it's anything you've initiated. I feel it's something someone else has initiated; and, it's more like you feel judged and put on the spot to prove yourself. . ."

Excerpted from a transcription of the tape recording made during my first session with Teresa Carol, Spring 1992

1: Eminent Consequence

Journal: June 6, 1995

I was on TV today. It was a crime drama so clichéd the tape keeps playing in my head. I wish I could turn it off. But, there I am again gazing southward, down two stories to the north corner of Pike Place Market and the afternoon's rosy orange dusted sunshine on Elliot Bay. Pulling my focus into the room I connect with the pseudo Victorian clock, complete with pendulum, hanging between the picture windows behind the desk of Dick Carville, attorney-at-law. His profile had looked most promising among the ads I found surrounding the Criminal Defense heading in the Seattle Yellow Pages two hours earlier. The clincher: he could see me right away.

While waiting for him to conclude his library search that will tell me what the laws are concerning my situation, my eyes peel away from the clock. Roaming along the wall perpendicular to the windows they come to rest on a display of impressive championship trophies heralding his achievements in Tae Kwon Do. Movement out of the corner of my eye makes me turn further to find him walking back toward his desk, silently reading the open book in his hands. I swing around but by the time he gets there my eyes are stuck on that clock. He declares, "Distribution of Marijuana to a Minor—a minimum of thirty-one months to fifteen years in state prison, depending on the number of counts or, in your case, on how many depositions are filed against you. There is a fine of up to twenty thousand dollars. It is a felony offense."

The clock is so damn loud TIC-TOC, TIC-TOC in my head. I know its only in my head because under it I hear my voice saying, "criminal defense attorney . . . thirty-one months minimum . . . fifteen years. How did I get here?" But, my lips aren't moving. My teeth are clenched. Perhaps it's my heart pounding and not the clock at all.

I think I was in a real cheesy crime drama on TV today. Please tell me I was. This can't be real. Oh, but it is, Beth. How did it come to me having to find a criminal defense attorney? Me! How did little old me from a nice family in the suburbs end up in Dick Carville's office? How could I be so stupid? Obviously, letting kids party at the house was against the law but I had no idea what the law actually was, nor how steep the consequences. My eyes had that clock in a stranglehold and it went silent—or maybe I stopped breathing. I'm not sure.

2: Clips On Cannabis and Concussion

I'll never forget the first time I got high on pot. That's not to say it was the first time I smoked it. It took a few times to get you in those days. We didn't have the high-tech, hybrid, high potency stuff that's grown now. Buds weren't available to us then, only the leafy stuff. I'd say it was my third or fourth time smoking. It was in September 1971.

Lokie, Laurel, and I smoked a joint on our way to the city park where some sort of peace gathering was happening. There were a bunch of people from school in one of the cabanas playing acoustic guitar and singing. The sun was low in the sky filtering through the trees, illuminating space between shadows on the heavily leaf laden lawn. The air was crisp and fresh. The crunch of the fallen yellow maple leaves beneath our feet was incredibly loud as we approached the gathering. We laughed at how loud the leaves were. As heads in the cabana turned our direction it occurred to us we were being loud. So, we tried to get small and unobtrusive by hunching over and ssshhh-ing each other with index fingers to lips which made us giggle even more.

We didn't join the songsters that afternoon. The swings, slippery slide, teeter-totters, and merry-go-round were more fun than they'd ever been before . . . or since, for that matter: pot as intensifier.

Poetry Class, Spring 1972

Teacher's note: "I enjoyed this poem very much"

The Purchase

The Glad-bag semi-full
brought to mind the bottle of oregano
among Mom's seasonings
both like dry lawn clippings crumbled
yet one to spice up your pizza
the other your evening
I poked my nose in the baggy greedily
as would a horse his feed bag
breathed deeply
lolling in the aroma of a hay mow
reaching into the bag sent me back
sunny dandelion picking days
slightly sticky, moist
"Try it?"
a dry sweetness
rolled over
my tongue
then three
or four
sudden snaps
like the first
few kernels
of corn to pop
       "Lots of seed.
       Ten dollars?
       I'll take it."

February 21, 1974

The show begins
good thing I'm a bookkeeper on the side
since my creativity glands can't abide
the winter
        I believe they've caught cold
I've been told that coffee stunts growth
groovin' on java while daylight climbs
the mountains Monday thru Friday
could do the trick
enough to make any one sick
I don't like bread-n-water
nice being an accountant's daughter
and keeping someone else's books
since I'm uninspired and can't
write my own
can't even remember the last time
a poem dropped in for tea   or   me
maybe Spring will bring one around
my creativity glands will get their feet on the ground
inspiration comes with the sun

When this poem was written I was nineteen and living in
a one bedroom apartment on the west rise of Capitol Hill on
Melrose overhanging Interstate 5 and downtown Seattle. My
place was on the back side of the building so I didn't have a
view unless I went to the roof. From there it was spectacular at
sunset looking west across the city and Elliot Bay, over to the
Olympic Mountains. I usually caught the bus at the corner of
Thomas and Bellevue to get to work downtown. Most of the
poem found its way to paper on the bus one morning after
standing on that corner waiting, watching the sun's glow ultimately reaching the mountains across the bay.

A twenty-six year old, blonde-haired, blue-eyed Ballardite
who I worked with, Janel, gave me a few of her credit cards
to take to the Department of Motor Vehicles so I could get a
fake ID. Saying I'd lost my driver license, I presented Janel's
credit cards as my own for proof of my identity. Security was

much looser back then. A valid Washington State Drivers License with all of Janel's statistics, which were close enough to mine, was issued with my photo and mailed to her address for me. I was now twenty-six and set to party down with my new namesake and fellow wild child.

Perhaps I should explain Ballardite. I recall enjoying a Sunday drive with my family when I was a young kid. We were headed north on Western Avenue leaving downtown Seattle and coming up on the Ballard Bridge when Dad tossed his head back while still watching the road to say loudly, "Hey! Hope you all have your passports!" He and Mom chuckled. Josh, my older brother, looked across the back seat to me with one eyebrow arched high in question. We didn't get the joke. Now I do, after years of listening to the plethora of *yah shoor* jokes Mom and Dad learned through decades of Minnesota life. Ballard is a neighborhood in Seattle where the largest population of Swedes and Norwegians have settled. The area does have a flavor all its own.

The youth of Ballard that I met were, indeed, another breed all together—enough so that I did mentally check for my passport a few times on the way to Janel's house. We'd go out to Parker's on Highway 99; always entering five or ten minutes apart so not to give away the fact the only difference between our drivers' licenses was the picture. We'd party until the wee hours then be at work by 8AM.

Janel and I started eating diet pills for breakfast; pharmaceutical speed that we called crisscross or little white ones. Later in the work day we would eat more for afternoon snack so to keep us perked for another night of partying. The only time we got more than two or three hours of sleep was on Sundays and then it was most of the day.

This pattern lasted a few months until one glorious September morning while driving southbound on Highway 99 to work from north suburbia, having slept away from home. I was indubitably exceeding the 40MPH limit when I broad sided a huge old Delta 88 type tank. It was heading northbound and made a left turn in front of me. In retrospect, I suppose I was putting on lipstick in the rearview mirror, tuning the radio, or engaging in some activity other than being a defensive driver.

Nonetheless, it took some time in victimhood before I could accept that I likely played an active role in the event.

I have zero recollection of the accident. I remember the sun warming my drive to work and, next, waking up in the hospital that night. Anything that happened in between has been told to me. I recall one of the doctors telling me this was my brain's way of protecting me from reliving the trauma.

While I was in the hospital Dad went to the wrecking yard and shot photos to show me what was left of my car. The front end of my peacock green Volkswagen Super Beetle named Cookie was now compressed to about a fourteen inch projectile beyond the windshield. The glass had an intricate spiderweb crack marking where my head made contact. The front bumper laid on the roof. And, there was a hole in the driver's side rear quarter-panel where they cut through to get me out of the car. One of the doctors told me, or it might have been the police-man who stopped by to see me that said, I wouldn't have been hurt nearly so bad if I'd been wearing my seat belt.

A police officer stood in the hall at my door saying he was glad to see I was awake. I invited him in the room. He told me he and his partner had been at the scene of the accident, and that it had taken a while to figure out who I was due to the two ID's in my wallet. Apparently, I was semi-coherent when they got to me through the metal and glass. When they asked me who they should call I repeatedly told them Mom's maiden name. (How's that for Freudian? It was during this time period that Dad's alcoholism had been escalating and I'd been coaxing Mom to divorce him, to get on with her life.) The cop also told me he'd given Mom the fake ID, the pot, and the speed he'd found in my purse. He said he figured I already had enough to deal with without also bringing the law in on that. I thanked him. He wished me well and left.

The injuries I incurred were diagnosed as severe concussion, sprained neck and ankle, multiple cuts and contusions. A goose egg protruded an inch or more above my right eye and temple that took better than two months to flatten out and normalize. Deeply blackened eyes gave me a raccoon appeal.

My right eye healed in conjunction with the lump. But,

my left eye remained black for another month. Headaches were constant as breathing. I wore a neck brace full-time and walked with crutches for over a month. When the neck brace prescription was reduced to "as needed," I attempted denial but the need won repeatedly.

Quoted here are selected passages from a well known medical reference book that describe my state of being:

"Head Injury: Concussion is characterized by transient post-traumatic loss of consciousness. . . More severe injuries may cause. . . uni- or bilaterally dilated and unreactive pupils; and, respiratory irregularity may result from internal brain herniation. . .

Treatment: . . .In the hospital, patients with concussion should be kept under close supervision. . . for at least twenty-four hours to be watched for complications. . .

Objective assessment of residual disability is important after severe head injury. Neuropsychological disturbances with impaired concentration, attention, and memory, plus a variety of mild to moderate personality changes are a more frequent cause of disability in social relations and employment than are specific neurologic impairments. . . Most recovery after severe head injury occurs in the adult within the first six months, with smaller adjustments continuing for perhaps as long as two years.

Post-Concussion Syndrome: . . .headache, dizziness, difficulty in concentration, variable amnesia, depression, apathy, and anxiety are common. . ."

From *The Merck Manual of Diagnosis and Therapy*, Edition 16, Edited by Robert Berkow, MD. Copyright 1992 by Merck & Co., Inc., Whitehouse Station, NJ. Please note *The Merck Manual of Diagnosis and Therapy* is now updated online at: www.MerckManuals.com.

My pupils were unevenly dilated for weeks. And they kept me in the hospital hooked up to intravenous hydration and oxygen for three full days after my day of admission. I was released to go home on the fourth day following the accident.

As I had no income nor a nest-egg for emergencies I stayed at Mom and Dad's. Josh went with Dad to my apartment and collected my meager belongings to store in Dad's garage. On many mornings I spent as long as I could concentrate and stay vertical on the phone dealing with my insurance company. The guy who turned left in front of me was uninsured, unemployed, and driving a friend's car. My uninsured motorist coverage was only marginally helpful. Before my claim was settled the company filed bankruptcy.

I reflected on what I'd been doing with my life and what I was going to change but I didn't get seriously introspective until after the Elton John concert. I wasn't getting high at all due to staying at Mom and Dad's. I had bought tickets prior to the accident.

The Monday morning tickets went on sale, September 9, 1974, our boss allowed me and Janel to take lunch first thing, over-lapping so to take turns standing in line with hopes we'd hold tickets for the Elton John concert by the time our lunches were over. The flipped coin indicated I would be second to walk several blocks to Fidelity Lane.

I saw a photographer standing at the corner half a block away, not knowing his huge lens was drawn to the Fidelity Lane sign behind me or perhaps to my hippiesque poncho. The following photo appeared in the front section of The Seattle Times that evening.

The concert day was long enough after the accident that I convinced my parents I was okay to go what with my friend, Lokie, doing the driving. I wore my neck brace and, with my ankle heftily bandaged, was still walking with crutches. Thank God, we had reserved seats above the floor of the arena and on an aisle so there was a place for my crutches; and, I could extend my leg.

Before the concert Lokie and I smoked out, my first bit of weed in a month. After the show we went to Denny's for munchies. As we reviewed the Elton extravaganza over a heap of fries, I started twigging out—afraid I'd never get well. The highness I felt was over-exaggerated for what we had smoked a few hours earlier. I told Lokie my post-accident brain was constantly in the downside realm of being high on pot. When having fun, difficulty carrying a thread of conversation can be laughed off. But, when not high, being unable to hold a line of

Around the block for rock

It wasn't just the young who lined up around a downtown block this morning to buy tickets for an October 12 concert at the Coliseum by Elton John, popular rock singer. It was a long wait that for some began as early as 7a.m. yesterday at the Fidelity Lane Ticket Office, 1622 Fourth Avenue.

Published 9/9/74 (Greg Gilbert / The Seattle Times)

thought for more than a few seconds is not a good time. We stayed at Denny's until four in the morning, until Lokie had convinced me I'd be alright.

The next day I was okay again — or, as okay as I'd been since the accident— not SUPER high like the night before. I began giving serious consideration to what I was going to do with my life when I got better. I've heard this type of introspection is common among people who have a brush with death. I was feeling lucky to be alive and motivated to move forward in a positive direction.

I became determined to get into college when I got well. It had been drilled into me that if I didn't go to college I wouldn't stand a chance in *the real world*. When I moved out of my parents' home in the middle of my senior year in high school, I knew I was on my own. That was what my parents threatened some time prior to my leaving, "If you run away, don't come looking to us for help - for college, for money, anything."

A month after I was deemed well enough to return to work I made an appointment with a neurologist. My boss and I were both concerned about my reduced ability to focus. And, I was embarrassed in my lack of conversational cohesion.

When I'd explained this to the doctor he said he thought I was doing fine along those lines adding, "You just imparted quite a lot of information to me very concisely."

I countered that I'd written down my little speech and practiced knowing his time for me would be limited — finishing with, "Most of life does not offer an opportunity for planning. Is there nothing you can do to help me?"

He had the nurse come in to prepare me for an EEG or electro encephalograph, a means of investigating the level of brain activity. She strategically planted several electrodes on my scalp with a gel to hold them in place. He then flipped on the machine and watched my brain waves as they printed out in graph format when I responded to his questions. After several minutes of this he turned off the machine and showed me what he saw on the print-out while explaining why it all looked good given the severity of my injuries. He told me that my brain was still badly bruised but functioning. He said it would heal in time as bruises do, but that brain tissue takes longer to heal than epidermis; that I may have difficulties for two to three years. He added that I must be patient; and, encouraged me to continue taking Valium to counteract my anxiety by giving me a new prescription which enabled refills for a full year. I left his office thinking, "Thanks, Doc! Now that there's no physical evidence of injury I just seem like an idiot to people. Great, I'll take drugs and be patient."

Soon after that appointment I moved in with roommates found in The Seattle Times classified ads, took a different bus to my bookkeeping grind, and stayed true to my conviction to get into college. I applied to Eastern Washington State College as they were known for a strong foreign language department. French had come easily to me in high school and I enjoyed the studies. I wasn't sure where I was going from there but figured I'd find direction as I went along.

Early on in my schooling, I all too readily accepted discouragement for pursuing my love of words and creative writing. Higher education along that course was not a consideration. In ninth grade one quarter of Social Studies was primarily dedicated to studying up on a chosen career. We'd then write a report and give an oral report. It would be the largest part of our quarterly grade.

When I got home from school and told Mom about the assignment she asked what career had my interest. I was surprised she had to ask, she who had spent years of rainy Sundays fostering my love of words by playing Scrabble or Perquacky with me. Without hesitation I told her I wanted to be a writer.

I was shocked at her response, "Ooh! You can't do that, it's too hard! You can't make any money being a writer. You should be an attorney. Yes, you'd make a great lawyer; and, even judge one day. Do your report on that." So, I did. It was interesting and I got an "A" that quarter but I knew it was not a career I'd engage in.

Inside the lid of the small wooden music box that sat on Mom's dresser all the years I was growing up, my name is printed in pencil. The letters appear inexperienced and it's apparent the time and care that went in to each line of each letter. I found room on the play list affixed inside the lid to squeeze "*Beth*" above "*Rigoletto*" and the "*ube Waltz*" portion of "*The Blue Danube Waltz.*" I remember I was scolded. But at age five this new skill was overwhelmingly powerful. I was in its grip and left my mark in unusual places.

Through high school I took a seventh period class every quarter, starting school an hour earlier than the bulk of the student body each morning. This way I could indulge myself scoring an A in every elective poetry and creative writing class offered while maintaining the classes more important to college entry such as advanced algebra and chemistry. After school I was an actress in the school play.

Where Writer has never been my title, writing has been integral to almost every profession I've pursued—from writing business correspondence to marketing materials to sales proposals; and, a comprehensive business and marketing plan for an invention I patented. As for any personal writing, for years it left my keeping as it went out to friends and family in other cities and states on a postcard or in an envelope with a stamp I licked.

Upon my acceptance at Eastern, I went to meet with the head of the Foreign Language Department; and, to consult with a counselor on curriculum. I was excited when I got back home, at least until I got notification I wasn't eligible for financial aid. Essentially, it said my father's income was too high. I didn't understand what that had to do with me for I was self-supporting. I went to talk to Dad about it. He didn't shed any light on the topic. It didn't occur to me until my Zoey was born some years later that he must have continued to claim me as a dependent on the 1040 when filing his income tax return.

Daily I scrutinized the *Help Wanted* column in The Seattle Times searching for a second job so to start saving money for college. One ad kept jumping out at me: **Dancers Wanted in Alaska.** I gave in to my curiosity one day, called the number in the ad, and was told that because the club was within the city limits of Fairbanks topless dancing was not legal. "The girls wear bikini-like costumes," the woman said.

The deal was decent given the completion of a minimum eight week tour. They would cover round-trip airfare, provide housing; and offered a salary of two hundred dollars per week plus tips—significantly more than my current earnings. I calculated one or two tours would allow me to save enough money to get started in school. Then I'd get a part-time job and start applying for scholarships and possibly grants.

I accepted the job and danced to my pick of jukebox songs on stage at The Flame Lounge. After three weeks of nightly gyrations, my left knee started acting up. I went to a doctor who, upon hearing of my occupation, recommended I go back home. I suppose he thought I was misplaced. Boy, was I.

In those three weeks of bunking with dancing veterans, I was educated in the activities my mom had no justification for talking of, given she had no experience with them. Nonetheless, she had instilled in my brain that kind of work is "what you don't want to grow up to be or do." Those would be "other-side-of-the-tracks" type people and jobs.

I took the doctor's advice and bought a return ticket to Seattle. Between ticketing day and my day of departure I met Riley. He came in to The Flame one night with a friend, the first guys my own age I'd seen thus far. Most of The Flame patrons were older men who'd been imported to build the Trans-Alaska Pipeline; like welders, engineers, etcetera. Riley asked if I'd like to go out with him after I got off work.

"Sure!" I hopped on the offer, relishing the prospect of a break from the sleazy environment. As we stepped out of the smoky cave at four in the morning, the late spring's midnight sun overwhelmed my vision. But not Riley, a Fairbanks native, as he'd already donned shades.

He took me to some of his favorite spots in the country-side. As we talked and laughed he, like the good doctor, knew I was out of my element at The Flame. We had a great time that night, the next night, and the night after that. I decided to give Riley my parents' phone number in Seattle as I was slated to leave the next morning.

Riley called daily trying to convince me to come back saying I could stay at his sister's home until I got a job and an apartment; that I could earn tuition by working on the pipeline and go to the University of Alaska after that if college was so important to me. I couldn't see what I was going to do back in Seattle considering Plan A had failed. I thought, "What the heck! Here's a Plan B."

Before I left for the dancing gig, my parents allowed me to store my stuff at their place again. After returning from Alaska I stayed with them too. But, they weren't keen on having a garage sale there. They wanted no part in my relocation to Alaska. Dad was still pissed off at me for his embarrassment when a coworker pointed out that Fairbanks has no fish canneries, given the town is hundreds of miles from any ocean. Of course, I'd lied about what work was in store for me in Alaska. I did confess upon my return and they were appalled at first but got over it. They still weren't offering up tuition though.

I was thankful Janel, my former fellow party animal, let me have the sale at her house. It took only two trips, with my car tightly packed, on the Friday night before the sale to transfer my household accoutrements to her garage. Next, we nailed signs on strategically located telephone poles to direct people to the sale.

Setting up my goods in Janel's garage and driveway, then getting it all priced went quickly Saturday morning. And, everything was sold before dinner that afternoon. Janel laughed at me when I gave every purchaser a tutorial specific to the care of each plant I bid fare well to. The hardest things for me to let go of were my precious potted plants. They were my pets.

Lastly, I sold my car. The funds I had raised afforded me a one-way ticket to Fairbanks and left three hundred dollars in my pocket. I boarded the plane that held two banana boxes containing what was left of my belongings stashed in the luggage bay. And I was off to a new adventure, my Plan B.

What was most different about me after the accident was that I started to take risks. I'm not saying I always made good choices or that I took particularly good risks. But, I could not continue to complacently watch while daybreak climbed the mountains Monday through Friday and be stuck drinking java at the desk where I kept someone else's books. I just knew I was going nowhere in that show and that I'd have to do something different than the *same old same old* unless I wanted to live in that same old way forever. I felt if I did that, I might just as well have died in that car wreck.

This is me with the only Cannabis Sativa crop I've ever grown. It was 1976, the year Alaska deemed it legal to grow and possess marijuana in quantities suitable for personal use. Riley and I grew ten plants along the banks of Moose Creek. The pot came to be known as Moose Creek Creeper. It was labelled as such by smokers who revelled in how the surprisingly good home grown buzz would creep up sneakily then explode into smiles and laughter.

3: The House Of The '90's

Journal: June 6, 1995 - continued
The moment I arrived home from Dick Carville's office I grabbed a garbage bag and started scouring the apartment for anything that could be construed as evidence—the bong, rolling papers, roach clips, and the like. Dick didn't suggest this but I know there is only one guarantee in life: You never know what might be coming next. With all the shit that has come down since May 17th -whoa- I haven't written about any of this! It has been insane. I would not be a bit surprised to get a knock on my door and open it to greet a cop with a search warrant.

Today was the third time I've gone into Zoey's room since the 17th. The first two were to bag up items to deliver to her dad. Eric called me on the 17th of May in the late afternoon at work to tell me, "I have taken Zoey to a lock-down drug rehabilitation facility out of state. You need to bag up a couple weeks worth of clothes and bring them to my office because I'm not telling you where she is."

This time I felt like an interloper in my daughter's room. I was invading Zoey's privacy as I scrutinized the contents of her closet and each drawer in her dresser. I searched for signs of what I had missed, that could give background to her changing behavior toward me—that would tell me what drugs she'd been taking on top of smoking too much pot.

In one drawer, written on her notebook paper and folded neatly, was a poem written by Zoey on May 10th entitled "Knots." My stomach was in knots as I read it through for the umpteenth time. I wondered if her metaphor referred to drug and alcohol use or if she was speaking of a relationship gone awry, or both. I am amazed by the depth of her words. It makes me feel small and saddened to learn that I do not know this Zoey. I am ashamed in that. And, if not for the fact I'm thankful it's over now, that the House of the '90's is a closed chapter, I would be afraid for her. Hell, I've been scared for her, by this whole situation! What a mess indeed.

[transcription formatted precisely as written]

KNOTS
 by Zoey   May 10th 1995
Isn't it funny how a seemingly trivial thing can
haunt someone for so long?
A voice, a name
    A memory, a face,
A situation can make you find yourself in a
world of pain as if it were never   lost?
Everything
    Has a way of getting twisted around
Everything
    Else to the point where you can't
    Read out your own life,
A story in itself.
And for some reason, the only ways to
get the knot untangled is to forget about
 it and lose it, or cut it.
But the knot is precious, Something
to hold onto, as loathsome as it may be.
So carefully you angle and bend, untwist
and untie, until you get yourself so caught
up, tight inside this knot that
You can't see anything else.
You can't hear anything else.
But the noise of this knot and
the sound of yourself, gasping for air.
You can't speak of anything else,
And all you can feel is the knot
    Tightening & Tightening
And you struggle to be free less & less, until the
Knot suffocates you.
So upwards your spirit flies from the mess,
And as you look back into the knot, searching
for your body, you see how you could have
saved yourself, prevented self-death;
By simply not buying the rope.

I continued my search and rounded up all the packets of photographs taken at parties in our apartment. When it came down to throwing them in the trash bag I thought it best to disguise them, to keep them separate from the most incriminating evidence. A cop with a warrant would likely look in the dumpster. I put all the photos in a plastic grocery bag and tied the handles tight in a knot. I then put that bundle in another bag just wrapping it tightly around the first—and then a third bag wrapped tightly around the second and a fourth on top of them all, knotted off like the first: no photos here. Paranoid? Yup.

All the while I was wondering if Zoey would ever speak to me again when she learns what I did with them. How she loves her pictures. I took the photo bundle and the trash bag down to the dumpster. After setting the trash bag down I climbed up on the side of the dumpster so I could reach in and bury the photos. Then I threw in the trash bag. Fifteen fucking years! With my luck they'll make me the new Poster C̶h̶i̶l̶d̶ Mom in support of the War on Drugs and nail me to the cross with the absolute max.

Before the quadruple bagging began I looked through the photos. The House of the 90's board hanging on the end wall in our kitchen got started about a week after we

21

moved in, Christmas Day 1994, during our celebration marking the first time Zoey and I have lived under the same roof at Christmas time since she was six years old. That night it was just our home. It wasn't dubbed The House of the 90's until several parties later. However, the tradition of all visitors being required to sign in on the board was instituted that night. All who entered were instructed to express them-selves, to leave their mark.

The photo of beer empties neatly lined up in rows overflowing from the recycle area conjured up the vision of Zoey's face smiling proudly at the gleaming tidy apartment and her Aunt Rosey's cheery face behind her as I walked in at about 2:30AM, both of them dying to tell me about the big bust. The cops came to break up the party I had forbidden but knew was likely to happen anyway.

The series of photos of one of Zoey's friends sleeping in a chair on a Saturday afternoon a handful of friends came over to watch movies sums up so much silliness. Zoey tried to wake him to no avail. There was no alcohol or weed in the house so I wondered what they'd been up to the night be-fore that he'd crash so hard. Following Zoey's lead, one of the

boys tossed a banana peel at him in an attempt to rouse him. Nothing. They were all giggling and proceeded to arrange a variety of items on his lap, his jacket and hat. The series of photos captured the build-up. They were looking forward to snapping a shot of his face when he'd awaken to find himself a multi-media sculpture.

And, there I am "lurking" with the boys, "hiding" behind our snack plates. It was easy to get caught up in the fun energy the kids brought to The House of the 90's. Fun—unlike when Zoey and her step-dad, Paul, found me with tears streaming down my face after their whirl on the big roll-ercoaster at the Orange County Fair, the last of the three rides we had money for. While waiting for them I watched pure joy emanating from the stage where cloggers stomped through their patterns with petticoats and full skirts flying, unaware of the tears. I envied the joy of those dancers and wondered if I would be fun again or if the strain of building two businesses would leave me forever fun-impaired. Thankfully, laughter found me as Paul and Zoey's grins turned to guffaws and they demanded, "What are you doing?"

How odd I should remember that at this moment, funny how my head works. I guess it's better than thinking about the ugliness at the top of today. Zoey's dad and his

wife, Crystal, showed up at my office just before noon saying they wanted to take me to lunch. It didn't surprise me
as I'm aware they've been researching other treatment
facilities for Zoey and figured they wanted to talk about
their findings. We'd been discussing her lack of progress at
the current lock-down treatment center. Since I have learned
of Zoey's whereabouts they've had no choice but to include me
in this decision making process.

We got in their car but Eric didn't put the keys in the
ignition. Instead, they both turned to face me in the back
seat to tell me about a program that takes kids on wilderness
survival treks. They showed me brochures from the facility
describing the benefits of the program and the associated
costs. They made their intention of signing Zoey up for the
next expedition clear, as well as their belief that payment is
my responsibility, that Zoey's condition is entirely my fault.

They then went on to illustrate that concept. They reminded me it had now come out in Zoey's answers to the
series of questionnaires that are a part of her treatment
program that I had supplied pot to the kids. They were looking for a confession. When I didn't furnish it, they went on
to tell me that some kids who frequented my house have
come forward to tell their parents about what went down
there; and, that those parents are willing to file depositions
against me based on their kids' testimonials.

Crystal's voice got louder and sterner as she pushed for
my confession. My mouth formed words on some impulse
that bypasses conscious thought apparently because I heard
myself saying, "I think I need to see an attorney." Crystal
nastily insisted that I just tell them the truth. I repeated
with conviction that I needed to see an attorney. The heave
of her shoulders and audible air intake brought Eric to grasp
her arm in calm authority. He told me to see an attorney
and to get back with them promptly, adding if he didn't
hear from me by tomorrow the depositions would be filed.

I went back in the office, told my boss I had a personal
emergency that must be dealt with immediately, that I needed
to leave. I assured him I'd be back in the morning, went to
my desk to grab my purse and left running on an adrenalin
sandwich for lunch. As soon as I got home I combed the listing
of criminal defense attorneys in the Yellow Pages.

My head is one huge jumble of whatthefuck! I miss Zoey so bad, my Lovebug. My dear daughter, how did it escalate from our first little celebration to me sitting across that mammoth desk from Dick Carville, all in five speed-of-sound months? I need to lie down and go to a peaceful place. Can I find one? Just breathe, Beth.

4: Matrimony and Me

Eric and I had lived together for a year and a half when he gave me a diamond solitaire ring. It was early December 1979 on my twenty-fifth birthday. The small box was wrapped like a gift and handed to me. There was no proposal. It was up to me to sheepishly ask what finger I was supposed to wear it on.

He laughed and replied, "What do you think?" I felt humiliated. We were at my parents' home for my birthday dinner and they were sharing the moment. They seemed embarrassed too. At home later that night, we consummated our engagement.

In late January, when my doctor confirmed the positive results of the self-pregnancy test I'd taken, Eric and I agreed that I must have conceived the night of my birthday. We hadn't stopped for the diaphragm. I was scared. He was excited.

We decided that our three week Mexican vacation in February, which had been booked for several months, would be our wedding trip. Mom and I hustled to plan a reception with a festive Mexican color scheme to take place soon after Eric and I returned. The fact that I worked for my parents in their interior design business made it possible for Mom and me to divert our energies toward pulling together all the details quickly and getting the invitations mailed.

On the morning of our departure, Dad drove me and Eric to the airport. After he and Eric cleared the trunk of our suitcases, Dad shook hands with Eric saying, "You two have a great time." He then turned and gave me a hug. With one arm still around me, he reached in his jacket, pulled an unsealed envelope from the inside pocket and placed it in my hands. He kissed my forehead and explained the contents were to help assure that we had a nice trip. While Eric watched attentively,

I opened it to find five crisp one hundred dollar bills. We both thanked him heartily and I gave him an extra hug.

As Eric and I were juggling our carry-on bags and settling into our seats on the plane he told me to give him the envelope. I replied, "No. Dad handed it to me." He insisted I give it to him for safe keeping. Not wanting to cause a scene, I pulled it out of my purse. That was the last time I held it. To assure my feelings remained unspoken with so many people nearby in close quarters, I opened a book. Eric chose the morning paper and pointed out the front page news to me gloomily. Mortgage rates were skyrocketing past eighteen percent.

On our way south, we had a short stop over in San Francisco. Eric's sister, whose ordination into the ministry we'd witnessed a few months earlier in the Bay Area, came to visit with us at the airport. As she approached us at the gate she was bubbling over with "You could be my first wedding if you want to get married right now. In the state of California there is a *Confidential Wedding* where we can do the paperwork later."

Paperwork? We hadn't given much consideration to what could be entailed in getting married in Mexico. It hit us that we weren't going to Las Vegas. Plus, it was easy to get caught up in her enthusiasm. We replied, "Why not? Sure! We'd love to be your first wedding."

She was happy with our choice and declared she'd buy a bottle of champagne to toast the occasion. In the Oyster Bar at the San Francisco International Airport, over a glass of champagne, I mentally prepared to become Eric's second wife.

Our minister suggested, "Before you exchange the traditional vows maybe you should share with each other your hopes and goals for the union."

Eric and I had never talked in those terms. I looked at him and said, "You go first." He seemed very focussed on the idea of working hard together. I remember hearing the word *work* several times. I did not hear him say the words *love* or *share* or *enjoy*. It was all oriented toward building a dynasty. My mind raced with: *Is that it? Is this what I want? Are these my goals?*

But, my mouth said words fashioned after all the romantic novels I'd read in my teen years. I spoke of the symbolism of the

ring I'd had crafted for him with the sun, the moon, and the stars. I thought of the seedling in my womb and the spirit awaiting entry. I saw Mom and Dad's faces—their excitement for their first grandchild—and thought of the invitations already sent out for the reception. My mouth moved at the appropriate times and I heard her saying, "I now pronounce you husband and wife."

The Pyramids,
outside Mexico City

The reception

Coming up on our first anniversary we were tight on cash having made a residential move recently and in light of building our new business. When the topic of affording gifts arose, I told Eric the nicest gift he could give me would be to sing me a love song. He played in a band occasionally so was paid to sing pop songs to people. Some of them were love songs. Seeing his blank face I added he could pick any song in his repertoire which expressed his feelings for me, that I wasn't asking him to write one. His face was still blank as he turned and left the room. When the day came there was no song.

The family unit   *Zoey and me*

Five years serving as a dynasty building partner, home-maker, and mother of our child—with no apparent love for me included—gave answers to the unvoiced questions in my head that day in the Oyster Bar before stating *I do*. No, I wanted love and affection too.

It's odd how minute the straw that breaks the camel's back can be compared to the weight of the full load. My straw came the night Eric ended an argument about me making a quick run to the convenience store for a pack of cigarettes insisting, "You are nothing. NOTHING!" How can anyone love nothing? I finally got it and those words changed everything.

We needed to get through the divorce without the expense of attorneys. Where we had assets our cash flow was poor. It was agreed that we had enough regard for each other and for our daughter to be able to amicably negotiate our terms. We decided on joint custody and drew up a detailed parenting plan where Zoey would alternately live with him then me, on a weekly basis at first. After a couple months of that we'd bump it up to a biweekly exchange; then, graduate to a monthly exchange by the time Zoey started Kindergarten. The every other month program would work for we lived in close proximity.

I knew if I put a dent of any proportion in Eric's wallet communications would cease to be friendly. With thirteen years of joint parenting ahead of us it seemed like a good idea to give him the house, the two rental properties, and the newer of the two cars. I made no bid for the business I'd helped him build. I was confident of my ability to succeed in a new life. I just wanted to get out of the marriage and get on with it.

The morning that Eric and I finalized our divorce the courtroom was packed. We were relieved to be the third or fourth case called to approach the bench until the judge scanned our paperwork, looked up, and told us to sit back down. She would hear our case when the courtroom was cleared. It was mid-afternoon when we were the only ones left and she called us back up to her bench. She looked me in the eyes and asked in a horrified tone, "You don't want the house? You don't want child support?" I was taken aback.

"We have an agreement," Eric quietly snarled at me out of the side of his mouth.

I wanted it to be over so replied to the judge, "No. I'll be fine." While shaking her head she signed and stamped the papers.

In the year following the divorce, I learned that the earlier confidence regarding my ability to earn an income sufficient to support Zoey and me was unfounded. A position in sales opened up where I worked as a customer service rep. I applied for it knowing my income would increase dramatically.

Even though I had a successful track record in retail sales and my department head could vouch for the quality of my work, I was informed by the Vice President of Dealer Sales that the wholesale level position would not be open to me. He told me I would first have to "pound the pavement" and sell directly to end-users before I would be considered for placement in Dealer Sales. To get that experience I would need to transfer to either the Chicago or Los Angeles office. Direct sales were not conducted from the Seattle office, only sales to dealers who in turn sold to the end user.

I loved working for a company that represented an innovative approach to music for business environments. It was a blast working in a rock-n-roll atmosphere for people that fostered company culture by hosting parties for every possible occasion. And, on Friday when the work day was done there was an in-house Happy Hour. I didn't want to give up this job with all the fun perks. But I did need to earn more money. And, at that point in my life, I also needed respite from the opinions on and expectations of who, what, and how I should be according to most of the people in my life. So, July 17, 1986 saw me landing in L.A. to work sales from the ground level.

It was understood all the way around, by Eric and Zoey in addition to my employer, that I'd be back in two years anticipating a slot in Dealer Sales. I was concerned to take Zoey with me to an unfamiliar and reputedly racy city where I had no support system to help me with her. I knew my schedule would be erratic. And, per the terms of our Joint Custody agreement, Eric could refuse to allow me to do so. That was that. I trusted all would work out for he'd been a better father to Zoey than a husband to me. We agreed she'd spend Christmas '86 with me at my parents' home. And, Zoey would have summers '87 and '88 with me in Los Angeles. We'd play Christmas '87 by ear.

I wrote letters to Zoey at least once a week and sent postcards and fun greeting cards in between. I called her as often as my phone budget would allow. As summer drew near all we talked about was our excitement for soon being together. Even so, I well remember her combined feelings of enthusiasm and angst for her first solo flight to Los Angeles. I wrote her a letter to explain that her dad would put her on the airplane; then stay near the door until he saw her plane take flight through the airport window. And, I assured her I would be at the airport in L.A. awaiting her arrival; that I'd come get her off the plane. When I wrote that promise I had no idea I was wrong.

On the day of Zoey's arrival I was at the gate plenty early and pacing anxiously. As the arrival of her flight was announced an airline attendant appeared to unlock the door to the ramp.

I told her my six-year-old daughter was alone on the flight and that I had promised to come on the plane to greet her. She informed me that was not possible; that I must wait there by the door and a flight attendant would deliver her to me.

I waited. The flow of disembarking passengers dwindled to nothing, and still no Zoey in sight. The woman who'd unlocked the door to the ramp was no longer around. I stood alone at the top watching and waiting.

As fear that something had gone awry knocked on my brain, I saw Zoey hesitantly starting up the ramp hand in hand with a flight attendant. When she saw me her pace picked up and her face brightened. I knelt down with outstretched arms and she broke grip from the flight attendant. She leapt into my embrace and I rose. With my arms encircling her, we whirled around and around and around. Her feet were flying with legs parallel to the floor. We giggled giddily and the flight attendant smiled with, "You must be Mom."

My paychecks from the branch office were not enough to live on in L.A. I had no resources to return to Seattle. Even if I had, the last thing I wanted was to return defeated, proving all the nay-sayers in my life correct in their assertions the move was a mistake.

I scored a District Sales Manager position with a company that knew me well for they were a top vendor to my parents' interior design business. I was well versed with their product line having sold all of it at retail. Where several years of working for my folks had been enough for me, I was thankful for the experience that gave entry to this new sales position. I'd put interiors behind me when telephone soliciting three nights per week for Eric's new business became full time hours in his office—for which I never saw a paycheck or even a peck on the cheek. Employment with the music company started after I'd grasped the only thing Eric loved about me was my ability to bring in business and I knew we were headed for divorce.

Soon after I started the new job I met Paul. We fell in love and two years I'd planned to be in L.A. turned into seven. We married just before Christmas in 1988 on Hermosa Pier, where we'd first crossed paths on The Strand, he on his bike and I on my skates. We rode there frequently together and loved that beach.

Zoey, who had flown in with my parents from Seattle, helped me tie balloon bouquets to the pier railings. Paul's folks were also in attendance and a justice of the peace indulged us our chosen location. After our *I do's* we untied the bouquets, watched as they floated far into the blue, then walked to a restaurant on the waterfront to share a celebratory lunch.

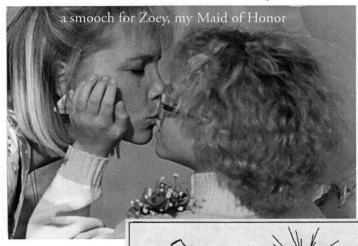

a smooch for Zoey, my Maid of Honor

the announcement card I made and sent to friends and family

In our favorite spot we tied the knot

Paul liked his work as an engineering tech in the aerospace industry but found he had no patience for the bureaucracy. I saw a demand for what could be a good niche for him so asked if he'd have interest in learning to install window blinds and draperies. He left his job and started a new business providing installation service to the loyal design clientele I'd built in my time as District Sales Manager.

After Paul had been busy installing for six months I gave

a notice of resignation to my employer and joined Paul full time. Management at the company where I'd worked offered encouragement and referred more business to us. Our service made my former sales territory stronger for them. We were their answer to the frequent request, "Do you know a good, reliable installer?"

We started out on a shoestring with no experience and no business plan. Though we were busy as could be, the cost of our learning curve was horrendous. Dad came to Redondo Beach to help us catch up our bookkeeping and do our income taxes for that first year of business. When he got to the bottom line, his tongue-in-cheek comment was, "I hope you kids are getting food stamps or something."

Not long before Paul and I married, Eric also wanted to remarry. He and his girlfriend, Crystal, planned a trip to Disneyland with her two sons and Zoey during the kids' 1988 Spring break. Eric called to tell me of their plan. He said they would bring Zoey to Paul's and my home at the end of their holiday. They were returning to Seattle mid-week but Zoey was allowed to stay with me and Paul for the balance of the week so long as we put her on the plane Sunday evening. That was the first and only time Eric paid the way for Zoey to see me in California. I should have guessed there was an ulterior motive but it did not occur to me until after they had departed.

Eric and Crystal followed the directions I'd given them to our apartment in Redondo Beach and on arrival Zoey showed them up the stairs to our door. The boys stayed in the car so the conversation that followed introductions was too brief to cut through the surface tension. I quickly showed them around our apartment and they left. That evening, after Zoey was asleep, Paul and I laid in bed and talked about the shared feeling that we had just been sized up.

Crystal confided to me long after their wedding that meeting me had been essential to her decision making process on whether to marry Eric. When she shared that fact, I could only surmise she had taken one look at me, the mother who would leave her child behind, and at my good looking surfer boyfriend who was ten years younger than me, and concluded that I would eventually go away or at least be a non-issue. She'd come to learn that initial assessment was in error, that Zoey and I shared a strong bond not to be undone.

A month or so after their visit, I learned of another prerequisite likely laid down by Crystal before marrying Eric. Documents arrived in the mail from Eric with his instruction for me to sign, notarize, and return. I was to sign residential custody of Zoey over to Eric if I expected him to put her on the plane to come spend the summer with me. I had already paid for Zoey's ticket and mailed it to him. He was fully aware I could afford only one so had no means to come get her. The *Stipulation* to our divorce decree would grant Eric residential custody of Zoey, and the annual dependent tax deduction which had alternated until then. It further stated that if or when I again became a resident of Washington State I would remain the visiting parent. I acquiesced, signed the document before a notary as mandated and mailed it back. I was not giving up my summertime with Zoey.

My parents later informed me of what they believed to be another of Crystal's prenuptial requirements. Zoey's little whisk broomish terrier was put to sleep; the dog Eric and his brother picked out at the pound six months or so prior to Zoey's arrival in our lives. When Eric told my folks the dog had some sort of tumor they sensed he wasn't telling the whole story. The next time Zoey stayed a weekend with her grandma and grandpa she told them her dad would not be getting another dog for her because one of her two new older brothers is allergic to dogs.

In the years following Eric and Crystal's wedding, my summers with Zoey grew shorter and shorter. Each year they had a reason for Zoey to return to Seattle before the end of summer. It seems nearly a year had elapsed since their wedding before Crystal placed her first phone call to me. I guess it took that long for her to figure out that I wasn't going to melt into the woodwork or simply go away and leave the mothering of Zoey entirely up to her. It was difficult for me to know what the dynamic truly was between her and Zoey as I heard different stories from each of them. Crystal was obviously very frustrated that dealing with Zoey was different from how she dealt with her sons. I had the impression Crystal held the opinion that most any tension existing in their home could be attributed to Zoey. One issue she had was Zoey not doing all of her household chores. I told her that I always made a little list for Zoey so she could tick off each chore as she completed them. It not only acted as reminder for what she needed to do next but it also showed her how much she had accomplished.

Crystal's response was, "I don't have time to make lists." I suggested she could have written a little list in the time we'd been on the phone. That didn't go over well. She didn't seem open to any of my suggestions. Perhaps she simply needed to vent and to do so on me seemed appropriate.

During one of Zoey's summers with me she told me Crystal had asked her to start calling her Mom. When I asked Zoey how she had replied she said, "I told her I already have a Mom."

That gave explanation for why on one phone call from Crystal she had asked me to stop referring to Zoey as *Lovebug*. I asked why she'd want me to do that and her reply was something about how it was too childish. I laughed with, "You've got to be kidding! It's a term of endearment and I will probably be calling Zoey Lovebug 'til I die."

On an ensuing call from Crystal she told me they were seeing a family counselor in an effort to smoothly blend their family unit of five. She added the counselor highly recommended Zoey's summers with me be shortened. I had a hard time believing a counselor would recommend a child spend less time with her mother and voiced just that. Crystal asked me if I'd go to an appointment with them the next time I came to Seattle. When my next trip was planned I told them and it was set. The counselor did indeed indicate it was in Zoey's best interest to spend more summer time with her new family unit to ease the blending process. She added that Zoey could then more readily let go of her California dreaming, her desire to live with me and Paul. I was dumbfounded and angry. Nonetheless I had little choice but to accept her explanation. Eric and Crystal held all the aces. He had residential custody and they paid the counselor's fee. Zoey's summers with me got short.

Then came the epiphany. One day I stood on the rooftop patio above our garage with arms spread wide, gazing up at the sky pleading for help, asking for a way to come up with the kind of cash needed to battle with Eric for residential custody of Zoey. That night, in my sleep, it came to me in something larger than a dream, a thunderous brainstorm of streaming mental video. Even after I awoke vivid color commercials for the next big thing in sunglasses continued.

Paul and I were excited to see Sundogz succeed. We naively believed our product would cause a huge wave in the sunglasses market. As such, while Paul and I continued to work in our primary business for the  needed income, we relentlessly pursued Sundogz. We ran with it at full throttle—heart and soul, credit cards and bank account, from prototyping through preliminary market exposure at the Action Sport Retailer Trade Show to the issuance of our patent.

Given I was the business head of our team it was me who pursued every avenue that might lead to the venture capital needed to get Sundogz manufactured and out to the retail marketplace. Unfortunately, all money roads ended at a brick wall. Potential investors were intrigued enough to meet with me and hear my pitch; glance over the prospectus I'd prepared which detailed my  marketing plan and their proposed share of projected profits. But, they were unimpressed by our prototypes being featured on the covers of and included in multi-product photo layouts in high profile trade magazines. They noted being news worthy did not demonstrate the product would sell through to the end user.

Every presentation went much the same. Paul and I went

further into debt and staved off discouragement. We were in so deep I felt driven to continue, to bring about the success that Paul and I initially saw as inevitable.

Factors we couldn't have foreseen or controlled were big bricks in the wall at the end of each road. The economy in greater Los Angeles hit sub-zero after thousands of local aerospace jobs were relocated to southeastern states for their more favorable corporate tax structure. At least, that's the reasoning a few of Paul's former coworkers suggested to us. The real estate market took a dive as homeowners walked away from their equity to move with their jobs; retail sales plummeted, and our installation business declined accordingly.

To top it all off, new federal tax laws inhibiting investment loss write-offs were instituted. I was told that was a result of the Silicon Valley computer start-up crazed venture capital glut. The combined factors gave cause for investors to hold tight to their purse strings.

Where I didn't tell Zoey that Sundogz were an inspiration born in my desire to gain residential custody of her she was, of course, in on the project from the get go. She thought Sundogz were super cool, couldn't wait to have a wardrobe of them, and was positive we would sell millions. While I saw no success in raising the near half million dollars needed to launch Sundogz with gusto, I was more so pained to watch Zoey's growing disappointment and waning interest.

I watched as my flawless credit history of seventeen years was gradually sucked down the drain and along with it my marriage to my best friend and lover, Paul. Being ten years younger than me, he didn't have the level of experience with difficult financial times that I did. He didn't take it well nor my inattentiveness to our relationship as I scrambled to hold our finances together, both our installation business—which now subsisted of the far and between high-end frosting on the cake jobs and the low-end rental market jobs, with the middle layer of bread-n-butter jobs nearly nonexistent—and the debt laden Sundogz project.

I'll not forget the sadness in Paul's eyes on the day he came to my desk in our dining room to ask if I'd join him for a bike ride and a skate. It was the last time he subjected himself to hearing, "Oh Honey, I just can't. I need to finish. . ." whatever it was that seemed more important than doing something fun with him.

That day was his straw. Paul withdrew, ceased to engage with me as my friend and lover. He also began to drink liquor to excess fairly frequently; and, at the drunkest of times, if there was cash in his pocket, he would make a cocaine connection. It was in this span of time—more than two years since the epiphany—that Crystal called me, frazzled and angry, to say, "Zoey can come live with you now."

The words I had long wanted to hear hit me hard. There was no way I could subject Zoey to Paul's behavior or to our circumstances. We were struggling to make rent on a one bed-room apartment. We watched our new bedroom set walk out the door for cash to pay one month's rent. As we adjusted to sleeping on foam pads on the floor, the elegant sofa covered in glove-soft leather we had gotten a good deal on with one of our designer clients became another month of rent paid. Pride would not allow me to share any of this information with Crystal; regardless of how I detested having to say these words, "Timing could not be worse, Crystal. She can't come live with us now."

I got a report from Crystal that Zoey, who was in middle school, had been caught sneaking alcohol from her and Eric's well-stocked bar. I realized it was time to return to Seattle. I needed to be a more constant influence in her life. In 1992, I was trying to relax and enjoy my usual every other year Christmas visit with Zoey at my parents' home. (In alternating years I flew Zoey to L.A. during her Christmas break.) One afternoon Zoey and her Grampa went to the neighboring town to do some last Christmas shopping. It was well after dark when they returned, much later than expected, because Zoey had been caught stealing make-up. That was the clincher: I *must* move back.

Paul and I temporarily stayed at my cousin's home in the Seattle area February 1993. Denny and his wife, Victoria, graciously gave us their family room until we were able to find jobs and an apartment. When we left L. A. we did not put in an address forward for we had no means of paying the collections notices that would follow us. We simply disconnected our phones, including the toll-free 800 number Zoey had called me on nearly daily for the last five years when she wasn't with me in California.

My sunny southern California steeped hubby did not last quite a year in the Pacific Northwest climate. The gloominess in the air further exacerbated our faltering communication and deteriorating relationship. In January 1994, Paul left Seattle and me for the sunshine of Kauai, Hawaii and to work with his brother in the last of post-hurricane construction.

August 1994 saw me heading to Kauai with hope of repairing the damage and restoring our marriage. It was to no avail. Paul, who had taught me how to unleash my sexuality, quickly made it clear things would not work out between us. I gave up hope on making love and quit trying to get him to go do fun things with me on his off hours. Instead, I found fun company in one of his house mates and some of his friends – mostly May, Max, and Julie. I started hanging out doing fun things with them on their days off.

Julie, an eighteen year old who was mature beyond her years, got how uncomfortable the scenario was for me at Paul's. She offered to let me stay at her family's home for the rest of my time on Kauai. She must have apprised her parents of my situation for they kindly embraced my presence and didn't act as though it was odd that their daughter should befriend, as a peer, a woman who'd soon turn forty.

The last three weeks of twelve total on the island were the best part of My Vacation of the Decade. I called it that as I took one week for every year that I didn't get a vacation due to surgeries eating paid vacation time, tending to a new business, or being too plain broke to take time off, plus two bonus weeks. Those weeks saw the end of my marriage and nearly two years of sexual drought. I reveled in being a kid with my new playmates, pushing woes and pressures off to the side, until the day before my departure.

I was at the beach alone that day feeling sad, replaying clips in my head on the highs and lows of life with Paul. I was recalling my frustration with the year or so before we left L. A., the apparent onset of my metamorphosis from sex-bomb-cuddle-babe to snuggle-bunny-only in Paul's mind, when who should walk up but Paul. He was also sad. But, neither of us could express that shared emotion. There were too many hurtful actions and words between us to find peace. We said goodbye.

Upon returning to Seattle at the end of October I camped on the sofa bed in my brother and sister-in-law's family room. This time I thanked the generosity of Josh and Rosey for a roof over my head. I was at the all time emotional low of my life to date having chalked up another failed marriage and a failed business venture that destroyed a working business. I feared the creditors would hunt me down. And, I worried for how I'd keep all of this safely away from Zoey. I was challenged to continue forward and be my best for her.

I had no idea a few short weeks would bring Zoey to sleep next to me and to help return our bed to its sofa function each morning, that Eric would give me custody. But I would soon discover, as a few months rushed by in a blur, how it feels to free fall past peaks of joy then panic as the darkest valley depth fast approaches while grappling for the ripcord tangled between my head and my heart only to crash on a ledge in Dick Carville's office with no parachute at all. The bottom was yet to come. One must land to bounce back.

5: Purring Motor Meets Need-To-Be-Mom

Every weeknight and again on Sunday mornings I scanned the *Help Wanted* columns in the Seattle Times hoping to find a job. I needed one that didn't require an upscale career wardrobe or a late model car for I no longer owned either. Paul and I had both worn tee-shirts with our company name and logo screen-printed on the front and nice shorts to work each day. The few summery dresses and suits I'd brought with me from L. A. were adequate and seasonally correct in the Seattle sales rep position I worked for a mere five months prior to being laid off due to corporate restrategizing. But those clothes weren't suitable for Seattle's fall and winter.

Before leaving for Kauai I sold the little truck I had driven up from California and put just enough cash into savings to buy an inexpensive car on my return. Josh was good at helping me find cheap but reliable cars. He always steered me toward the one he wouldn't mind working on if necessary. This time it was an American made, small squared off wagon with a hatch-back. The prior owner had installed a moon-roof and being a soft golden yellow color Zoey was inspired to name it Sunbeam Moondancer. She liked our little car.

One evening, shortly after my return from Kauai, I thought Josh and Rosey might enjoy having the house to themselves after their three girls were in bed. Plus, I was feeling restless and bored. I had two good reasons to go out for some music. Different acquaintances Paul and I'd made in our jobs suggested Seattle bands we should see and the best clubs to take them in at. We had enjoyed checking out the Seattle scene a few times before Paul left for Kauai.

There were two clubs in downtown Seattle I particularly liked. They were close to the I-5 freeway and around the corner from one another: the Off Ramp and RKCNDY (rock candy). When the band in one club finished their set, it was a quick walk to see what was happening in the other.

It was at the Off Ramp that I first saw the Band I'm Not to Mention. A young woman that worked for a paint store in my sales territory had invited Paul and me to go with her saying we should definitely see this band as they had a hit song getting heavy rotation on MTV and were likely to be the next big band out of Seattle. She had the hots for the lead singer so I paid particular attention to his performance and understood the attraction. He had an unusual charisma and fun stage presence.

Paul introduced me to big hair rock and heavy metal in the 80's. It was quite a switch from the comparatively bland pop music, classic rock and light jazz that had been standard fare for Eric and me. Rolling from the likes of George Benson and Billy Joel to Motley Crue and Metallica was a dramatic yet welcome transition. Paul and I had frequented the clubs on Sunset in Hollywood checking out up and coming bands like Warrant, Ugly Kid Joe, and Red Hot Chili Peppers. In larger stadium and arena shows we took in Scorpions, Dokken, Van Halen, White Snake, Judas Priest, Megadeth, Guns-n-Roses, Aerosmith, and so many more.

At the top of the 90's Seattle Grunge made its way out of the Pacific Northwest. Our favorite radio station in Los Angeles, KNAC out of Long Beach, was playing Mother Lovebone (while lamenting the death of lead singer Andrew Wood), Nirvana, Alice in Chains, Soundgarden, and, later, Pearl Jam. By the time Paul and I hit Seattle in 1993 all of those big name bands were on major tours. We missed seeing them play in the clubs by a long shot, relocating to Seattle only in time to catch all the wannabes. And, there were still plenty of good bands playing in the clubs wanting to be the next big thing.

This midweek night in early November I picked the Off Ramp. I had no idea what band would be playing and didn't care. The Off Ramp was like a neighborhood bar on week nights. There seemed to be a regular crowd for people greeted each other and eased into conversation. I walked in the door a bit before 9PM to find the dozen or so tables and handful of booths in the front room sparsely populated, making it easy to see beyond the open space to the bar at the back. I glanced to my left to find the showroom was not yet lighted so sauntered back to the bar, happily hopped up on one of the two remaining stools, and ordered amber ale on tap.

As I sipped my brew I took in all activity surrounding me via the mirrored wall behind the bar. The front door opened and in walked a tall young guy in motorcycle leathers. He removed his helmet to reveal a mohawk like I'd never seen before. About a three inch wide strip of straight, silky and fine, near-black hair ran from his brow to his nape and falling past his shoulders. He set his helmet and jacket on the table of an empty booth then proceeded to strip off the leather pants. The lithe and lanky frame that emerged was sexy as they come. He gathered up his gear to then stash it in a small cubby-like area where a vertical post met a wall at the bar just behind me. Next he flashed his best feature at me, a gorgeous smile beaming warmth, good cheer, and just a titch of devilishness; and asked, "Did you like that?"

I laughed, "Could you tell?"

"You were looking pretty interested."

"I am," and I returned the smile. "That's quite a striking hairdo you're sporting and I'm thinking you've got to be hearty as hell to be riding a bike in this weather. My name's Beth," as I offered my hand, "Care to join me?"

"I'm Jay," as he took my hand, turned it and drew it to his lips while dropping his butt onto the stool next to me, "Glad to meet you." He smiled looking directly through the windows to my soul. I held his eyes in mine while thinking I had judged wrongly, that indeed those deep crystal blue pools were his finest feature.

Jay ordered a beer and we proceeded to play Get to Know You. We talked and laughed and talked and laughed some more. His mind turned me on as much as his body, eyes, and smile. Somewhere between comparing favorite bands, favorite books, and favorite pastimes came the topic of pot which was more than a pastime to Jay. Pot bordered religion with him. He said he had studied Rastafarianism and attempted to hold true to the course but that some of the practices were too stringent for him.

Sharing this information with me led to the topic of tattoos. To validate his passion for pot he stood and pulled up his tee-shirt. Centered on his rib cage and stomach there was a slender line drawing of a cannabis sativa plant, precisely as it would be depicted in a botanical journal. The top of the plant lay slightly below his collar bone and the roots dangled around his navel. I told him I've had thoughts of getting a tattoo but I can't think of what symbol means enough to me to permanently commit it to my body. And, where would I put it?

All of a sudden the house lights came up to bright indicating it was a few minutes to closing time. We hadn't even heard "Last call." Nor had we noticed that the Off Ramp was by then nearly full of people. He asked if I'd like to get together again, would I give him my number. I rummaged in my purse for a pen and scrap of paper then wrote down Josh's number. I reminded him that I'm temporarily living at my brother's home so he should know I might not be the one to answer the phone, that it might be one of my nieces.

We walked out of the Off Ramp together after he was zipped back into his leathers. It turned out his bike was parked by my front bumper. We laughed at the convenience as he placed his helmet on the seat. He then planted his hands on my shoulders, pulled me toward him, and covered my mouth with his. We kissed deeply with limbs wrapped so tightly around one another it felt we were fused. As we plunged further into the kiss, some people leaving the club began to cheer and applaud. When we opened our eyes and realized we were the subject of the enthusiasm we drew apart and laughed and the group laughed with us. Jay took a small bow and I curtsied, then a quick peck lips to lips. He put on his helmet and mounted his bike as I got in my car.

All the way home I thought about how much I looked forward to another one of those kisses and whatever else might follow. And, I looked forward to sharing the experience with Rosey. I knew she'd love it, a juicy story.

45

Just a couple days after meeting Jay, Zoey was with me at Josh and Rosey's for the weekend. On Saturday morning we watched cartoons with Zoey's two younger cousins. Later the four of us played Monopoly until Rosey told the girls to get their coats and boots on if they wanted to go to the store with her. Josh was in his hobby shop in the attic working on an airplane model, leaving me and Zoey in the house alone to our own devices for entertainment.

Zoey told me how much she wished she could come live with me when I got in my own apartment again. I asked her to write out a list of PRO's and CON's to that scenario, to seriously consider everything she might gain or lose by that move. Here's what she wrote:

"PRO'S:
1) We have a certain trust-love bond
2) We can talk about anything with no fear of each other's reactions
3) I'd be able to learn a more real-life way of having responsibilities for myself
4) Instead of starting a "clean slate" with no trust and building it, I'd start with complete trust
5) I'd have more freedom as in what is accepted for clothing - thrift shops
6) Likes and accepts my friends by who they are as a person not how they look, i.e. - nose rings, shaved heads, dyed hair, people's clothes
7) Doesn't put me down but still shares her feelings about me with me
8) We know how to have fun together and still be safe
9) Sunbeam / Moondancer
10) Doesn't think my music is shit - it's "the shit"
11) Doesn't get violent - tries to talk thru things
12) Doesn't have pointless power trips
13) Thinks of me as a person, a human -- not a possession or a "trainee"
14) We don't need to yell and argue to get the point of a conversation across
15) We are easy to please - cheap entertainment!

16) Knows tactics on how to "survive the wild" in an apartment
17) My pals like her
18) Mom's very logical, sensitive, and understanding
19) Willing to help me with things: school work, social problems, guy things, transportation
20) Tries hard to make me happy and herself too
21) Thinks about often and respects all those she loves
22) Loyal
23) Doesn't worry unnecessarily
24) More time with mom's side of the family

CON'S:

1) Dad would be on our butts like glue
2) Having to take care of all my own things even if half way - I'm not used to that
3) Won't have my own TV, phone, or maybe stereo or even room -sleep on couch- mattress on the floor, preferably
4) No fancy appliances - may have to do dishes by hand? laundromat?
5) I'd have to learn how to do laundry
6) Maybe no ski school or camp
7) May have to start making meals, learn to cook real food, work with mom's odd work hours
8) I'll miss my brother and my cat"

Zoey wrote the above list shortly before "The New Rules" were handed down.

November 1994: "The New Rules" per Eric

1) Beth can have Zoey with her on most any weekend she wishes provided that it's cleared through Eric at the office. All phone calls come to the office - not at home. Weekends run from Friday after school to Sunday at 8:00 p.m.
2) Beth won't call Zoey at the house and talk with Zoey during the week (Sunday night to Friday afternoon). Zoey won't call Beth.
3) Zoey's room must be clean when she leaves for the weekend OR Eric & Crystal will clean it to their satisfaction.
4) Rules at Eric & Crystal's may differ from those at Beth's, but the rules at Eric & Crystal's apply only while Zoey is at home. Beth's rules

apply at Beth's house. Eric & Crystal won't ask
Beth to enforce their rules. Beth won't ask Eric &
Crystal to enforce hers.

5) All clothes & jewelry etc. that are from Beth
stay at Beth's. If they come home, they are automatically trash. None of the clothes from home can
be modified.

6) Exceptions to the rules must be mutually
agreed upon - if not, this entire agreement is off
until Eric & Crystal decide it is back on.

7) Zoey must maintain a B average in all academic classes at school.

8) Only Beth can pick-up or drop-off Zoey from
orto home.

9) No dyed hair, piercings, or tattoos. No permanent changes.

10) Money earned with Eric & Crystal stays with
Eric & Crystal family.

December 5, 1994 - a letter from me

Eric, while going through miles of files recently, I
stumbled upon our divorce decree and the stipulation to
it. After reading them I feel compelled to discuss a couple
of things. Please read the attached copies, particularly the
highlighted areas.

I have gone along with you and Crystal straight down
the line; allowing you to control custody and visitation issues because as each occasion for discussion arose the
deviations from the decree and the stipulation that you
requested (or flat out stated, "This is how it will be.")
seemed to be at least as much for Zoey's welfare as it was
for yours. This is not the case with this new set of rules you
have handed down. I signed the silly thing with the statement, "We understand each other." In actuality, I can only
speak for myself. I understand that:

(A) You are indulging your NEED TO CONTROL on me
and Zoey, both.

(B) You and Crystal don't want any unnecessary contact with me. You don't concur with my recent suggestion
that we work on being a team in parenting Zoey.

(C) You are burnt out on whatever level of friction/
hassle in your household that is accountable to Zoey. So,
you have decided to continue to survey (and attempt to
control) her during the week then free up your weekends by

having me take her off your hands.

I have gone along with your New Rules thus far because I enjoy every minute I can have with Zoey. There is little to zero friction between her and me because we understand each other and respect each other. I love and appreciate most of the things about her that you would prefer to stifle. I digress. My point is that having Zoey every weekend at the present time is (and has been) difficult. When I am head of my own household we can reevaluate, however, for now we will need to adhere to the terms that we have set forth and agreed to in the Stipulation to the Divorce Decree. I have told Zoey that she would be with me this coming weekend; but, if you would like to check your calendar and give me a call regarding when you'd like to begin alternating weekends again I can certainly go either way. I will be reachable only in the evening for a while as I begin a new job tomorrow.

Additionally, I am requesting that you remove the telephone ban. I will not call your house to chat with Zoey but there are times I need to communicate with her or with you outside of your office hours. The key thing is that Zoey be able to call me when she has the desire to do so.   Beth

December 7, 1994 – Eric's reply:

Beth, since you've chosen to communicate with me in written form, I'll respond in same. I'll respond to the issues you raise, in the order you've raised them, and then raise a few of my own. I presume you have a copy of your letter. . . You are absolutely correct in asserting that I am in control of the visitation and custody of Zoey. And, you are again correct in recognizing that Zoey's best interest is the basis of my decisions. We disagree the "new" set of rules is no longer in Zoey's best interest. I think we do understand each other,

A.) I don't have an inherent "need" to control Zoey, despite what you and/or she may think. I don't care what you do. I do care what you do with Zoey, but per our understanding, I gave up the controls that I have in the past tried to levy on you both. I agreed to this because the controls didn't work, You did what you wanted to do anyway and it put an unfair responsibility on Zoey to try to deceive or withhold information from me.

B.) Based on weeks, months, and years of history,

you and I are not, have not, and most likely will not be a "team" in parenting Zoey. A team does things the same way to achieve an objective. You and I disagree on parenting styles, methods, and objectives. It is exactly for this reason that the new set of "rules" created an understanding that when Zoey was with me my rules applied, and when she was with you your rules applied. When the captains of the team are playing with different rules, the players get confused, get mixed signals, and seldom win the game. I wish that you and I operated under more similar sets of rules, but the fact is that we don't. While I recognize that we have different sets of rules, I agreed per our "understanding", to stay out of your life when Zoey is with you and you are to do the same when Zoey is with me. My opinion is that Zoey has and will suffer as a result of this dilemma.

C.) I have been under the impression since you've moved back this time that you wanted to have Zoey as much as possible, and that you and I were having a problem because I was hesitant to let you have her as often as you would like. Again, per the new understanding, you could have her as often as every weekend, but were not obligated in any way to take her every weekend. I thought that this was made clear at the time of the understanding. This was never a "take her off my hands" kind of arrangement. Yes, I do continue to try to keep close tabs on what she does during the week, and I'm quite certain that like any teenager her age, there is probably a lot that goes by without my knowledge. Regardless, I have a duty to try to not bury my head in the sand, and hope that all will work out OK.

I'm glad that you enjoy your time with Zoey, and I am clearly aware that you and Zoey see things in much the same way. This is probably why you have so little friction. From my point of view, this isn't such a proud position to find yourself. I do not want to stifle positive things in Zoey's personality, but I can identify several areas that need some work, or some might say, some discipline, some strong parenting, some guidance, and yes even some control.

I am so tired of you telling me what I am and am not, when you have been so completely irresponsible in doing your part over the last 10 years. I'm not really very sympathetic when you say it is so difficult to take Zoey...what is it... three weekends in a row???? When you are head of your household, when you get your next job, when you get settled.... when you this.... when you that.... when you....I'll have to owe you....etc. etc. etc. when will you wake up and realize that you are 40 and not 14? You have a responsibility to Zoey, and to a lesser degree, to me. Zoey will always be your daughter, but I've been the one to accept responsibility for her. It's not an opinion, it's not judgmental, it's just fact.

When and if you are ready to be a Partner in raising Zoey, I'll treat you as a team member. When is the last time you bought a lunch ticket, an ASB card, a yearbook, a pair of contacts, a health insurance premium, a ski lift ticket, a set of sheets for her bed, paid a dentist bill, a doctor bill, had the vice principal call you, the last time you were lied to straight to your face, on and on ad nauseum.

My point is that I can't control you or your actions. I can't really control Zoey very much either. But I am responsible for virtually every other aspect of her day to day living. For those things that I don't absolutely have responsibility for, I feel some responsibility for, and at the very least a duty to set as good an example as I can.

As far as the divorce decree, I've never interfered with YOUR "social development" in any way, or your relationship with Zoey. On the contrary, it is clear to me that Zoey has a very high affection for you. An argument could be made that YOU have been having conversations with Zoey that could be "frustrating" Zoey's and my relationship. If the test of this concept is the "feeling of affection" between parents, it seems that Zoey's affection for me is at an all time low over the last several weeks.

I'm happy to alternate weekends, at your pleasure. Just call me by Thursday night. My position on the phone is unchanged. Per our conversation at Thanksgiving, I expect Zoey to be with me on Christmas Eve. If you want to celebrate Christmas with her, she can leave after school Friday, and she needs to be back at my house by 4:00pm Saturday.

we have never been a team raising Zoey. When it has been convenient for you, or inconvenient for you, it becomes an issue. Strangely enough, this time it's difficult because every weekend is too much. In a few more years, you'll be able to look back and wish things had been different, but in the final analysis it won't have been my fault. I know that you feel that there are reasons, circumstances, excuses, and conditions but it just doesn't matter to me whether you think I'm fair or not.   Eric

With his letter he enclosed a copy of the results of a test that Zoey was given nearing six years of age, to see if she qualified for the First Grade Challenge Program. It reported that she has a DIQ of 131, placing her in the 97th Percentile, and expounded:

". . .approximately 2% will obtain DIQs above 132; 14% will obtain DIQs between 116 and 132. . ."

He clipped a note to it: "This is why C's are not acceptable."

Journal: December 26, 1994

I can't believe what a mind boggling whirlwind the past two and a half weeks have been. Zoey is here with me, in OUR apartment. Wow! Where do I begin? I started my new job on December 6th. I have not worked for money this low in over ten years. But, at least it's something until I can get a real job. The bright side is I don't need to dress for success or commute.

Eric called me at work in the afternoon of Friday the 9th to tell me to stop by his office on my way home to get Zoey. He informed, "She is coming to live with you now." Those are the words I've wanted to hear for so-o-o fucking long but, geez, the circumstances suck. They had a knock down drag out fight at his office over Zoey's interim Grade Report. He had her locked in the bathroom. She obviously had been crying her eyes out.

When we got in the car she handed me a note she'd written to me on a trail of toilet paper! God, thank you for bringing her to me at last! We put the office scene behind us fast and moved forward with jubilation for the gift that we are now together. In fact, the three of us—Zoey, her Auntie Rosey and me—were reminiscent of the little munchkins in Wizard of Oz singing "Ding Dong, the witch is dead..."

Rosey had a Visa card that Josh didn't know about. She took out a cash advance on it to loan to me for use as deposit and first month's rent. Thank God, I found a place in Zoey's school district that's on my way to work and is dirt cheap. It's cheesy, but I should be able to make rent, even while giving one hundred dollars a month to Rosey on the loan. Amazingly enough, the guy wanted it rented before Christmas. With Josh's help, he is the best brother, we emptied my storage unit and Zoey and I were moved in on Saturday the 17th.

Josh, Rosey, and my sweet nieces were great putting up with me and Zoey sleeping on the sofa bed in the family room and vying for bathroom time for a whole week on top of me having already been there for a month and a half! Fuckin' Eric! He knows I have no money, reeling in the financial devastation of Sundogz and my looming divorce from Paul, that I'm less than a month into a new job and sleeping on my bro's couch. He decides to now make my dream come true, to give me Zoey. God knows I'm not complaining. I'm just saying. . . sheesh.

Last night Zoey was calling everyone she knows it seems, to inform them of the fact that she and I are together in our own place. It was so cool. She was so excited, not that I wasn't! But, she was so cute going on with her friends. Being Christmas Day night, they all seemed to have time on their hands and Zoey kept asking "Is it okay if so-and-so comes over?" It started out with just a handful of kids coming over but, the next thing you know, we had a pretty big party going. There were a bunch of kids I met for the first time, from freshmen up to seniors, as well as the ones I already know and love. At one point, I went to the bathroom and smelled pot smoke coming out of Zoey's room. So I checked in to see what-the-hell? I decided to let it slide. It was too happy an occasion to have conflict. Everyone was obviously having a mellow good time. It was cool. Zoey looked to be in seventh heaven and I suppose I did too.

Lonni, along with a couple suitcases and boxes, is moving in with me and Zoey this week. She and her hub are splitting and she really needs to be in a space away but preferably not all alone. WOW! I haven't talked about Lonni. She and I clicked immediately. I share an office with Lonni at my new job. Our employers, a husband/wife team, own a company that distribute the baseball and golf caps manufactured in his family's factory in China. Lonni and I each make a minimum of fifty outbound phone calls per day to advertising specialty companies across the U.S. to promote our line of caps and custom logo embroidery services and scrambling for sales.

Thinking about the first day of work makes me think of my birthday weekend. Friday December 2nd, right after picking Zoey up after school, she and I took off for Portland to go see May, who I met in Kauai while on my fruitless put-it-back-together-with-Paul quest. Damn mmm that makes me think of that little hot-stuff, Max—friend of May, Julie and the gang on Kauai—who turned my motor back on. Nothing like hanging out and playing with eighteen to twenty-four year old kids to snap me back to life! After two years of being Paul's teddybearblanket with no sex included, Max got my motor purring again.

Back to the Portland trip, Saturday night we three girls went to an 18-and-over club called LaLuna to see the band Jesus Lizard. They let Zoey in since she was with her mom. It was such a good time! May was not imbibing in smoke but had one beer. I let Zoey have one beer also thinking what the hell, it was the night before my 40th Birthday! I smoked enough weed for both me and May, who was driving, and we squirreled around downtown Portland, going back and forth over the network of bridges that cross the rivers. Ultimately, we found LaLuna and had a great time. The band lived up to their reputation and Zoey loved it.

Zoey and I headed home around noon on Sunday. It was a mellow and fun road trip. We took turns being "DJ" alternately playing our choice of CD's in the player all the way to Seattle.

After I took her back to her Dad's, I went down to spend the night with Jay, which is why I told my new boss I'd start on Tuesday the 6th. Jay has Mondays off and I wanted Monday morning to chill with him, not to have to dash forty miles to Everett by 6AM from the south end of Seattle when I'd just turned forty years old. Gotta sleep. I am beat.

Journal: December 28. 1994

I started reading the book Jay brought over last week and got caught up in it. It's about "the hemp and marijuana conspiracy." The book is called *The Emperor Wears No Clothes* and was written by Jack Herer. Now I understand why Jay brought it over. The history of how and why pot came to be illegal is dense; far more than can be communicated in casual conversation. I had no idea hemp has so many industrial uses, that any petroleum based product can be made with hemp seed oil. In fact I didn't really know much about hemp at all. It's bizarre that the American people bought in on all the corporate and governmental propaganda for demonizing marijuana so that the cannabis species could be deemed illegal thereby keeping hemp goods—like fabric, paper, fuel, building materials, and even super healthy food products—from competing in the marketplace. What a crock.

6: Freefalling

Dear Jay, since I'm not certain if I'm writing these words for your benefit or mine, I'm writing in my journal for future reference—so that I can pick up my journal when I'm feeling weak and say to myself, "See, you already learned this. You don't need to go here again." Jay, I'm going to tell you something you can learn from being acquainted with me. It's pretty universal but I think it becomes more apparent with experience, years ... age. Here's a little tip you can take now should you choose to benefit from my years of experience. But first, let me tell you what I really learned because I didn't express it correctly when we were talking on the phone. I learned that I can't handle a for-sex-only relationship. If I could I might as well be a call girl and make bucks at it. I can definitely handle a for-friends-only relationship with a man but, for me, sex wouldn't enter into it. If you're having great sex and you're great friends you have a firm foundation for a lasting, loving relationship. This is something I want but keep telling myself I don't need and don't want to be open to because of the potential for pain.

11ᴀᴍ (home for lunch now) Jay, you told me you're interested in older women because they tend to be more self-assured. The continual practice of assuring self falls into the category of attitude maintenance. I know these things to be true of me: reasonably attractive, in relatively good shape for a woman my age, intelligent, good sense of humor (though sometimes a little too sensitive), a good and kind person. I believe these could be considered appreciable attributes.

In the times we had together, not once did you say to me, "You look great tonight, Beth" or "You feel good" or "I'm glad you're here, thanks for coming." I don't believe there is one human being on Earth who can honestly say they don't

56

like to be appreciated. So, here's your tip: when you meet up with your older, self-assured woman who is happy with a for-sex-only relationship, appreciate her. She will expect it. This ties in with my statement that a relationship with a younger man seems like self-destructive behavior. I wake up now and thank God for another day of living. You appreciate more as you go along. It is self-destructive to put myself in a position where I wake up in the morning and worry about how puffy my eyes are or if my laugh lines are deeply pressed in. Do I look old? This is what is. I shouldn't be feeling insecure about it. Why am I drawn to younger men then? I love raw energy, rebelliousness, lack of inhibition, and so much that comes with them. Why did I get so sprung over you, Jay? Because the more time I spent with you the more I saw in you all that I love.

5ish pm (home from work now) A key point is that I can draw on my vocabulary and you know what the hell I'm saying. I cherish intelligence. I appreciate you're searching spiritually - not quite as good as being spiritually grounded, but at least you're seeking a path. Ha! I can't believe my tone! Who appointed me Goddess of Grounded? You turn me on totally not just sexually, although you do a fine job of that too. Okay, so it seems to me you didn't even really want to be friends. Friends communicate. I asked to hear about the "complexities" you claimed to be in your life and you gave me a bullshit answer. Instead of telling me about what was going on with you the night of the Rolling Stones concert, you just "took it out on" me. Have you got some big hairy skeleton hanging at the back of your closet that you're afraid for me to know about? Or, what? Things and issues don't scare me.

Hurting scares the hell out of me. I just really have no capacity to hurt right now. In that sense I'm a little fragile. But, now, as I think all of this through and write it out, I'm feeling much freer and stronger. And I'm still monstrously attracted to you. So what is it with you? Do you have super high hurt barriers up based on some past experience? Do you just find emotional investment in me to be a wasted effort because of our age difference? Or does my discovery that I don't make a good fuck buddy just screw up what could have been a good thing from your point of view? Actually my discovery rather disappoints me. It's such an uncomplicated viewpoint - so seemingly effortless. Emotional investment requires effort but I am too much of a lover to detach emotion from sex. I love to love and be loved. I have a lot to give, but I've learned that paradox: if giving your heart, get one in return. When I called you yesterday morning all of my words were fear based. I'm not feeling so skitchy now. Perhaps I was a bit hasty in not giving you a chance to say anything. If you'd like to be friends (platonic) I'm up for that because I think you are a hell of a lot of fun. If you are open to being loved and willing to be responsible to it I'm up for that too. If neither of those works for you then I guess it is goodbye. With love,   Beth

On another note: I finally made my first sale today! Yes! 1,600 caps = $4,600+ sale!

Journal: January 21, 1995

It was such a phenomenal day yesterday. Magical. Sunshiny! Mountains gleaming all around. Cruised straight to the bubbles in K-Mart and through check-out in two minutes max! On the way to Jay's God was smiling on me, Zoey, and Lonni in a big way. The state patrol officer who pulled me over saw most of what occurred that found us suddenly accelerated to 93MPH in fairly thick traffic on I-5 southbound. So, when she saw how genuinely panicked I was and I filled her in on what she hadn't seen, she was so cool! No ticket! And, no wreck! What's with people who ignore merging traffic? I don't get it.

We went to the Pike Place Market and bought a very little rhino Zoey wanted, put a down payment on the faery I must have, raised a little havoc in Pipe Palace, and then blew bubbles onto Western Avenue from the Market Mezzanine stairwell. We relocated to Myrtle Edwards Park and blew bubbles into the sunset across Elliott Bay to the Olympics while watching the last golden glimmer go down. We listened to "Pan Man" play his centaur's flute as the sun sank into the mountains behind him. Got home with new smoking tools to assemble and a pizza; thinking to stay home and chill but, NO. Rorschach Test was playing at The Colourbox in Pioneer Square. It was packed. I got more bruises but that's the risk one takes hopping into a mosh pit!

Journal: January 23, 1995

Fuckin-A I say fuck a lot lately! How fucked up is that? When I first started hanging out with Jay I was pretty taken back by his extensive conjugation and use of the word - seems every other sentence contained a form of it. I mentally winced at the profusion. But, the more I've heard it in all its multiple uses, the more I've assimilated it. What the fuck? Haha – I just got a clip on Mom, the first time I heard her use The F word. It was the day I took the cab from the airport so I could surprise her – coming home from Alaska to stay finally. I had barely arrived. We were in the kitchen hugging and gabbing a million miles a minute when loud barking outside the window caused her to fly out the door I had just entered shouting, "Stop it, Lady! Fucking dog! Leave my squirrels alone!" The neighbor's terrier backed away from the tree housing the platform where Mom laid out nuts for the squirrels and dashed home. I was in such shock to hear Mom say "fuck" I busted a gut. When she came back in I had to tell her why I was laughing and she started to laugh too. Between sniggles and snorts I pointed out the irony in first hearing her use of fuck aimed at a dog, Mom—the ultimate lover of canine kind. We laughed 'til we gasped. It was in that moment that I became an adult in her reality. She laid down her Mom role and we were just people.

Journal: January 24, 1995

Jay - I'm sorry I've been so self-centered about MY needs, MY fears of being hurt. Maybe if I had seemed like I had the capacity to be a friend to you, you would have been more willing to share more openly all that was going on with you so that I could have been a better friend to you. Maybe. B.

Journal: January 28, 1995 Saturday

THANK YOU, GOD, FOR WAKING ME UP TODAY! Aaargh! I can't believe it. My right pupil is dilated about forty percent larger than my left one, following a severe blow to the head. Gee, what could that mean? Fuck! After talking with Zoey and Lonni, filling in the gaps between what I remember, I feel so lucky I woke up. Lonni and I got home from the big trade show in Dallas at about 11pm Thursday. We had a great time but that's entirely another story. We did learn that Deep Ellum in Dallas is nothing like Seattle's rock scene. So, last night we were feeling like getting out for a little mosh and who should be playing at Jimmy Z but Sweaty Nipples? Neither Lonni or I had seen them and that seemed almost criminal since they're practically an institution in the NW music scene.

We smoked a bowl on the way to Everett and just caught a buzz, nothing major. The place was packed except for the dance floor. There was only a handful of the burliest, sweatiest, naked-from-the-waist-up type moshers tearing it up. As we were thirsting for a good bounce-n-whirl, we decided to check it out any way, not to be intimidated by a dozen or so gnarly, muscle-bound, sweat-balls. I had a really good bounce-n-whirl across the floor through the middle, with only a passing nudge to some guy. I landed on the other side, was barely becoming still and catching a breath when some guy (the one I nudged?) landed behind me and shoved me with such force that in a split second—I mean in the blink of an eye!—I'd flown probably fifteen feet through the air, landing on my knees with my head bashing the corner of the speaker! GOD! I saw stars! I was all twirly when I stood up. The guy I had originally landed next to, having exited the pit unscathed, dashed over to see if I was okay. I told him I was and went to look for Lonni. We stayed until the music was over. I had a third beer.

This is where Lonni's account adds to the picture for me. She told me I seemed okay until we got on I-5 South. I insisted she was going the wrong way; so much so that she got off the freeway, looped over it and got back on going the other direction. As we passed a couple signs for Everett exits I realized she was right. We were now headed north; spooky. Having placated me, she hit the off ramp again and got back on the freeway homebound. I passed out asleep in the car. Lonni said when we arrived home she went inside for Zoey to help get me up the stairs. I get clips of them, one on each arm, supporting me, half carrying me up to our apartment. They tell me the moment they dropped me on my bed I was out again. They undressed me and tucked me in. Thanks, God, for waking me up this morning! WOW!

So, here I am with a concussion. This is not a good thing. Lonni and Zoey think I should go to a doctor. But what's the point? That'll take cash I don't have or choose to spare on it when I know he's just going to confirm what I already know by experience. I have a bruised brain. There is nothing they can do for it. When it heals, it heals. Until then, I just need to take care of myself and remember my brain is injured. Based on experience, I better reduce my pot intake dramatically. Ha! I can *just say no* to the kids. I must and I will.

Journal: February 22, 1995 Wed. eve

Well, this Jay thing is drawn to a close as of this evening I believe. Seems funny that just Saturday when Lonni, Zoey and I stopped by to see him at work Jay came out of the kitchen and sat and visited with us at our booth three times. It was nice. It's so weird. It's like I was nothing to Jay and yet very much something. I can be certain of absolutely nothing when it comes to Jay. What was all that?   Gotta go to sleep.

Journal: March 2, 1995

Stapled to the page: photocopy of a greeting card bearing a photo of a smiling pig wearing cow-head slippers on every hoof and the caption - "Moo-shoe pork". I thought moo-shoe pork would nicely compliment friendly dog salad. Inside and flowing onto the back of the card I hand wrote: No, no...thank you! So very much! You guys are too much! Hi! I'm Beth who you guys thanked on the inside cover of the red "Friendly Dog Salad" CD that Susan, from your label, asked you to sign at RCKNDY last Saturday, the 25th. I hope you heard me yell "Thank you!" through a split in the roar of the crowd a couple of times. Black Happy is such a special band to me! And you all come across as special people - warm! The vibe at your shows is so loving and peaceful, even in all the bouncing and grand rowdiness we love so much.

You guys were three BIG firsts for me. The first time I saw and heard you was at the Mural Wall at the Bite of Seattle a couple of summers ago. The sun broke through just for Black Happy and your fans. I'll never forget the happy, fun feeling in the crowd. I moshed for the first time, after years of being an "on-the-side, push-'em-back-in" kind of spectator in the clubs on Sunset in Hollywood. And, it was solely due to chasing after my, then, twelve year old daughter who hopped into the pit against my orders. Having no choice but to bounce with the crowd in order to get through it to her, instant addict, gotta bounce.

Many shows later, New Year's Eve '95 at Under the Rail, I first crowd surfed to your music. My friend, Lonni, went straight from first mosh to stage diving that night! The photo with two ladies is me and Lonni right before leaving for the show. Then, on February 4th at the King Performance Center, Zoey-my daughter, two of her friends, and I all followed Lonni's example. What a fun dancing time! ALL of our 1st stage dive! The other photo is just before leaving for that show.

Most recently, at your *Last Ever Show*, you may have noticed me in the chopped Crossbone River t-shirt momentarily stuck in front of your monitor with a stage angel on each arm. I was the one that the crowd held up for the longest time on fully extended arms right up by the stage. I'm just now coming off the hum, the sensation that created.

What a chronicle! Thank you all. We've had some great times together and have not even met. I hope that will be remedied. Please keep us posted as to when you'll be playing out again. We'd love to come see you and support your new projects. Or, if you're ever in the area and feeling up for anything, give us a call. My CD is such a treasure. God bless. Love, peace and happiness to you all, Beth

PS – The Friendly Dog Salad CD cover design has been cause for such much laughter in my house. So cool.

<u>Journal March 3, 1995</u>

Writing to Black Happy about my first moshing experience within two sentences does not do the scene justice. It's not one I'll ever forget. Paul, Zoey and I were at The Bite of Seattle at the Seattle Center. We were at the Mural Wall waiting in a throng of people for the next band to start when Paul said he was going to the beer garden and would be back shortly. Right after he wandered away the band started to play some fun upbeat music.

Zoey pleaded, "Come on, Mom. Let's move up closer to the band."

"A little closer but stick with me. I want to hang back from the mosh pit," I told her. There was a human wall a few dozen bodies deep amassed around the stage. All were pogo-ing shoulder to shoulder in time with the happy pulse of punk meets reggae with brass. Zoey didn't hold back long. She deftly wove through the thin layer of observers standing between us and those bouncing big until she was bouncing tight in the thick of it. The only way to catch her without being trounced was to bounce and advance simultaneously. By the time I could grab her arm I was panicked and pissed. But the sun glinting off that silky blond hair as it whipped around was no match for the sunshine in the smile that followed.

"Come on, Mom. This is fun," Zoey shouted over horns layered on fuzz-box laden guitars and voices harmonizing about a three day weekend. "Mom, lighten up," she added when she saw my squinched face behind her. "Come and dance. We're just dancing."

A tribal tattooed tricep and elbow came at Zoey's face but she threw up a quick block and gave a friendly shove, her arm then continuing around to encircle my shoulder. A salty wet, naked-from-the-waste-up mosher emerged from the heart of the pit with a black tire boot tread imprinted on his face. He was grinning like a corsaged kid at prom. We both exploded into laughter. Bounce, bounce, bounce all the way to the end of the set.

"Mom, was that cool?"

"Yeah, that was fun."

"Hey, can I get one of those?" as a sopping wet Black Happy tee shirt passed by, "Quick, look at the back."

It read *The geek shall inherit the earth.* I had to laugh then conceded, "Only if I can borrow it."

Journal March 12, 1995 - 10:30pm Sunday

I don't know what last Sunday was about with Jay. He was being sweet and actually trying to be friend-like. For some unknown reason he wants to stay in contact with me. I imagine after meeting with him yesterday that he wants to stay in touch with me via bud so he can continue to skim off the top of everything I get. Also, maybe to keep the connection open in case something goes haywire with him and his girlfriend-roommate. I hope to set up a reliable north end herb person so I won't need to see Jay anymore. On Thursday night I invited him and his girlfriend to our party. He declined saying he had to work at 6AM next day. I feel I've done all I need to do for the care of my karma in this situation. It's time to quietly bail out without closing any doors or burning any bridges.

I finally got it together with the manager of the Off Ramp. I went home with him last night. We walked from the street where I parked to his apartment and stopped along the way at his neighbor's to hop in on the tail end of their 70's party. It was fun. We didn't get to his place until probably 4:30AM or so. He gave me a big t-shirt and left the room so I could undress. I crawled in bed, planning to go to sleep, but he kept touching and hugging and smooching on me. We both came twice without having intercourse. It was very sensual. (I was in heavy flow mode so was not about to for the first time and he was very cool with that.) He says he's thirty-four and commented something to the affect that I am the older woman doing the younger man. Ha! If he only knew he is one of the two men that I've been with in the last nearly ten years whose double digit age started with a number higher than two.

Journal: March 13, 1995

Now that I am becoming fairly regular about writing in my journal - thanks to Jay - I think I should cover a broader range of topics than the men in my life and the clubs I get out to for bands and shows. Wow! It's 11PM! 4:30 is coming fast! Gotta go. Thank you, God, for my many blessings - for seeing me through another day. Thank you for getting Zoey to me. Please help me to be strong and patient and loving.

Journal: March 23, 1995

I'm feeling so lost, so out of touch with God and faith that it all works out. I can't really get into it now but so wish for warm, masculine arms to be around me all night. I feel so isolated. What parent can I possibly talk to about what's going on?

Posted on the wall between the kitchen and living room:

Rules for Going Out - Beginning TODAY March 30, 1995

[1] Inform Mom of where you're going, how you're getting there and with whom. Mom has veto power. All points are subject to approval.

[2] Curfew will be established (based on company and activity) prior to going out.. . .to be continued

IF YOU WANT TO GO OUT
the Overall Rules, House/Chore Rules, and
the Phone Rules must have been adhered to all week.

Overall Rules:

[1] Mom rules. Don't BS her. Stay out of Mom's room!
. . .to be continued

House/Chore Rules:

Every day, NO PHONE until the following are finished:

[1] Do the dishes - whatever needs to be done, do it - load the dishwasher, unload the dishwasher, wipe down counters and stove, whatever. Just do it.

[2] Pick up the living room. Put anything belonging to me by my door. Make sure your room is tidy. Get your bathroom stuff into the basket in your room. Wipe down the bathroom counter. Do homework. ...to be continued

Journal: April Fools 1995

Shit! I wish the $93.86 plumbing bill handed to me today for unclogging the toilet was an April Fools Day joke. I wish the whole nightmare of last night was a bad joke. Things are getting so fucking out of control! It's getting scary, God. Fact is, I'm out-of-control as much as the kids are. So, what can I expect?

On one hand I knew I should have stayed home last night. But, on the other hand, I was afraid to! I could see the handwriting on the wall, that it was going to get out of control. So instead of staying home, being firm, and not allowing things to get out of control, it seemed to make more sense to leave and let it run its course. That way I could supposedly have no knowledge of it and therefore, not be responsible to it. I can't handle all the conflict with Zoey. I don't know how to handle it.

I told Zoey on Monday she could have a few girlfriends stay over on Friday night to celebrate a fifteenth birthday. Lonni and I were going out with Susan that we met at that Black Happy show. She was coming here so we could all go in one car.

While waiting for Susan to arrive, kids that weren't on the invitation list started to arrive. Some were kids I'd never even seen before. When I greeted them at the door and told them, "There is no party," they looked at me like

"Who in the hell are you?" Zoey was arguing with me, demanding they could come in. She was on edge and getting in my face so I told them they could stay until I left. Then they would have to go also.

Susan arrived. So, I started rounding up kids and ushering them to the door despite too much fucking resistance! It turned into quite a scene. It also became clear that word had gotten out there was a party at Zoey's place tonight because there was an electric-like energy in all the girls, that anticipatory kind of buzz. Zoey was acting so cocky, like Queen of the Rodeo or Ringmaster. She was not surprised to see all these different people showing up. More kids, for me to turn away, walked in our door before Lonni, Susan and I could leave on the heels of the kids I had just un-invited.

It went through my head that I better stay home. Instead, I reiterated to Zoey that there must be no more than six girls in the apartment for the night; and, we left anyway. Just before we got to the freeway I asked Lonni to turn around and go back. I ran up the stairs and, sure as shit, all the kids I'd just thrown out and more were filling up the place. Zoey looked at me almost menacingly. I took her aside and told her, "This is bullshit!"

She started getting real snotty with me. As her voice rose, the birthday girl came over to level the situation and assure me that it was cool, that there wouldn't be any trouble. I threw up my hands and left.

When Lonni and I got home at about 2AM, every light in the house was on. Every window was open. Five or six cases of empty beer bottles and a big black garbage sack full of empty beer cans were stashed behind the front door in the recycling-center-hold. The carpet had obviously been freshly vacuumed. Ashtrays were emptied, tables wiped down and the place was as tidy as ever. Zoey and Rosey were sitting at the kitchen bar talking.

When the cops showed up at about midnight (in response to a neighbor's call) to break up the party they had asked Zoey, "Who and where is the responsible adult of the household?" She told them her mom was out for the evening. They told her they'd stay until I got home unless she knew an adult to call who would come over to supervise the situation.

She told them, "Call my Auntie Rosey."

Both Zoey and Rosey were smiling and bubbly as they recounted to me the evening's events, acting like it was cool, not a big, bad deal. It sounds like *The Party of the Year* happened at our apartment last night. And, it seems that due to this, Zoey has attained some level of celebrity, which she is presently reveling in! What next?

I assume that the woman in the four-plex next to ours is the one who called the cops because she made a point of calling me this morning to be sure I was aware of what had gone down. She informed me that she'd counted over seventy kids filing out of our apartment last night when the cops came to break it up. I'm amazed seventy people could fit in here! Well, I guess if you count standing space on the sun deck. . . .wow. It looks like they all tried to cram into the bathroom at the same time because the shower curtain is ripped off three or four of the rings, the poster hanging in there is torn, and God knows what they tried to cram down the toilet or what fell in. The plumber couldn't tell but said it was tough to snake through—*ninety-four dollars* worth of tough! Someone stole the watch Mom and Dad gave me for Christmas.

A card to me from Zoey:

"BIRTHDAYS KEEP COMING WHETHER YOU LIKE IT OR NOT. THERE'S NOTHING YOU CAN DO TO STOP THEM."

Written in Zoey's hand, added to the front:

I know it's not your birthday, but this card is wonderful!

Text inside:

"KINDA LIKE WHEN THE TOILET STARTS TO OVERFLOW BUT YOU'RE NOT SURE SO YOU WATCH IT FOR A WHILE, THEN YOU SEE IT'S NOT GOING DOWN, SO YOU DROP TO THE FLOOR TO TWIST THE WATER VALVE BUT IT'S STUCK AND THE WA-TER LEVEL KEEPS RISING AND YOU KEEP TRYING TO TURN THE VALVE BUT IT WON'T BUDGE, SO YOU RUN TO FIND A WRENCH AND THE WATER BEGINS TO POUR OVER THE BOWL ONTO THE FLOOR . . ."

And Zoey, inside left and flowing onto the back:

Mom . . . ironic it seems to me that I come home to find your note, because I got this card to kinda say I'm sorry. I really truthfully honestly don't know why I went on like that. I realize it was un-called-for. I guess I was just being snotty because I had been waiting for my ride to come, and I was ready to leave. I don't mean to be snotty, but I feel awful when you do that to my friends, because in Melinda's words, "Oh, it's okay, she just makes me feel like shit when she does that." I realize you're concerned and just looking out for my friends, but you're my parent and not theirs. You did the same thing to John that one time. He said the same thing Melinda did. And don't take this as being rude - but you're my (and only my) mom. Don't parent my friends. I'm sure they get enough of that at home. It's their trouble. Let them handle it. I'll keep myself out of the bad situations on my own, and so will they. I love you, so don't think I don't, okay? And I'm sorry I've been being the bitch (actually, we both play our parts). I think I should thank you for putting up with me. I know I've given you a lot of stress, but I still have a lot of shit of my own I gotta sort out.

I love you, okay? ♥ Zoey

Journal: April 14, 1995

Well, well, well! Quite a few notable occasions since last writing! Had a meeting with Zoey, her counselor, all of her teachers, Eric and I, plus the vice principal, who called us all together. Zoey is flunking three classes, marginally getting by in the others, and has a full page listing of tardies and absences. Of course, I knew nothing about this until the meeting because Zoey has snagged the notices they've mailed out of the mailbox before I got home from work. I have told her that she must average the semester out to a 2.5 GPA, no more absences or tardies. If not, she can rerun ninth grade in a new school.

Lonni couldn't take it anymore. It was getting too crazy for her so she moved into a spare room in the home of another of our coworkers and her husband.

Night before last, I went to get a stash from Jay. Among lots of comfortable talking, laughing, and toking, he says to me something like, "Beth, you know I find you attractive. You still turn me on."

I said "You still turn me on, Jay."

He replied, more or less, "Well that's all good so long as we're on the level..." I know I had a question-mark look on my face mixed with a bit of disbelief as in 'Like I wasn't?' And he goes, "No. . . no, that's not what I mean".

I suggested, "You mean so long as we're both in the same place with it."

"Yeah! That's it exactly!"

Journal April 18, 1995 Tuesday 5:20am

The above entry was preempted by a small party (under twenty kids) that spontaneously came together here at the house, all with my approval though. It was fun.

So, to continue, Saturday morning Zoey, her friend, Ginger, and I went downtown to Westlake Center Ticketmaster to buy End It tickets—Beastie Boys et al at Kitsap County Fairgrounds, Monday May 29th. Then we went to the Hurricane Café to flash all six of them at Jay and let him know that one is still available. He juggled eggs for us and begged his boss for the day off (to no avail). I gave him a cool "Woodchuck" brushed cotton cap saying "You can take this as one of two things at your option, a present or a trade for some of your home-brewed extra pale cranberry ale." After a bit we left for Green Lake and I skated a quick lap while the girls. . .?... hung out. Then Zoey and I went to Mom and Dad's for Easter.

Same day - 4/18 Last night I had Zoey spend the night with Ginger in hopes of bringing Jay home with me but, NO. All I brought home was a bag and the feeling that he's playing with me again. I cannot begin to guess what pleasure he derives from keeping me on a string. It surely can't be just to keep my business. No, it must be an ego feed of some sort. I just spent the last ten minutes with my eyes closed viewing body-tingling fantasies. Yikes! whew Need to get horizontal. Now. Does he know that I think of him constantly? Nah. But he probably suspects it, just not to what degree I suppose. I need to either be with him and get into it with him both verbally and physically or distance myself dramatically.

Notes to myself on a page from the phone message pad following a call from Ms. G, Zoey's stress management group counselor at school:

★ Zoey missed group 2nd Period Tues. 4/18 ★
Appointment: 2PM May 4th Thurs with Arla for assessment
60 day Intensive In-Patient Program

★ Lakeside Rehab Center - Lake City ★
★ Girls and Boys kept separate ★ 6 months after care ★
★ Ms. G. referred ★

Journal: May 1, 1995

Happy May Day! Right. It's not a happy day when I know my daughter is in trouble but I feel powerless to do anything about it. I called Lakeside today to cancel her assessment appointment. I have no way of paying for Zoey to go into a 60-day treatment program. I sure as hell can't talk to Eric about it. He's not only NOT going to help but he'll want her back. She would feel so betrayed. I can't do that to her. I've tried to talk to her, to be reasonable. All the years in L.A. -the summer and holiday visits- have left me not knowing how to be the everyday parent to her. I know the "Do as I say, not as I do" approach that Mom crammed down my throat didn't work on me so why try it on Zoey? I didn't want to be a hypocrite. Now I don't know how to undo the pace that's set. Please, God, what do I do?

Journal: May 7, 1995 Sunday AM

Okay, so a little background to the Jack thing. No, first let's finish off Jay. On Friday 4/28 I went down to get herb from Jay and to talk. He was trying to avoid the talk part so, by hurrying me, I didn't get everything said in the words that I wanted. But the gist of it got out there. I told him I didn't want to be a customer as he is much better at the mental distancing thing than I am. "Don't call my house. I don't need any pot." It seemed he couldn't get out of the car fast enough when I dropped him off. So it goes back to the closure on my letter to him of 1-20-95 (over three fucking months ago!), "maybe this will have been one of those brief, though not chance, meetings that you just always remember." And so it is.

I looked back through my entries and find that I've made no mention of Jack. Hmmm. . . I guess I didn't expect it to go anywhere, so it didn't seem worthy of mention. Now I know it's going nowhere but it's interesting how it got to here so I should talk about this.

Lonni and I were at the Off Ramp one night back in January and Jack was there celebrating the birthday of one of his band-mates. He came over to me, said "Hello," and

70

asked how I was doing. Then he bounced back to where he'd been hanging out across the flow-of-traffic-aisle from me. Later I went over to where he was and struck up a conversation. When the lights came up as the bar prepared to close, he informed me he was coming home with me. Wanting the distraction from thoughts of Jay, I went with it. We had great lusty sex and in the middle of the night he told me he was taking a taxi home. He couldn't sleep because I was snoring. He left his pager number. I paged him a few days later. He called back a few days later. We made a plan to get together the following weekend. He didn't call.

Lonni and I went to hear his band one night at the Lake Union Pub. We had lusty sex again. He came over a couple of times when there was a house full of kids and then I didn't hear from him. A couple months went by and I paged Jack one night when I was looking for smoke. He called me the next day saying he'd been thinking about me. I told him why I'd paged and that it was handled now. He suggested we get together and we've been doing so ever since.

When I went back to bed last night Jack was facing my side of the bed and gave me a quickie, nice considering how horny I was. But, I gather it was a gratuitous thing, like he figured I was pissed when I got out of bed and was slamming stuff around in the kitchen after he ignored my advances. I suppose he was correct. I don't take it well considering the culmination of Paul's *Beth-as-teddy-bear* phase and Eric's many rejections before that. How do I forget the time I was so starved for some lovemaking that I attempted to create an alluring atmosphere in the bedroom with scented candles matching the aroma of the shower gel still lingering under the lacy lingerie I modeled atop the bed? How do I forget the crush of Eric's laughter and words when he entered the room, "Ha! You must want sex," and the fact that he blew out the candles, got in bed, and went straight to sleep? What magic makes that go away?

Letter from Eric, May 18, 1995

Beth,

(1) Zoey is in a safe place, under the care of licensed psychiatrists and physicians.

(2) The events of the last 48 hours have been very stressful, and I am not prepared to discuss

them with you at this time.

(3) I am thoroughly disgusted with you, as I am now aware that on at least two separate occasions over the last 5 months, school officials have asked you to take action regarding Zoey's drug use and you have failed to notify me. The school had become so frustrated with you that they asked me to become involved. Your main concern, based on what has been stated to me as well as on your behavior, was not Zoey's welfare, but rather if (A) I would find out and (B) How Zoey's downward spiral would reflect upon you. Then when I did take action, you say "thank you, thank you, thank you".

(4) You too are a drug user, and it has affected your ability to make decisions, and use good judgment. You should seek treatment.

(5) I'm now aware that you have actually supplied Zoey with pot, and have smoked pot with her at concerts.

(6) I'm not willing to make any further agreements with you, as you are not willing to honor them.

    Eric

Within a day or two of Zoey's admittance she heard a girl was being released to go home. Zoey gave the girl my number, begging her to call and tell me where she is. Thankfully, she did. The woman who answered the phone at the center asked me for my code when I asked to speak to Zoey. I told her I didn't know a code. She would not let me speak to Zoey, adding she had already said more than she should have—I guess by letting me know Zoey was, in fact, there. I verbalized everything in the attached letter to the woman. She gave me their address telling me to write a letter reflecting my statements and send documentation.

May 20, 1995, my letter. . .

To: Youth Drug Rehab Facility in Oregon
Re: Patient, Zoey - admitted 5/17

To Whom It May Concern,

    Please find copies of my divorce decree enclosed; and, the stipulation to it. Specifically, Agreement 12 covers the issue of Joint Custody. Zoey's residence alternated periodically for approximately two years until I relocated (out of state) for the purpose of increasing my earnings and career status. A year after I moved, the stipulation regarding Zoey's residence was formalized. This stipulation regarding residence in no way alters the Joint Custody aspect. As you can see by the way they are listed they are two separate issues. I am entitled to knowledge of the whereabouts and health and well-being of my child. Eric is wrongfully withholding information which allows me access to my child. As is often the case between divorced parents, we do not always communicate well.

I have been back in the area for over two years and Zoey has been residing with me for the last five months. Eric has been in contact with his daughter approximately six times during this period. Because I didn't immediately act upon the suggestion of Zoey's group counselor at school to get her into an in-patient treatment facility he assumes I am her enabler. I am totally supportive and thankful for Zoey to be receiving treatment. Why I chose a different route of action and did not apprise Eric of the problem is moot at this point. The bottom line is I want access to my daughter and information on her treatment and progress. I'll be out of town on business until May 26th but will be in contact before then to confirm receipt of this letter.

Please tell Zoey I love her with all of my heart, I miss her beyond belief, to be brave and to listen—and to pray, to give her worries and fears to God.

Thank you, Beth Rice

7: A Lot A Little Too Late

June 10, 1995: Letter to my criminal defense attorney

Dear Dick,

I have had to prioritize my available time such that the listing you requested of me is not yet finished. In actuality, I could never complete a thorough list because I don't remember all of the kids who have come through my door, don't remember or never knew their last names, have had little or no contact with most of their parents. If indeed The Anonymous Caller's kid was at my home last Friday night then you have all the info you need on the following page. There is the chance that The Caller just heard through her kid, a friend of one of those listed, that there was "a party" at my house that night. Or that could've been just Crystal's choice of verbiage in relaying the story of The Caller to me. MY POINT BEING that there are two kids who were not present that night whose parents I could envision being The Caller. I will cite them below. I do have a listing of the entire student body at Zoey's school complete with phone numbers. I will copy it and highlight all known pertinent names.

After much self-analysis and soul searching, I have concluded that I must talk to Zoey straight out about ALL that is coming down before she leaves on her wilderness trek. In order to keep the oratory focused and concise I have written her a letter which I plan to read to her tomorrow morning, Sunday June 11, '95. I will then put the letter in my purse and bring it back with me. Only you get to have a copy (enclosed) so you know what I have attested to in Eric and Crystal's presence.

I've no plan for any confessions or apologies beyond dealing with the needs of my own child. I will do whatever I can to avoid prison except for leaving any deceit in place among Zoey's family or running from the situation. I was a contributor over a very short span of time. I was never the cause or the instigator of any kids' drug use. As I told you, every one of the kids who partied at my house were users before they met me. Their parents need to take responsibility for their trip.

Regards, Beth Rice

June 10, 1995 – Letter I read to Zoey

as referenced above to Dick Carville

Zoey,

There are so many things I want to say to you that I hardly know where to begin. That is why I am writing this, so that the key points can be made concisely and without sidetracking.

In the first three weeks that you've been away I've gone through an incredible range of feelings from rage at your father for handling things the way he did (although I now accept that he did the only thing he could do and it was the right thing), to total heart-sickness at watching you be caught in the middle of the lies I've created for fear of losing all contact with you, to a half-assed acceptance that my pot smoking over this last year and a half has reached problematic proportions but still holding an unwillingness to do anything about it.

You have said that you need to have some sort of negative experience happen before you'll be willing to be clean and sober. Well, this last Tuesday, thanks to Crystal (and I do mean sincerely, *Thank you*) I have had this kind of experience, the kind that snaps your head around and makes you ask yourself "What on earth are you doing?"

It started last Saturday, Zoey, when Crystal got an anonymous phone call from a woman who said that her child had told her not only do I smoke pot but that I have provided pot and alcohol to you, her kid and others. Crystal called to talk to me about it and I continued to deny it. Crystal, in her persistence in caring for you, started contacting parents in an attempt to get to the bottom of it. That is why last Sunday, in our family therapy meeting; the first question the counselor asked you was, "Have you ever smoked pot with your mom?" And the knife twisted around in my heart while you lied to all of them because of my presence. But, I thank you, Zoey, for your honesty in speaking out in your group session back in lock-down.

On Tuesday your dad and Crystal and I got together at lunch to go over some details in preparation of your wilderness trek. They again confronted me with the question of my usage and my contributing and I again denied. Crystal then informed me that there are a number of angry parents and their kids who will come forth with depositions and that if I do not come clean about the situation, be honest, she and your dad would file charges against me. Zoey, the dictionary definition of deposition is the testimony of a witness made under oath, but not in open court, and written down to be used when the case comes to trial. Needless to say, I got very scared and decided to immediately see an attorney.

The attorney read the law straight out of the law books to me: if found guilty, I would serve a minimum sentence of thirty-one months in prison. The sentence, or total prison term, would depend on how many parents and kids came forward, each one being a "count," with a possible maximum of up to fifteen years. The attorney told me (since it's his job to keep me out of prison) "Do not confess anything to anybody." And I said to him, "But my daughter is stuck in the middle of all this and she's not going to get well if I don't come forward and put it all to rest." So Dick, the attorney, called your dad and they had a long talk. Dick called me back and said "They have no desire to press charges. They just have Zoey's best interest at heart and want you to confess to her that you have a drug problem and that you are taking steps to get well."

I have been doing a lot of self-analysis and soul searching since Tuesday. I feel like I have been walking around in a stupor, zombie-like, for the last few months and someone just passed smelling salts under my nose on Tuesday. Up until last Saturday your dad and Crystal and I were beginning to communicate well and were getting clear on truly being a team in parenting. All of us would work together to lay down the rules that we could and would all enforce in the same way in both households. I now realize that unless I come completely clean, you, Zoey, and I will know that we still have a line of lies out there, that we are still being deceitful. I can't be on the same page with Eric and Crystal and share a lie with you. I can't teach you to accept that there are rules we must abide by if I am breaking them. I have broken the law. I am not an anarchist. I believe that we have laws and rules for the better of all. This doesn't mean that they are always fair or maybe even right, but they are there for a reason and must be abided by until they have been changed by popular vote or by the officials we have elected to represent us.

Zoey, I am saying to you again, loud and clear, I have a drug problem. It is a serious problem. I have smoked enough pot over the last year and a half to cloud my thinking enough that I had actually justified in my mind breaking the law in a big way on top of the fact that I was already breaking the law just by smoking the stuff. At the time I thought I could hardly preach to you not to do that which I myself do. So rather than change my ways and do right, I not only allowed you to break the law I participated with you. I feel absolutely sick when I think about the example I have set for you.

Look at yourself, Zoey. Think about some of your actions. Tell me drugs haven't clouded your sense of right and wrong, your ability to make a good decision. You cannot tell me that we aren't sick. We are. And we need to take the steps to get well. I am going into therapy, Zoey, and I am excited about it. I can't wait for my first session next Tuesday. I want to get well. I do not want to live with all this hanging over me anymore – the guilt.

I am finally ready to accept that drugs have clouded too many of the big decisions that I've made in my life. Therefore I have made bad choices. Every time there has been a major crisis in my life I have turned to drugs to numb the pain or make me happy and all it did was cause me to make a wrong decision that ultimately led to more pain. When I made the decision to go to L.A. and leave my beautiful little girl behind my thinking was clouded by pot and dabbling with cocaine. I was using to ease the agony of divorce and the loneliness. Zoey, I am so sorry.

Life is good but it's not always fair. Things don't always go the way we want them to or even the way they should. But the only way to deal with any of it is with the knowing that everything happens for a reason, faith that everything turns out in the end and by keeping a clear head so to learn the lesson that has been presented to us.

You are going back to live with Eric and Crystal when you come back from your vision quest. They have better parenting skills than me at this point. Plan that this living arrangement will be in force until your eighteenth birthday. We are going to participate in parenting classes together and we are going to stick together. We're all playing by the same rules. I will be here for you. I'm not going anywhere. Your dad, Crystal, and I are all willing to say that we have made mistakes in parenting you, Zoey. But if we are to go by "the rules," Rule #3 For Being Human is "There are no mistakes only lessons. Growth is a process of trial and error, experimentation. The "failed" experiments are as much a part of the process as the experiment that ultimately works."

We are all growing and we all need to communicate clearly to one another but since we've been growing and learning for at least twenty-five more years than you, Zoey, we will make the rules. We will parent you. Your job while you're out there on the trail is to learn and accept that you have a lot to learn.

Remember when I asked my psychic self-empowerment counselor, Teresa, why I chose Mom and Dad? She told me that mainly I chose Dad because I needed to learn about addictions and obsessive behavior. Well maybe that is why you chose me to be your mom. So let's learn from it and move on to the next lesson!

Journal: June 12, 1995

Zoey is now out in the wilderness with a backpack, a bag of trail mix they call gorp, a counselor, and several other kids. Each kid got a bag of gorp and it's the only food that went out on the trek. The counselor will teach them how to survive on what the desert provides for sustenance. The philosophy is for the kids to learn basic survival skills so they will return with a strong sense of empowerment. A natural course to that end is to strip them of all walls and barriers so that in group discussions they talk about their experience, what brought them to substance abuse and how they acted in it. Then they are mandated to time in isolation to process what they've learned about themselves. More group discussion ensues.

Eric, Crystal, and his mom went to get Zoey out of the

lock-down place on Friday; then drove down to be near the offices of the wilderness trek treatment program and spent the night in a motel. I drove down early Saturday morning to join them all in seeing Zoey off on this new leg of treatment, which her dad has so rosily dubbed her "vision quest." There is and has been so much going on I'm not sure where to start in the telling of it all. And, more so, I don't think I can possibly describe the confusion of emotions I'm feeling. I'm not sure if I'm as remorseful as my letter to Zoey says I am, if I'm being brainwashed by Eric and Crystal's tactics, or if I'm saying a lot of stuff they want to hear so to keep my ass out of prison. OR, is it the fear of being murdered? How about the combo of it all?

It is safe to say that I have had all I can take of Crystal. Those two are a perfect match. One judgmental, money-monging, manipulative, control freak deserves another. I just want to puke when I think of the conversations she and I have had over the years where she was clearly looking down her nose at me while explaining with a smile how she had found solutions for situations similar to mine that allowed her to be a better mother. Why is it I have not once said to her, "Maybe so, but you are not me nor were you wearing my shoes walking on the path I was on." WHY? It's so damn weird. There were times where it seemed like we were getting along fine. She made an effort to include me in things that were going on with Zoey, besides drama. Then just the basic differences in who we each are as individuals would get in the way. It's clear to me that any niceness that came my way was motivated by her hope that if she could like me it would help her and Zoey get along better; and, that's certainly why I made an effort to like her as well. Obviously, all of that is long behind us now! Now it feels like it's all about what she can get me to admit to.

I do believe my pot smoking, since meeting Jay, reached seriously problematic proportions. I know both he and Zoey heard me parrot, "I have smoked more pot in the last month than the last ten years put together!" Then it was, ". . . in the last two months" and then, "three months" etc. until they both rolled their eyes at me and finished my sentence. I know from each of the times I've quit smoking pot over all the years since my first time smoking at age sixteen that too much too often can become a problem. Over-usage has, at times, caused me to be lethargic, apathetic, less ambitious—or more so—less apt to act upon my ambitions. I recall becoming paranoid in certain situations, questioning people's motives and the like. I've experienced all of that. And, that's why I've gone blocks of years without smoking weed and why I've had zero trouble quitting when I realized it was no longer benefitting me; was detrimental to my goals and best interests. The idea of me going for drug treatment is ridiculous. Pot is not physically addictive. Besides, I'm living in shock therapy.

I look forward to counseling to help me muddle through all this muck; and all that I've been through before it. I've booked an appointment with a psychiatrist because this is the only option where I can speak freely of all that has gone down, as only an MD can be held to confidentiality. I don't know how I'll be able to afford even one visit per month considering the hourly rate. But, I have to find a way as Eric and Crystal have put an ultimatum on it. Basically, its get help or else. I spoke with a certified counselor saying that I'd broken the law and it involved my daughter. I asked specifically if I would be able to talk about the issue without fear and she told me that if it had to do with child abuse in any form she would have to report it to the police. What can be considered child abuse is pretty subjective and I just can't take that risk.

I've been going over to Eric and Crystal's fairly frequently and we have been having talks. I am too damn honest and there were times I caught myself saying far more than I should have. I know what a master manipulator Eric is but I found myself opening up to their questions because they were sounding so reasonable and understanding.

In all their cordialness they shared a pretty fucked up story with me. Crystal brought up a couple of kids, a brother and sister, who were among those that partied at my home. The boy was never an issue but the girl struck me as trouble from the git-go. I simply did not like her. She had a vibe that made me very uncomfortable. Zoey'd told me she had just gotten out of drug rehab fairly recently the first time she came to our apartment. I asked, "Then what in the hell is she doing here hanging out with all of you potheads?" Zoey simply shrugged. I recall when Zoey introduced me to the boy the first time. She had added quite matter-of-factly, "His mother was murdered." He seemed to accept that addition to the intro with no problem. Crystal has now filled me in on details.

Apparently this boy's father had been a member of a cult or some such that supposedly was an offshoot from Mormonism. Within this group of people quite a number of deaths occurred in which there were homicide investigations but never any convictions. Crystal told me the book titled *The Prophet of Blood* was written about this group and the mysterious deaths; that the man is both discussed and photographed in the book. She and Eric became acquainted with the man through a club they belong to and were getting friendly when another member of the group took them aside to warn them of him, saying that he'd gained his wealth at the cost of people well acquainted with. Crystal said she got the book. They're being cordial with the guy as necessary, since apparently his son has befriended one of Crystal's boys, but Eric and Crystal are backing away.

So, this guy, the father of two kids who have hung at The House of the 90's, says to Crystal about that, "Just want me to off her?" meaning me! I could see she enjoyed telling me this. Holy crap! Then she added, "I told him no, that we're working it out."

Okay, a couple nights later I came home from work and that last golden light before sundown was in my parking lot glinting off the nymph-like hood ornament of a white Rolls Royce or Bentley or some such. Behind the wheel was a large set man and I thought, "Is that the guy in the photo in the book?" My gut said, "Yes." No shit! What in the hell would that car be doing in my apartment building's parking lot in this dumpy neighborhood? He sat there and blatantly watched me get out of my dumpy little car and walk into the stairwell.

When I got in my door I was shaking, totally freaking out. I wondered if the car was still in the lot so I crossed the hall and asked my neighbor to look out his window and tell me if it's still there. He said, "No, but it sounds just like the car that was here earlier today." He goes on to tell me that in the afternoon a guy was here in a work van measuring

81

up an area of siding on our building in need of repair. The heavy set guy in the white car watched and made notes. Then when the van left, he got out with a tape measure and mimicked the actual repair guy like he was doing a bid on the job too. My neighbor didn't know if the Rolls guy stayed the whole time until I got home or if he left and came back. In any case, I repeat what the hell!?!

The next time I talked with Crystal I asked her if that guy owned this type of car. Of course, she wondered why I asked. So, I told her and she confirmed it was likely him.

I'm still freaked out. I am getting out of this apartment. At $8.50 per hour I can't pay rent, make payments to Eric to reimburse my half of the cost of Zoey's treatment, and pay for a psychiatrist. Plus, I don't want this guy to know where I live. I'll throw stuff in storage and keep my clothes in a wardrobe box and my dresser, plus other necessities in the drawers, up front next to the door so I can get to them easily. Then I'll get some big Tupperware bins for clothes, toiletries, a couple towels, and my pillow to put in the trunk of my car. Throw in my sleeping bag and go. I'll get a membership at that gym near the office for showering. I'll have to sleep in my car for a while until money is on a more even keel again. The thought of it makes me sick. It sounds scary, like I won't get much sleep being on watch. But, ya gotta do whatcha gotta do! The storage and gym will cost me a third of what the rent is here. And, when I leave work each night I'll take a different route to preclude anyone following me and figuring out my car is home.

I haven't written about going to see Zoey in lock down. The weekend after I got back from the regional trade show in upstate New York I drove the three hours to go see her. I confirmed by phone a couple days earlier that the treatment center had received my letter and documentation and would abide by my legal rights. It got to where the little leak of transmission fluid that I've been nursing along became a solid flow. On the way home I had to stop and pour in fluid about every ten to fifteen miles, depending on conditions. So, Monday in to the shop it went; and, there went most of my rent money after adding on gas for multiple round trips to Oregon to the cost of repairs. I finally made commissions and got my first check for eleven hundred dollars. But that money, plus half of one of my twice monthly paychecks, promptly went to paying Dick Carville's retainer fee.

Getting back to Zoey, I can't think how to describe our first couple visits. As always, on one level we were co-conspirators, both of us very pissed off at her dad. On another level, I was trying to Mom her; to impart some wisdom, food for thought, hope, and lots of love. Damn! I want to scream. This is all so unreal. I need to go to bed. I don't think I want to write about it. I wonder how I'll ever not think about it. I don't need to write it.

However, I do want to make note of the precious gift Zoey made for me in arts and crafts. It is a darling little marshmallowy dragon made of pale purple clay with soft yellow wings accented in baby blue. The toes are blue and little tail spikes are yellow. He has yellow and baby blue spots for scales, each perfectly rounded. He's got big blue eyes atop his head and a sweet little smile. The flawless detail she put into it is amazing. When she gave it to me she was proud of her work. She seemed like such a child in that moment. It felt like a peace offering of sorts. I absolutely love it and will keep it forever.

One more thing, I had a consultation with Teresa. I got to her office early so browsed through a notebook in her waiting room while she finished the appointment ahead of me. It was in that notebook that I saw "The Ten Rules For Being Human." They were simply typewritten and tucked into a vinyl sleeve with no author credited. Tears washed my cheeks as the words balmed my soul. I took a blank piece of paper from the notebook and started writing verbatim. "The Rules" were stashed in my purse when Teresa walked out with her client. I'm stapling it to the next page here in my journal.

The Ten Rules For Being Human

1. You will receive a body. You may like it or hate it, but it will be yours for the entire period this time around.

2. You will learn lessons. You are enrolled in a full-time informal school called life. Each day in this school you will have the opportunity to learn lessons. You may like the lessons or think them irrelevant and stupid. It makes no difference. You will learn lessons.

3. There are no mistakes, only lessons. Growth is a process of trial and error, experimentation. The "failed" experiments are as much a part of the process as the experiment that ultimately works.

4. A lesson is repeated until learned. A lesson will be presented to you in various forms until you have learned it. When you have learned it you can then go on to the next lesson.

5. Learning lessons does not end. There is no part of life that does not contain its lessons. If you are alive there are lessons to be learned.

6. "There" is no better than "here". When your "there" has become a "here" you will simply obtain another "there" that will, again, look better than "here."

7. Others are merely mirrors of you. You cannot love or hate something about another person unless it reflects to you something you love or hate about yourself.

8. What you make of life is up to you. You have all the tools and resources that you need. What you do with them is up to you. The choice is yours.

9. The answers lie inside of you. The answers to life's questions lie inside of you. All you need to do is look, listen, and trust.

10. You will forget all this.

June 16, 1995 - a letter from me
Dear Dad and Mom –

I've been swamped at work and haven't had a chance to send these pages as it's peak season for caps and our fax has been going non-stop. But here they are now, my letter I read to Zoey before she left on her wilderness trek follows this note.

Regarding Father's Day on Sunday, under ordinary circumstances I, of course, would be coming over to spend the day with you. But, things being as they are, I don't imagine either of us would enjoy the time. I love you and know you love me but I am as disgusted with me as you must be and I'm not emotionally prepared to spend time with you guys right now.

Additionally, I am far more broke (dollar-wise) than my usual state and can afford neither the ferry nor extra gas expense at this time. One or two round-trips to Oregon three weekends in a row have bitten into the paycheck I haven't received yet via a loan from Eric. He has my post-dated check for the loan plus my first installment toward my share of Zoey's treatment expense. The Pontiac repair ran one hundred and sixty dollars; and, I might or might not get your dealer, who initially did the work that caused the problem, to reimburse me. Additionally, one hundred dollars is out to my psychiatrist in a post-dated check.

I've given notice to be out of my apartment by June 30, will put everything in storage and get a cheap room for a while plus a second job at a burger joint or sub shop or whatever from five to ten at night. Thank you for letting me continue to use the Pontiac. I am sorry you got such a fuck-up for a kid. And, Mom, I'm sorry this all hits at a time when you're not doing so well to begin with. Everything will not only be fine but probably better (wiser for the lessons learned) eventually.

I love you both more than you can know.

Beth

Journal: June 30, 1995

I got a call from the wilderness trek treatment facility. They do not want me to be there tomorrow to greet Zoey on her return. They wouldn't offer much of an explanation but said that information has come out that leads them to feel my presence is not in her best interest.

I haven't mentioned that Zoey told them she is not ready to come home yet. So, on Sunday, she is going out on a second three week trek. I guess this one will be in a mountain environment. I wrote a letter to Zoey and am giving it to Eric to deliver to her. I hope he does. I was so looking forward to seeing and hugging her.

June 30, 1995 - the letter I hope Eric delivered

Dear Zoey,

I wish I could be there to see you, hug you hard, and hear about the second leg of your journey. But I feel I can't. I hear you've been hanging on to something I said to you back in the lock-down facility, back at the beginning of all this, when I was hyperemotional and very angry with your dad. I had completely forgotten about it because we've come so far since then. Zoey, get clear on these three things:

You and I are not running away to Kauai or anywhere else. We are going to deal with the problems we have created for ourselves right here.

I am choosing to get into therapy with a psychiatrist as soon as my health insurance kicks in on July 1st. I am off pot and plan to stay off all drugs. I have been sick at heart for far too long and mentally twisted due to the drugs. I want to put an end to it and live out the rest of my life recovering and finding the peaceful place inside of me.

Your dad and Crystal and I are all on the same team, your team. We are your team of parents, the people who love you the most. We are working to compromise our differences to a meeting point in the middle that we can all live with, agree on and stick to.

How about you, Zoey? What are you working on? Have you been working on any of the things I asked you to? I hear you're beginning to accept that you have some problems. That's a start. Now you need to start working on them. I'm very happy to hear you've become sensitive to not wanting to steamroller us anymore. That's a great one to start with. Manipulating us, your friends, *the system* (school or otherwise), may bring short term gain but is a losing proposition in the long run. I know you have experienced this. Please learn from it!

I miss so much of you, my dear daughter. You are on my mind constantly and I find myself wondering how, where and what you're doing. As your counselor suggested before you left on your trek, I have placed my fingers to my jugular pulse at these times; and, have indeed felt calmer and closer to you. But, Zoey, I shudder to think of you coming back with no change in attitude. I am not daring enough to seek out alone time with you unless I can be assured you are committed to staying off drugs and alcohol, and to working on getting beyond all of the havoc it has caused. I love you.
Mom

I wrote out for Zoey the complete ". . .Rules For Being Human." I also wrote the following on a recipe card and put both items in the envelope with my letter for her to take on the next leg of her journey:

Mom's List of Things for Zoey to Think About and Work On:

- That you have a lot to learn and to adopt an attitude of willingness to learn.
- Acceptance of Rules and willingness to abide by them.
- Accountability, willingness to be responsible for your actions and accepting of the consequences.
- Appreciation
- Appropriateness
- Abandonment. Get over it. I am so sorry. But, it is done. I can't change it. I am here for you now. Let's live from today forward.

On the other side of the card I wrote:

Today is a new day.

Today is the first day of the rest of my life.

I choose to make the most of today.

I choose to be happy.

8: Hiding Out

<u>Journal: July 2, 1995</u>

The House of the 90's is gone but thanks to Susan (with Black Happy's label), I am not living in my car. When it came down to actually doing it the first night I was scared shitless. Under less extraordinary circumstances I'd call Josh or a cousin to ask if I could camp for a bit but I'm just not up for it, for being judged and lectured. I'm doing a great job of beating myself up. I don't need more. And, in light of the situation, I don't know that I'd be welcomed any way. So, I called Susan to ask if there was any chance I could sleep on her floor for a week or two. I told her I have my own bed roll and that I intended to join the gym so would not vie for bathroom time, that I just needed a place to crash that was fairly close to work. Even though I promised I'd come only to sleep, that I wouldn't be hanging out, she said her studio apartment was just too small and she wasn't in a good place mentally/emotionally, that she was going through some stuff and needed quiet. However, she told me she has a friend who's looking to rent a room and added that I should come over to talk about it.

When I got there she asked me what was up so I told her the whole story – why I have no money for rent and why I need to hide out for a while to perhaps avoid being "offed." She knows of the man! How freakin' wild is that? She was working for the company he bought, apparently what brought him to Washington. She said when he took it over all employees were offered to stay in their jobs or take a severance package. One of her coworkers had read "The Prophet of Blood" and told everyone about his story, his inclusion in the book. Susan said a lot of the staff took the severance package, including her and she still hasn't found a new job. I hadn't realized the record label gig isn't fulltime.

She called her friend and told him what was going on with me. He said for me to come over. So, I got directions and went. And, I'm staying. Joe is great – pretty funny though that I now have three "J" guys in my life. He knows I'm in a pinch and is willing to let me pay just a hundred dollars a month in July and August. He has a beautiful home in a nice neighborhood in Mukilteo, close to my work. It's also not a likely place to look for me based on the dumpish neighborhood that guy just saw me in. I am so thankful not to be sleeping in my car!

July 7, 1995 – a note to Mom and Dad

Hi – I absolutely refused to pack up my sewing projects one more time so I worked on these instead of packing. It made for a bit of a pinch at the end of the move but was sure satisfying just to complete something. I have something for you too, Dad, but will have to do it by hand since my sewing machine is in storage now.

Through a friend of a friend, I have rented a nice room in a lovely Sound view home (very cheap thank heaven). I don't know how long it'll be available to me but sure beats my back seat.

Zoey has started a third three week stint of treatment. She is in the mountains this time. Her attitude seems to be turning around.

I'm anxiously awaiting receipt of info from my health insurance company so I can get into serious treatment.

It's best to call me at work if you need me for anything. I hope all is well with you.   Love, Beth

July 9, 1995 – Sunday, 7:20pm

– sent to the treatment center to be delivered on Zoey's return

My dear Zoey –

I know you're not overly fond of surprises when it comes to major changes. So, I want you to know that I have moved. Most everything is in storage right now. I am renting a room in a lovely home that is convenient to work (our new office location – work moved also! about six weeks ago – shortly after you went on your first leg of treatment). I have two house mates, Joe, who owns the home, and another lady renting a room.

There are no drugs in this house or anywhere near this

house. We're in a very nice family neighborhood. It's nice not to be alone and yet everyone is respectful of each other's space. Completely changing my environment and disassociating myself from the influences (people) of before has been a real positive move for me.

I think of you every day. Today I was sitting on the front porch having a smoke and it started to rain. I wondered if it was raining where you're at. I wonder how you're doing with one pair of panties. I wonder how you're doing –period– all the way around. I was so happy to hear you had a big hug for your dad and Crystal last week. I WAS SO PROUD OF YOU in hearing you came back with all your gorp! That took some serious will power. I miss you so much and love you even more. I look back on the last six months and it's like looking at a movie — not something I lived. . . or like a dream. . . ? . . . a nightmare. Not just that time really but all the way back to when Paul left for Hawaii, when it really started.

On the fifth of July (immediately following the four day holiday) I called to make an appointment with my Primary Care Physician through my health plan. In order to get help dollar-wise for psychiatric help my P.C.P. has to refer me to the psychiatrist. (Without insurance help I'm looking at one hundred dollars for each visit.) Well, come to find the P.C.P. I selected, out of the book they gave me when I signed up, is no longer taking on new patients! So, I've requested a current 1995 book to be sent to me so I can select a new doctor and get an appointment and get into therapy. In the mean time I'm reading a book called "The Inner Child of Your Past" and another that Eric and Crystal's counselor recommended to me, "Unconditional Love and Forgiveness." I have been doing a lot of self-analysis and been generally coming down on myself awfully hard. Reading the books is helping me to be not quite so angry with myself, not quite so sad and useless feeling. I've decided to step out from under all of the fear I've felt trapped by. No sense in allowing fear to dictate my days. What will be, will be. It's highly unlikely I can change anything along those lines so will just figure on dealing with things as or if they arise.

I am very hopeful that you and I both will remain successfully in a state of recovery. We have a lot of hard work ahead of us but a whole lifetime to enjoy the "fruits of our labor."

I can't wait to see you. Zoey, I'm so sorry I have failed to be a good mom to you. I can't change the past but I can sure work on the present and set attainable goals for our future. I hope you can forgive me for all my bad decisions. I hope you're as clear as I am about working for a bright future.

All my heart, Mom

<u>July 9, 1995 – a letter to . . .</u>

Eric & Crystal –

I just finished a letter to Zoey and feel compelled to jot off a note to you. I have not been able to quit thinking about the other evening. But, I don't feel comfortable with talking with you right now.

Crystal, I apologize for going off like I did. You have stresses I can't count or know. You can't possibly feel the stresses I am experiencing. I am sorry that I have dented any thread of confidence you may have been grasping on to in regard to me "saying things [I] don't mean." I told you at the beginning of the discussions on this subject matter that I do not feel safe going into a group therapy/treatment scenario. I told you what the sequential steps are to getting myself into one-on-one therapy through my health insurance. I told you I'm taking the steps. Why back me into a corner with statements of how I'm not meeting up to your expectation of what I should be doing?

I am asking you both for the last time, do you want me out of the picture? Do you think Zoey will benefit from this? If we cannot get along I do not believe my being here for Zoey will be beneficial. It will be the same old tug-of-war. I feel firmly that Zoey needs me, that removing me from the picture will be damaging, but, honestly, not as destructive as us being on different "pages" with her in the middle feeling either loyalty torn or positioned for playing us against each other.

The other night you clearly expressed your disbelief that I was doing all in my power to expedite my therapy before I "fessed up" to the fact that I have no intentions of going into a group setting. As I said then, I told you I would look into a group simply because I could feel your pressure, your expectation, and I am in a very vulnerable, powerless position right now. I feel like any wrong move and it's all over for me. Can you understand this? I feel like I am at all times one breath away from losing all contact with Zoey, perhaps losing my life, or my freedom to incarceration, or my mind in light of the weight of it all.

Well, I am no longer going to live with these fears. Whatever happens I've apparently asked for it and there is no sense in concerning myself about it until it hits me in the face. The key point of this letter however is that unless we TRUST each other regarding the fact that Zoey's best interest is in our hearts and that we are doing all we can to be on the same page—the middle page, not your page, not my page—the one where we meet up and work on bridging the differences and compromise to where it's workable for all, then it's not going to work for anyone – you, me, or Zoey. It seems to me that the only way this is a real possibility is if we take counsel together regularly. Are you willing?

If you inherently dislike me then you have the most work cut out for you because unless you can get past it and genuinely find something likeable to cling to, Zoey will sense the conflict still exists and we are right back where we started. It is obviously your call.

I have to get to bed. I guess we'll be talking soon.
Beth

An undated note from Eric:

Beth – Zoey is very anxious about getting her CD's out of pawn. We don't know which CD's are hers or yours but she's upset that they are in pawn. If you can't get them out of pawn please let her buy them out. In order to do this we would need the pawn tickets involved. She seems to think she knows which ones are yours and hers . . .
Thanks, Eric

August 4, 1995 – my reply:

Eric – I received your letter today regarding Zoey's CD's. I just got back from a business trip to Chicago. I got the CD's out of pawn before I left as the ticket was due August 2nd. It cost sixty dollars I may or may not have in my budget right now. Even with help from health insurance the psychiatrist is sixty dollars per visit. Call or write me to tell me a neutral zone where I can leave them for you to pick up. Also, I have a little book for Zoey. She is on my mind constantly. This is the longest we have ever gone with no contact and I am having great difficulty with it. Now I have to borrow money to pay an attorney to represent me in your new line of exercises for me. Does she know what's going on? Well. . . no doubt she has your perspective on it. Or maybe not. Does she know about the restraining order? To get a hearing date on August 2nd you must have been working on all of this some time ago. Let me know about the CD's.   Beth

I came to severely regret sending my letter of July 9 to Eric and Crystal. The actions they took were not what I had in mind. It seems the restraining order was just to keep me away while they had their lawyer draw up the papers for regaining residential custody of Zoey. As soon as I was served with a date to appear in court I was back in the Yellow Pages; this time looking for a family attorney that offers a free thirty minute initial consultation. Again, I found one such attorney who could see me right away, at lunch that day.

When I had briefed her on the scenario she told me I must keep it out of court. She said if a prosecuting attorney with a bent against pot, or even just time on his hands, caught wind of the case it would become the State of Washington vs. Beth Rice. She reminded me that there was a war on drugs going on. Then, she added that the court would likely appoint a representative for Zoey and that I needed to think about how all of this would impact my daughter—hearing my and her dad's testimony and arguments; her own testimony presented if necessary.

I went back to work in a daze. After an hour or so of pretending to work I got on the phone again. I found another attorney who offered a freebie consultation and could see me after work. I laid it out for him precisely as I had done at lunch. His words to me varied little from what the first attorney had said. He was very clear I needed to keep it out of court.

So, I had two identical opinions. The next day I called Dick Carville and asked if I had enough retainer left that he could now act as a family attorney for me. I told him what my free consultations rendered. He called Eric to apprise him that I'd like to settle the matter out of court. When Dick called me some days later to tell me what day we'd all meet at his office, I told him to tell Eric that I would not be at the meeting unless he came without Crystal, that it was between the two of us as Zoey's parents.

There I was in that TV show again—the final episode. I stared out the now familiar picture windows into the cool morning sun and waited for Eric and his attorney to arrive. When three people entered the office, Crystal rounding out the set, it hit me like I'd licked my fingers and inserted them in an electrical socket. I started walking out the door past them but Dick was fast on my heels and convinced me to come back with the idea that the three could go to his inner office and I could be in the conference room. He would be the runner. From the moment I settled in by the conference room window to again get lost in the sun on Puget Sound I was a walking electrical charge.

When Dick came in to present the papers I was to sign he explained they were a new proposal and that I'd best read them over. I got as far as the top of page two and declared, "I'm not signing this!" He wanted to know what I objected to.

On the template for the "Final Parenting Plan," as an amendment to our divorce decree, there was a check in the box indicating my conduct as a parent included "Physical, sexual or a pattern of emotional abuse of a child."

My adamant "I will not sign this! Get rid of that clause! It's ridiculous!" had Dick headed back to his office. Minutes later he returned to show me a large black felt marker had concealed those lines. Now the clause above it had an "X" in the adjacent box, "Willful abandonment that continues for an extended period of time or substantial refusal to perform parenting functions."

"I have never *abandoned* Zoey and I'm not signing that either." Dick reminded me that I needed to keep this out of court so I'd have to sign something. I ultimately settled for the phrase peeking out between black marker lines, "substantial refusal to perform parenting functions."

In the next paragraph, "Other Factors," boxes were checked off to form the statement: The mother's involvement or conduct may have an adverse effect on the child's best interests because of the existence of the factors which follow:

[X] Neglect or substantial nonperformance of parental functions.

[X] A long term impairment resulting from drug, alcohol, or other substance abuse that interferes with the performance of parenting functions.

At that my fight took flight. I had no charge remaining. Gravity took over as the weight of the words bore down. I looked over the "Residential Schedule" which gave every day of every year solely to Eric.

The second to last paragraph on page eight held this "other provision:" Mother should have no contact with father or child until she successfully completes drug rehabilitation treatment program and then only through supervised visitation approved by court. Mother required to reimburse father for expenses of daughter's drug rehabilitation program.

I voluntarily signed the document which deemed me a non-parent in every way; and, as an individual with a serious drug abuse problem. And, I agreed to a Judgment for over thirteen thousand dollars plus interest. I must reimburse Eric for every penny of all three of Zoey's three week stints of treatment.

When it was time to leave, I found Eric and Crystal standing in the reception area waiting for me to emerge from the conference room. It seems they had words for me beyond these but they are the only ones I remember, Eric telling me he wouldn't record the judgment so long as I kept *my agreement* and made timely payments.

The camera zoomed out until I was invisible. I was so small as to be nonexistent. Nevertheless, the Bad Mom Syndrome sniffed me out and I was promptly infected before "It's a wrap!" was called.

Part 2: Floundering In The Wake

". . .You're a little bit of a tomboy. There's a sense of, "I can do it all. Don't put me in my place. Don't tell me how it is." Yet, you're very feminine without being delicate. There's a very wholesome energy, very feminine. . . but a little tomboyish.

You often put yourself in situations where you have to work from your own inner male energy and that often creates a misalignment of energy. This is not a negative thing but I do see a new opportunity that comes up where you may find yourself in a traditionally male role, having to really push yourself because you don't want to lose your own feminine balance... and having to come to a place where you can work well as one of the guys without losing your sense of identity and your femininity..."

Excerpted from a transcription of the tape recording made during my first session with Teresa Carol, Spring 1992

9: Revelations

November 8, 1995
Fax to: Mr. Attorney-at-law
From: Beth Rice
Re: Your client, Eric

Dear Mr. Attorney,

My and your client's daughter, Zoey, has a very ill grandfather at the University Hospital in Seattle. On November sixth he underwent a near fourteen hour surgery to remove cancerous organs. He is now in the intensive care unit and improving but his condition is tenuous. Zoey and he are quite close and I believe she would want to see him and shine some love on him. My mother, needless to say, is not comfortable contacting your client in the present state of affairs nor is she capable of offering to transport Zoey to see her grandfather without the assistance of my brother or sister-in-law, who I believe are off-limits to Zoey. Would you please inform your client of this situation and ask if he would please contact my mother at my brother's home to make an agreeable arrangement for Zoey's transport. He need not be inconvenienced if my brother or sister-in-law are acceptable to him as chauffeur in this scenario. Of course, Zoey's grandmother will also be along for the ride and I will stay away during this time.

Thank you,
Beth Rice

cc: Dick Carville, Attorney-at-law

P.S. - If there is need to contact me please do so via fax c/o Dick Carville. Again, thank you.

November 15, 1995 – letter from Jeb
(who I thought was likely a one-night-stand)

Hey, Beth, what's up? Just got back to Tennessee. Wow, I already miss Seattle. I think I am going to move there. I must first apologize for not calling you back when you called. I came down with the worst case of strep throat; I could barely talk or move the last day there. Much better now, my blood stream is teaming with antibiotics.

How is the hat biz doing? I must say I love the cap you gave me. I've been wearing it almost every day. Also thinking of our evening... I think it could have not gone better, you are wonderful.

Well, I must say that Seattle seems to be the place to be. A couple of days before I got sick, I was walking in Queen Anne and a car slammed on its breaks and a man yells "Jebbah!!" It was the last place on earth I thought I would hear my name. Well, it turns out to be one of my college buddies that graduated with me that I have not seen in years. He lives in Queen Anne and has been in Seattle ever since graduation. What a small world.

Well, drop me a line and let me know how you are. I would love to hear from you and hear more about Seattle and you.

Talk to ya soon, Jeb

November 17, 1995

Fax to: Mr. Attorney-at-law
From: Beth Rice
Re: Your client, Eric - Two issues:
[1] A message to your client in follow-up to my fax of 11-8-95
[2] Something YOU should know
[1] I thank your client for getting Zoey to see her grandfather. I saw Zoey's "I love you" card, in which she stated she'd come visit him when he comes home from the hospital. Well, he underwent another four and a half hours of surgery this week; and, is likely to go in to surgery again in the next few days. I seriously question whether he is going to make it home. I feel Zoey should be made aware of this and offered another opportunity to see him. Again, your client need not be inconvenienced. He can utilize the avenue presented in my last fax. I will not violate our bilateral no-contact agreement.

[2] Your client is in violation of the above mentioned agreement/order. On November 13th or 14th, a police officer called me at my place of employment to question me about a Missing Persons Report filed on Zoey November 11th. If your client can wait two or three days to get word to me of an emergency regarding Zoey he can wait one more and reach me through the proper channels. Had he called my brother on November 11th I could have been reached and offered assistance immediately.

If your client has *any* third party contact me at work again other than my attorney, Dick Carville, or one of my immediate family members: my mother, brother, or sister-in-law, this will be considered harassment and endangerment of my ability to earn an income and I will press charges.
Thank you, Beth Rice
Cc: Dick Carville, Attorney-at-law

The psyche is mysterious. I vaguely recall, upon seeing the last "other provision," saying to Carville to tell Eric he was not to contact me either, that it must be a street blocked in both directions. I don't find it written anywhere in my miles of files; but, somehow my mind grabbed on to my provision as reality —"bilateral no-contact agreement." What? I suppose if I could hold onto that I would feel somewhat empowered in the scenario.

Journal: November 27, 1995

Some big truths were realized last night. Mom and Dad each had moments with me in which truths dawned. I am so thankful for last night.

Mom, Josh and I were visiting with Dad until Mom needed to go lie down. She's staying at her dear friend Jenny's home so to be close to the hospital. Josh drove her back to Jenny's. I stayed with Dad.

We were sitting there in quiet for a while when out of the blue Dad said to me, "I'm sorry I wasn't such a good father."

I replied, "I'm sorry I haven't been such a good daughter."

"I should have gotten you to college. I'm sorry I didn't."

I thanked him for saying so. I am so thankful he told me that. He atoned. I wonder if that's why he dropped out of Alcoholics Anonymous so soon after he got out of treatment all those years ago. Maybe when they got to the step about making amends he wasn't ready to go there. But, after fourteen years of sobriety and with death looming I guess he figured it was time.

Earlier in the evening Mom and I had dinner at a diner near the hospital. Josh joined us later. Aaargh – this is such a long story. But, if I don't write it now when will I? It's about the jade ring that Dad bought for Mom in Hong Kong back in the 70's when he was working in Viet Nam and Mom, Josh, and I lived in Singapore. I know I've never written about this so I must start at the beginning:

One Christmas a few years back, when I was up from L.A., Zoey, Josh, Rosey, their girls and I were all staying at Mom and Dad's house to share the holiday. The fact I was *visiting* from L.A. apparently rekindled in Mom her ire in that I'd moved away from her and Dad and, above all, did not have Zoey living with me.

After dinner one evening while Dad, Josh, and the kids were all watching a movie in the family room, Mom, Rosey and I were in the living room visiting. I don't recall what prompted the action but Mom started bringing out the beautiful silk dresses and pant suits she designed and had custom tailored in Singapore, as well as the Asian style silk outfits that Dad had bought for her. She said they no longer fit her but that someone should be getting use out of them.

She held up a long white silk brocade fitted sheath with a mandarin collar and those beautiful frog closures, glanced at me and said, "You couldn't get into this." She then turned to Rosey and offered it to her with, "But, I'm sure it'll fit you." Rosey was taken aback but accepted it with grace. Next Mom held up a darling pant suit in that kind of silk woven with two different colors for each the warp and the weft so the color of the fabric appears different given the lighting and angle of view. This silk was woven in a vibrant pink and sort of an orangey gold. I had always loved this outfit but Mom repeated her earlier action with a similar cutting remark to me. Rosey looked at me uncomfortably but, again, said nothing beyond, "Thank you," and accepted the gift. I was just plain speechless.

Mom continued on through to the last outfit in much the same manner and Rosey finally expressed her thoughts with, "I'm sure Beth would love to have some of these."

Mom told Rosey something to the affect, "You're in the family now, mother to two of my granddaughters and I'd like for you to have the outfits. Besides, Beth could never squeeze her hips into them." She then held out her hand to Rosey adding, "Here's one last thing. See if it fits." Rosey held up her hand and Mom dropped the jade ring onto her open palm. I couldn't believe it. It was apparent by the look on Rosey's face that she couldn't either. Rosey looked mortified and turned to me wide eyed with lips zipped. I imagine my face mirrored hers.

Right about then Zoey and her cousins bounced into the room wondering what we were up to. I was thankful for the interruption as the Bash Beth Give-Away drew to a close with no further discussion. A dagger had just been planted in my heart and given several sharp twists. Nonetheless, I was silent for I didn't want my sister-in-law to feel I was resentful of her. It was obvious Rosey also welcomed an opportunity for the scene to be over as she diverted her attention to the girls.

Now, fast forward to me staying with Josh and Rosey after my unsuccessful put-it-back-together-with-Paul trip to Hawaii. One afternoon while the girls were playing in the back yard, Rosey and I were talking over coffee at the kitchen table. This was before I got my new job and before Zoey came to live there too. Rosey got up saying, "Come here," and walked down the hall. I followed her into the master bedroom where she was lifting the lid of her jewelry box. She turned to me saying, "Open your hand." She dropped the jade ring onto my palm saying, "You should have this."

"But, Mom gave it to you," I replied.

"She shouldn't have and I didn't know how to say so at the time. I want you to have it now. Besides, it's too big for my tastes. You know me. Look at all my tiny rings," and she pointed into her jewelry box.

I thanked her; both for the acknowledgment of my unvoiced feelings and for giving me the ring. I then gave her a hug. It did not fit the ring finger on my right hand but it did fit the finger that no longer held my wedding ring. I laughed. When Rosey gave me a questioning look I told her, "It's a perfect expression of how jaded I feel about marriage."

Fast forward again to the diner where Mom and I were

eating while waiting for Josh to meet up with us for the hospital's evening visiting hours. Mom was talking about all the horrific mistakes the hospital staff has made and the anxiety it's caused for Dad—such as the tube that was stuffed down his throat for a full day between Mom's visits but was not connected to anything so performed no function STOP! I can't get started on that load of crap now—when all of a sudden she interrupts herself with, "I'm so glad to see you're finally wearing the jade ring!"

"What do you mean "finally"? Rosey just gave it to me a few months ago, when I was living with her and Josh."

"What are you talking about? I gave you the jade ring."

"No you didn't. You gave it to Rosey and she gave it to me."

At that Mom hesitated; but then persisted with, "I gave you that ring! Your father gave it to me and I gave it to you, as should be."

"I hate to break it to you, Mom, but you gave it to Rosey several Christmases ago when I was up from L.A."

As her eyes began to glaze over with the remembrance of this truth, Josh showed up. Ha! Saved by the bro! That was the end of the jade ring discussion, thank God. I also thank God for those moments though. What I take away from that experience is that she was acting irrationally in anger at the time the ring was gifted to Rosey. In her heart she wanted it to be with me, that her intent was for me to have it. I am so thankful to Rosey for buffing Mom's comfort zone, for undoing the action Mom couldn't undo herself. Wow! What a night of revelations.

November 27, 1995 – a letter to...

Hi Jeb!

How nice to hear from you! Bit of a surprise it was, since you hadn't called back. And, now I know why. I hope you got all of your auditions in before the strep hit you. How did all of that go, by the way?

So you think Seattle might be the place to be, huh? I'm lying on my stomach in bed so please excuse the scrawl. Well, you have at least two friends here, me and your college buddy, so it wouldn't be like starting from ground zero. I really enjoyed your company and think we'd have great fun doing cool things like Pike Place Market on Saturday mornings, the best day for street musicians; and blowing bubbles off the top of the tower in Volunteer Park, etcetera. I am so stoked! Sunday December 3rd I'm moving into a great new apartment at Green Lake, my favorite place to skate aside from Hermosa Beach, California.

11-28-95 - Jeb - It's a new day! Boy my life has been such a jumble these last 3 weeks. To tell you the truth, I don't precisely recall when our evening together fit in there. Fact is you were a marvelous distraction. My father has been in the hospital for just over three weeks. He underwent a 14 hour surgery to remove cancerous parts and tissue and then another surgery about a week later, due to complications, and a third surgery on Sunday (2 days ago) that will hopefully be the last and see him on to the road recovery. But once we get him home it'll be just a month or so til he starts chemotherapy and...well, if you've known anyone who has gone through this... We know he's going to die due to cancer, it's just a matter of how long does he have and how much will he have to endure. Sometimes I ache for a good "spoon".

And the hat business! Well, you know how the old snow-ball effect works. 1995 is going to conveniently disappear out of my reality until such time as I can write my book and sort through the muck in a detached manner. Some stuff has come down in our company (due to my boss, the owner, allowing his dick to make some bad decisions for him) that will either put me on top of a bad situation with tremendous personal gain OR cause me to update my resume and be seeking new employment. It's funny how one day things are moving along and the next day your whole world is spinning out of control.

I need to get ready for work but certainly don't want to end on such a downer note. Life goes on and I must say that with each passing event I become much duckier, much better at letting it roll off my back. I am very much looking forward to moving into my own home, getting back in touch with my things, like my art, my polar bear collection, *my* bed.

In the week between Christmas and New Years our office will be closed so nine or ten days in a row OFF. I'm going to spend the time settling into my place and sorting through my life which is now jumbled up in a lot of boxes. I'm going to get rid of the bad, the excess baggage; and

organize the good, the warm memorables and the evil necessities like tax records, and get ready to ring in 1996 with renewed faith and hope and a higher level of inner peace. WHEW! I ramble. I'm glad you like your cap and I hope I will see you again.
Beth

Journal: November 28, 1995

Ha! About that higher level of inner peace I spoke of with Jeb; its probably a good idea I got my first ever, and hopefully only, anxiety attack out of the way before New Years. Yesterday at work while talking on the phone with one of my fave customers I started losing it. I went kookoo. He asked me how I was doing and I said something humorously bland and fairly impersonal. He laughed and then said something like, "But, really, how are you doing? We haven't had a good chat for a while." I went blank and wondered what I could say to him. I started to laugh, out of nervousness I guess, but very quickly my laughter became a choke in my throat and tears came to my eyes. I started to cry. Then I started to laugh again and commented in the phone something to the effect, "How silly! I guess I laughed until I cried." At that I started sobbing, told him as best possible that I'd call him again real soon and hung up.

A tap on my shoulder had me turning to find Lonni staring at me. Again I started to laugh, like this was normal. When she asked if I was okay my laughter again became sobs. The fact was I could hardly catch my breath and I said, "Lonni, please go tell David *(our boss)* we're going to lunch and take me to the urgent care clinic. I don't know what's going on with me."

So Lonni took me to the clinic that's several blocks up the street from our office. I alternately laughed and cried in ten second spurts all the way. They took one look at me and immediately lead me into a private room. The nurse or the doctor, I don't know, someone in a uniform, asked what's going on in my life. In between sobs I told her I had not seen my fourteen year old daughter for months, my father is in the hospital and we don't know if he'll make it out alive, things are all screwed up at work, then added, "And I'm a terrible mother, bad mom." She jabbed a needle into my arm and afterward told me to breathe into the paper bag she was handing to me. She explained I was hyperventilating, that breathing into the bag would help level me out. She left the room. Within what seemed like mere seconds I felt absolutely euphoric and wonderfully at peace with the world.

I was still breathing into the bag when the nurse or doctor came back. She handed me a prescription saying it was for the pill version of the medication I'd just received via injection; told me that I was to get it filled, go home and take one pill, then take another before bed. She said I should stay home tomorrow, take one pill after breakfast and the last pill after dinner. I told her I needed to talk to my friend in the waiting room and was informed Lonni had gone back to work quite a while ago. It seems I was in a bit of a time warp. She asked if I knew anyone else who could come get me and take me home. I gave her Rosey and Josh's phone number and thankfully Rosey was there to get the call. She came and got me.

We stopped at a grocery store and sat in the waiting area near the pharmacy department while the prescription was being filled. I felt like I was in a movie that I was watching. I felt so detached from the setting, so other-worldly. I don't know how to describe it, like I was on the other side of the rainbow or something. Rosey was cheerfully chattering at me but I didn't hear her words and she didn't seem to mind.

When we pulled into my driveway she asked if I wanted her to come in and stay with me a while but I told her I'd be okay. I took a pill as directed, laid on the couch to watch TV and fell asleep almost immediately. I woke up at about 10PM in a dark house, took another pill and crawled into bed.

I called work this morning to let them know I wouldn't be in. Lonni got on the phone saying she already told David what the folks at the clinic recommended, that all was cool. So, I am taking it easy today, focusing on positivity and counting my blessings. I looked at the pill bottle as I ate my Cheerios and learned I was taking Xanax. I took one and seeing one last pill in the bottle brought to mind the day I dumped a couple dozen Valium in the toilet. I was living with Riley out by Moose Creek in Alaska at the time. There was still a couple months left to refill that prescription the neurologist in Seattle had written for me in follow up to my car accident. But on that day it hit me I didn't need them anymore and didn't see why I should keep taking them. Considering how strong the Xanax is I can see why they only gave me four. Damn, it would be easy to get hooked on feeling this relaxed, like peace in a bottle.

TO: KISW Radio	DATE: December 1, 1995
ATTN: Anyone helpful & nice	FAX #:
RE: Last night's broadcast	TOTAL PAGES: one

Fax Message

Hello! My friend and co-worker, Lonni, informed me that I missed an in-studio interview with one of my all-time favorite bands last night, [the Band I'm Not to Mention = BINM]. I think BINM's [most recent CD] is brilliant. I get out to see and hear them play at every opportunity. And, I always listen to KISW so I don't know how I missed this! Is there any chance I could get a recording of this show? Pretty please? I'll offer up a bribe! I'll trade you a very cool custom cap (we manufacture caps). By the way, I bought tickets for Saturday night's show as soon as they went on sale. Lonni & I will be there celebrating my birthday. If you can't get me a tape of the Mad Season/ BINM/Screaming Trees show maybe you could arrange for that hot singer, T., to come home with me to help celebrate! See what you can do, please. Need 2 or 3 caps?

Beth Rice, Director Sport Fashion Division
The Cap Company

Journal: December 9, 1995

Last night Dad called me quite late. It was apparent he was inebriated by pain medication. He said he's going home, that he'll "just sit on the porch with [his] morphine bag and when it's over, it's over". We talked quite a while and out of the blue he asked, "Have you seen Zoey lately?"

"Dad, you know I haven't. But since you're going home I bet she can visit."

"Will you ask Eric if you can be there too?"

I told him I would.

I kept my promise and drafted a letter to Eric regarding Zoey and I having Christmas with him and Mom together. I intended to fax it to his office tomorrow but I got carried away, it got far too long and sidetracked in an angry way.

A suggestion that Teresa, my psychic self-empowerment counselor, had given to me at my consultation in the summer rang out in my brain, "Write letters. Write, write, write! But, don't send them." If I had heeded that warning last summer things might not be where they are now. I called Mom and Rosey and read it to each of them. Of course, they both said "Don't send it." Mom said, "I'll call and talk to him." So, I did not send the letter. She told me his response to her was, "It's not up to me. It's up to the court." What a fucking crock! "The court" had nothing to do with anything. Among our circle of family and friends, I doubt any would make a dash to call the police to inform them of the violation. Zoey will be allowed to go visit with Mom and Dad between Christmas and New Years when I am not there.

December 14, 1995 – a letter from Jeb

Hey Ms. Beth! I have a great late Christmas gift for you. Can you guess what it is? You should get it around January 20th and it will be . . . the best spoon you ever had!! So get ready.

I'm so happy for you to get your own place on Green Lake. That is one of the spots I want to look into moving to when I get there. Being a personal trainer, that track around the lake sounds very nice. Thanks for offering to be a friend when I get there. It's great to know somebody in Seattle. This is a very big move and it's kind of scary!

Sorry to hear about your dad and cancer. I did not want to bog you down with my problems on our wonderful night together; but, I must let you in on a little secret now. Yes, I have a college buddy there in the city, but I also have a mother and grandmother in Kirkland. One of the big reasons I'm moving out there is my mom has cancer (in remission now, thank God) but my grandmother has been diagnosed terminal, and has less than a year to live. I'm moving out to give my love and support to my family and help bring closure to my mom's relationship with my grandmother. So, I know what you are going through.

109

We can climb that hill together. I hope you have a great X-mas and New Year. If you like, call me. I will be leaving Tennessee mid-January. Take care.   Jeb

---

KISW
9 9 . 9 F M
Steve Gardner
Promotion Coordinator

Beth:

Here is the aircheck of the
Mad Season/BINM/Screaming Trees interview.
I'll give you a call about the hats next week!

Steve

TO: KISW Radio   DATE: December 22, 1995
ATTN: Steve Gardner   FAX #:
RE: My fax of 12-1-95   TOTAL PAGES: two
(follows this page as reminder)   (including this cover page)

Fax Message

Thanks so much for sending me the requested tape! I have some cool caps picked out for you and would love to bring them by. I live at Green Lake so could hop in at the drop of a hat (ha!) I'm usually home by 5PM so call me when it works for you.

Have a very Merry Christmas!
Best regards, Beth

December 26, 1995 - In the drawer at Gramma's

My dear Zoey,

We are survivors. I have just made it through the most painful Christmas ever and, thank God, am nearing the closure of the worst year of my life. I won't add "so far" because I hope that was it. I can't imagine it being or getting any worse than 1995. I guess what keeps me going is knowing that you need me, even still, and that we will find our ways through this and come out the other side being stronger and wiser. Also, I hold firm to my belief that we are here on earth to learn and that it <u>is</u> true that "the failed experiments" are all a part of the process. I miss you so unbelievably bad. I just ache to hold you in a good spoon, to hear your laughter and see your beautiful smile.

From what I heard from Lonni (she told me of running into you) I sense that you have been given a fairly distorted view of some of the events around our present circumstance and that many truths have not been given to you at all. It was fear and pure adrenaline that kept me going for a while and then I threw myself headlong into work as a survival tactic. Then work became part of (a factor in) the awfulness of 1995 and, of course, now the roller-coaster ride between hope and reality regarding Dad's life and impending death.

And through it all <u>not one day</u> has gone by that I haven't thought of you <u>in depth</u> - wondered how you are? What are you thinking? What are you feeling? Is school going OK? Are Eric and Crystal treating you well? Are they giving you space to be Zoey - to write your poetry and to draw? Are they learning to appreciate you or are they still trying to make you an Eric/Crystal clone? I do know, without a doubt, that at least they are parenting you and whether right or wrong, good or bad, your father loves you and you do need to be parented. It won't be long and you will be eighteen, of legal age, and able to make your own choices and decisions. Its through the parenting you receive until that time that, hopefully, you'll have learned how to make decisions that will best serve your needs and hopes and desires—the essence of you.

When I go home today I am going to start making phone calls until I find a treatment plan that will fit both my budget and schedule so that I can take the steps necessary to

111

earn the ability to have some input into your parenting. Obviously, not with or alongside Eric and Crystal, but to at least have an opportunity to see you, talk with you, and share some of what I've learned and also to learn from you. It is fear that has kept me from taking this step until now - not fear of treatment, as I have been clean for months. I can explain this fear to you when I see you or maybe not. Maybe it won't matter. It is going to take time, Zoey but know that I am in process and that you will certainly know when I've made it.

I am looking forward to 1996. I view it as an opportunity for a fresh start. The high point of my life right now is my new apartment - my new *home*. I will be there a long time so you will see it (maybe even live there) one day. On December third I finally got into my own home again. You will love it. I sure do. You are everywhere, in every room. I have a big box of your art, poems, and favorite things waiting for you. And I continue to pick up little things for you. There will be an interesting collection waiting for you. The little gold ring that came from Gramma and Grampa at Christmas-time I bought for you in Hong Kong (a work trip). I hope you will wear it every day and be reminded of my love for you.

For now, my dear daughter, let me just say that I hope you will view all people with love in your heart—that includes *you*, above all. I have concluded that this is life's biggest challenge and the most important lesson we have to learn. Play by the rules, Sweetie Heart, and I'll be seeing you as soon as possible.

All my love, *always*Mom

P. S. - The other high point of my life right now is knowing that I am well loved, that I have a wonderful family who have forgiven me my blunders and love and support me. I don't know for sure where you are at on this note. I know you love me. We have a bond that will never be broken. If not now, some day you may find yourself very angry with me about all of this and it will be justified and okay if that happens. My only hope is that if or when that happens you will eventually work through it and come back, or better, evolve to a new and higher love. You are such a beautiful person inside and out. I have tremendous faith in you, Zoey.

December 27, 1995 - a note from my new upstairs neighbors

Beth, the incense both have frankincense in them. Several of my "teachers" have told me that it is good to burn frankincense or sage when one moves into a new space as it will cleanse the energy of the space & make it <u>yours</u> !

The Pooh book is from a used book sale. I know that Pooh is not a polar bear, BUT the first story in the book is about building a house; maybe it will warm your home...

Enjoy ! I'm glad we've met . . .

Here's to warm houses for all of us!

Love, Holly & Marcus

December 29, 1995 - my letter to. . .

Hey Billy!

Sure enjoyed talking to you the other night. I hope your collar bone eases up on the pain factor soon. What a bum deal!

New Year's Eve BINM is opening for Candlebox at a small arena here in town. I haven't decided for sure but think I'll go since I love both bands. Hate the idea of no alcohol though so will probably vacillate until it's sold out.

Let me know what you think of the tape. It'd be cool if you could use one of my friend Jack's songs in your next video. The video you gave me rocks! I'm glad for you that Abacus is doing so well and am looking forward to seeing you in just a month.

Peace,
Beth

Journal: December 30, 1995

I paged Jack and much to my surprise he called back. I apologized for saying stupid shit. I told him that was my maligned self defense system at work: If something starts to feel nice, do something to fuck it up.

9: Rolling In, Over, and On

January 1996 Calendar:
  6th: Gruntruck @ The Crocodile Cafe
  8th: Steve Gardner @ KISW – 6PM - doors will be locked
                                          so knock loud
  25th: Inflatable Soule @ The Crocodile
  27th: The Last Ever Pleasure Elite Show @ the Fenix – 9pm
  30th: Leave for Dallas tradeshow - early am

January 2, 1996 4 am

Howdy Billy!

  I'm amazed I should get back on my regular work day schedule so easily considering that many mornings of this last nine days I was just going to bed at this time! Well, I went to get tickets for the BINM and Candlebox show only to find that it was at a big arena and nosebleed seats were all that was left. So I went to see 7 Year Bitch (they fucking rock!) at a club downtown: RKCNDY (pronounced: rock candy). I drank too much to drive and didn't have enough cash left on me for cab fare so got a ride home from some nice guys I'd been rocking out with. I invited them in for munchies and soda to drive home on since there were roadblocks set up all over. They gave me their number telling me to call the next day and they'd take me back to my car. So I did and they did--a great way to start the New Year.

  Hope you have a Happy New Year! Beth

Journal: January 9, 1996

  At 11:20pm I was washing the ashtray Zoey made for me in pottery class and was consumed by deep Zoey vibes—like she was in me, yet surrounded me. *Hero* by Mariah Carey played on the radio and I thought of how she never wanted to hear that song. Like me at that age, she'd prefer someone else to take the hero role rather than finding her own inner strength and trusting that she would be her own best hero.

114

January 17, 1996 – a letter in the drawer at Gramma's
Hi Sweetie Heart!

I was so anxious to talk to Rosey last Friday (the 12th) to hear whatever I could about you. She said you had a great time at Chuck E. Cheese playing with your cousins. And then she also told me some stuff that distresses me, my worst fears realized. In fact, it is the exact fear I mentioned but didn't explain in my letter of December 26, 1995, the first one that I left for you here at Gramma's.

As I have told you, I've been clean since May 17, 1995, the day your father took you to the lock-down rehab facility. So, getting into a treatment program has not been a concern to me for my benefit. But since my "completion of a Drug and Alcohol Treatment Program" has become the key to my ability to see you, getting enrolled has been on my mind heavily. I believe Lonni told you about the extensive traveling I was doing for a while there (for work) and, as always, cash flow is a serious problem. I've got about an $800 repair coming up on my car at the end of this month. Thank heaven Mom and Dad are going to pay it and I will make payments to them. The last week of this month I'll be in Dallas for a Trade Show and then February 9 thru 13 in L.A. for another one. All of the treatment programs I've checked into demand continuous attendance. The Milam program is the cram course that would suit me best, Monday thru Friday 6PM to 9:30PM for four weeks with an AA meeting every Saturday and Sunday. Since I'm going in clean I should "graduate" after that Basic Training but even if I get help with health insurance my share out-of-pocket will still be five or six hundred dollars. And, I'd still have this big fear to deal with:

Rosey tells me that you are now drinking and getting high "*in moderation.*" Zoey, you're getting away with it for now but sooner or later Eric and Crystal are going to pull their heads out of the sand (where they now have them conveniently buried since only they and you can be accountable for your actions at this time—they don't have me to blame it on). If we start having supervised visits with the court of the State of Washington's blessing (which will be a major process to get through and "supervisors" don't come cheap) you know as well as I do that they will start watch-

115

ing you more closely. If they decide to run a urine analysis on you I will, again, become the scapegoat. You don't know all that went on this last spring and summer, Zoey. Your dad and Crystal knew they had me over a barrel. They milked the circumstances and me for everything they could. I made it very convenient for them to have everything about your behavior be all my fault.

Being separated from you until your eighteenth birthday is painful enough. But if they decide to demonstrate how really awful I am and how this is all my fault they can file criminal charges on me, the State of Washington picks up the tab for prosecuting me (because criminal charges are always the State versus the Defendant) and I either risk going to prison (not county jail) by going with a Public Defender or end up on the streets trying to pay for a good criminal attorney, maybe lose my job. What a damn mess!

Zoey, if you can promise me that you'll get clean and stay clean I'll go through the process to see you. When you are eighteen you can choose moderation if that's what you want but right now it's a big *big* mistake. If I get put away it'll be long after your eighteenth birthday before we can be together. You and I both know what a good actress you can be when you put your mind to it. Until your eighteenth birthday you have to play the role of the Zoey that they want you to be. Act respectful toward them and their values. Your life and my life for this next thirty-one months will be much easier. I love you so very much Zoey and I miss you beyond belief but I don't need any more pain in my life. *Please*, Sweetie Heart, clean it up! Thank you for getting good grades. Rosey told me that too.

All my heart, *always*Mom

February 1996 Calendar:

2nd = Inflatable Soule @ Shark Club in Kirkland
3rd = Gruntruck @ Moe -AND- Jeb here
8th = Leave for L.A.
17th = Home Alive CD Release Party @ Moe - BINM, Dancing
     French Liberals of '48, Anne & Nancy Wilson of Heart
27th = Leave for L.A.

February 17, 1996 – a note in her 1996 Bag

Zoey - I was telling Holly, my neighbor/friend, about

my purple dragon (the one you made for me) and, again, I had the most incredible overwhelming, all-senses (like the Kauai wave embrace) sense of you and then the emptiness of missing you SO FUCKING BAD! And, as always, the remorse tagged along.   Love, Mom

<u>February 24, 1996 Saturday 9a.m. - In Zoey 's Bag</u>

Hi Love!

I picked up these postcards at a place on First Avenue called The Lux. It's a couple doors down from Casa Ubetcha, where my new friend, Jeb, and I'd planned to go for Valentine's dinner. We got a late start because I am so swamped trying to settle all my personal STUFF into my apartment while getting rid of reams of paper, in trying to condense and incorporate all of the "portable files" that developed while I took my Kauai trip... slept on Josh's couch... never got settled into *our* apartment... threw everything back into storage for five months while staying at Joe's in Mukilteo... and haven't had a chance to sort out since my recent move to Green Lake because of business travel and spending every possible moment with Dad... all while setting up my new in-home office that there is no room for until I get the personal stuff settled!.

The kitchen at Casa Ubetcha was closed so we wandered down the sidewalk and stumbled on The Lux. This place was too cool. You'd love it. It's a coffee house with a one-table-nonsmoking-section which, of course, is one of the features I liked best. You'd love the decor and the mochas, as did I! The owner, Lisa Marie ("just like Elvis' daughter" she told us), makes not only the most delicious mocha I've ever drunk, but also the most artistic. She paints pictures with the milk foam on top! I got a leaf and Jeb got a Valentine heart.

Speaking of reams of paper, I am writing a book. You know I have talked about this for a long time. Different unique phases of my life have each inspired a drive to write a book about the experience. But now I am totally compelled to tell the story that brings us to where we, you and I, are today. I am writing the book for several reasons:

[1] For me, because I need for you understand the full dynamic of the "relationship" between me, your dad, and Crystal; and, how it has all come to have such a profound

effect on you.

[2] For you, in hopes that it will clear up a bunch of *STUFF* such that you can look at it, digest it, then release it and get on with your life.

[3] For others who have been through or are now experiencing similar trauma that they might find comfort in knowing they aren't alone.

I love you, Zoey and miss you so very much. I am not putting this in the drawer at Gramma's house for you to read now or soon (as I had planned when I started writing) for I fear that it would add fuel to the internal flame that is you -your essence- and cause you to stir when you should be settling. Right now and until your eighteenth birthday it would be best *UNFUCKINGFORTUNATELY!* for you to stifle your rebel/peaceful/abstract essence in order to cruise through life with Eric and Crystal as unscathed as possible. WOW what a weird paradox. Life is weird. So I'm taking this home with me and putting it in your 1996 bag-of-things-I'm-collecting-to-give-you-later, on your eighteenth birthday, to be precise.

For now, I'll write another simple note to put in the drawer at Mom's for you. . .continued. . .

February 24, 1996 - In The Drawer At Gramma's

Dear Zoey, love of my life and ray of light beaming to see me through, I'm enclosing our astrological forecasts for 1996 as published in a calendar book entitled *WE'MOON 1996 - GAIA Rhythms For Womyn - Earth Matters.* This book was given to my new neighbor and friend, Holly, as a Christmas gift from one of her friends; and she, in turn, shared it with me. I think you will identify with what the forecasts say. I sure do. I hope you enjoy and, hopefully, heed.

I have concluded that it is in both our best interests to accept this separation and leave it in place. Remember how we used to count down the months, weeks, and then days until we'd bridge the geographical gap between L.A. and Seattle, until we would be together? Well, *this* separation will ultimately span a total of 38 months. We are now down to 30 months to go. After that we have the whole rest of our lives to be together unfettered, as ourselves, as we choose. You are strong, beautiful inside and out, smart, and creative and oh how I love you and miss you. But we will come through, me and you.

Use your smarts. Express yourself in your art. Get into the Drama program at school or some forum for expression that doesn't set you up for trouble with your dad and Crystal. Keep *you* intact with care and with consideration of/for these current circumstances. Be good. I am so very proud of you. Keep smiling and keep loving.

My dear daughter, I often feel you with me and I know you must feel my love and presence also. Please leave these letters here or best give them to Gramma for safekeeping. Do not take them with you for, if found, the consequences will be so severe. Trust me. You will be able to read the whole story when we reach the end of this segment of our lives and can move forward into a new day in a new way.

Love always and forever, Mom

March 1996 Calendar:

14th = White Zombie with Gary
30th = Tony Hawk/BOARD STIFF @ Snoqualmie Pass with Jeb

March 8, 1996 – on my kitchen table

Beth,

I hope you don't mind but I brought your mail in and watered a couple of the plants in the window as they looked droopy and sad – I talked with them in the hopes of cheering them!   Holly

P.S. We have a new toy and I need to
ask you a favor in order to use it.

March 8, 1996 – a note in her 1996 bag

Zoey - I just got back from another week in L.A. Holly and I are hanging in my kitchen yacking and you have woven in and out of the conversation. I just had to stop in the middle to write down what I was voicing to Holly... that I miss you so bad and that I think of you every day ... several times a day. I love you. Mom

Journal: March 13, 1996

I wish Zoey would get over to her Gramma & Grampa's to get my letters. It's hard to believe we're coming up on the one year anniversary of the day her dad snagged her out of school. So much stuff has happened - if I just let loose and scribble events as they occur to me. . .

119

I've been to upstate New York - Chicago - Las Vegas - L.A. 4 or 5 times – Canton (Guangzhou), China - Hong Kong - Las Vegas again for 2 or 3 hours -Toledo - St. Louis - Lansing - Detroit - Dallas. I've met Joe, Jeb, Gary, Deke, Mark - - Still see both Jay and Jack on occasion. Met Marcus and Holly - good thing.

I met Cindy Hammond (from KISW). It is, literally, BINM that brought us together and, wouldn't you know, over hats the first time. I took some cool caps to the station in exchange for a tape of the BINM interview I'd missed. Then, while I was waiting to board the plane to L.A. on this last trip, she was too. I struck up a conversation with her. She was pretty friendly, told me she was on her way to do an interview with Ozzy Osborne that would be syndicated along with the live broadcast of his concert there. We got to talking about the local music scene and she was telling me all about the early days hanging at NAF (a place where bands practice) when Alice In Chains, Soundgarden and others were still up-and-coming.

As soon as I got home from L.A., Marcus, from upstairs, told me he heard BINM would be playing somewhere around town that night; but, he couldn't remember in which club. He thought he'd heard it on The End that day. It wasn't listed in the Rocket so I called The End to ask which club. Geez, it took forfuckingever for them to answer the phone and then the DJ knew nothing about it!

I was listening to KISW and heard Cindy on-air so thought I'll call KISW and see if anyone there knows. I wasn't looking forward to letting it ring 50 times before someone picked up so I looked in the phone book to see if there was another number to call besides the Request Line. The business office was closed so I thought what-the-hell and dialed 421-rock. As it started to ring, I was thinking "Okay Cindy, pick it up. . .pick it up" and, much to my surprise, on the third ring *she did!* I willed her to answer the phone! I said, "Hi, it's Beth, the HatLady. How ya doin'? How'd your trip and the interview go?" She was really cool and we chatted a bit. When I asked about BINM playing she told me they'd be at RKCNDY; and, in fact, that she would be announcing. She told me to come over and talk to her if I was going. I did go but didn't hang over at the side of the stage where I could have talked to her because I wouldn't have seen the performance well from there.

I've seen BINM two or three times in the last couple of months. I've talked, briefly, with T. twice. And, last Friday I had quite the nice chat with his mom. She's a very nice lady. While we were talking, after their set, he walked out the back door and I asked her if that was his girlfriend leaving with him. She responded, "I hope not. He's married." This was good to learn. I will now put thoughts of taking him home one night into the *total fantasy* category, take it off the *hopeful* list. He just seems so delightfully abstract, not to mention incredibly gifted, as is the band as a whole.

I had quite an unusual experience last night. Holly was here and I was going to tell her about BINM and talking to T.'s mom when I had an aggressive visual thought. I've recognized that when I have visual memories I seem to see them up and center in the total of my range of vision or the movie screen in my head. This animated computer graphic type character telescoped up to me, or my center screen, from the lower left corner and it lunged at my thought to share BINM news, as if in an attempt to push it away. It was 3D-ish, like an extrusion. Wow, it was very intense and startling. Holly wondered why I jumped. I think it was easier to explain it to her than write it because I could use my hands.

I've been promoted to Director of the Sport Fashion Division with The Cap Company. But my boss started screwing the witch of the office and asked his wife, Evie, for a divorce. Evie, being the Financial Officer of the Corporation, emptied the company bank account into her brother's account in Hong Kong (so David, my boss said) then took off for L.A. As a result, the office witch came into power as The Boss's Babe. What a fucking nightmare.

My whole program that I'd just spent two weeks on the road promoting following our return from Hong Kong and China was scrapped. But not until we really pissed off the owner of Fresh Jive. He had placed close to a fourteen thousand dollar end of season filler order with us under the new program. Two weeks after the order had been sent to the factory they finally ceased to evade our requests for status and informed us they were not interested in running the order! That made for one hat-buying company who'll never talk to me again.

Late in January, just before I left for the Dallas trade show, I got a call from Evie asking if I wanted to come to work for her. It turns out that she has three siblings; all with very successful, totally autonomous cap/hat companies. They're like Hats R Us! So, now I am working in an in-home office, in the apartment here at Green Lake (that I love so much) working for Evie. Our main office is in L.A. I'm the only person in the company remote from the office. Have I mentioned I got a healthy raise?

I called Tony at Abacus today to say hi. I told him about my plan to go to Board Stiff, the rock-n-roll snowboarding event that The End produces up at Snoqualmie Pass. And, I told him I was going for a quick lap around the lake for lunch being its a nice sunny, blue sky day. He was very cordial.

I've dressed up planter boxes for my greenhouse window. I've seen Gruntruck play three times in the last seven weeks. So much more but I'm falling asleep.

March 13, 1996, a letter to a DJ at KISW radio

Hi Cindy -

So, you had also sensed we'd meet up again. Have you read the Celestine Prophecy? I think it's the first insight which states that there are no coincidences - that people come into your life for a reason and you'll never know that reason unless you are open to listen and share.

You, no doubt, have plenty of friends since you've always lived in Seattle. I, however, have had much stuff to deal with in the three years that I've been back in the area, after seven years in Los Angeles. I've had little time to be social or develop relationships. I found quickly that I've little in common with the people I used to know. Hey! I've got forty-one years of experience and facial lines with the interests, attitude and energy of a twenty-three year old. What can I say?

My point to this discourse is that if you'd like to catch a mocha at Vivace's or The Lux with me some time I'm totally up for it. I have enclosed my card. If it's sometime in May that you find yourself drumming your fingers on the desk wanting to go do something but having no one to hang with you, pull out my card and give me a call. I empathize with busy schedules, having one myself. As I said, you seem like a real nice person and like you'd be fun. Not to worry. I'm not a celebrity stalker. I just have an incredible love for Rock n Roll - new or old, in all its formats. I'm creative and rather abstract myself so find myself drawn toward artistic people. Frankly, I'm a frustrated musician and skateboarder wannabe with a high IQ & executive-type presentation, as needed. How's that for an interesting dichotomy? And I'm friend worthy. So... see ya!

Beth

Enclosures: 2 blank tapes: one for Ozzy interview,
one to replace the BINM interview tape

Journal: March 16, 1996 Saturday

As I read back over the part about my aggressive visual thought I am recalling an acid trip I took twenty-three years ago. I was living with Denny and Victoria at the time. We had gone down to Renton to visit friends of theirs. The host split a 4-way hit of Orange Sunshine with me. It was the first time I did acid and didn't know that consuming it at about 8 or 9PM was too late in the evening. We had eaten some sort of shellfish for dinner, scallops or shrimp, and Denny broke out in hives.

At the time that we left for home, midnight or so, I was just going beyond the getting off stage and then went into full launch sitting in the dark in the back of the van on the way home. At home, Denny and Victoria went to bed after tucking in 3 year old Will and I hung out alone in the living room tripping. I remember being real fuzz mouthed, and thirsty, and polishing off about a quart of grape juice. There were footsteps coming through the ceiling in the kitchen. Since they were obviously still up, I paid a visit to the upstairs neighbors in hopes they'd have some pot.

I had been there just a few minutes when I excused myself, went into their bathroom and proceeded to embrace the head while extricating grape juice and remnants of dinner from my stomach. I became totally engrossed in all of the pretty purple patterns swirling atop the toilet water, rested my chin on the seat and gazed at the spectacle. I know not how much time elapsed but ultimately a knock at the bathroom door whipped me back to reality, or at least a semblance of real time. I flushed the toilet as my face flushed red with embarrassment. I opened the door to find a concerned look on my neighbor's face. He asked me, "Are you okay?" I apologized and retreated down the stairs.

Back in our apartment, where I shared a room with Will, I flopped on the floor of the living room not wanting to risk waking the toddler as it was only a few hours from day-break. My body was so tired. It begged my brain for sleep. But, no, my brain was busy, very busy, frying on acid.

I firmly believe that video games were invented by a computer-jock-gone-acid-head. That morning, as I lay on the floor unable to keep my eyelids open, I experienced what I now realize was a preview or premonition of a primitive version of a video game on my mental movie screen. In fact, I think it was on this occasion that I first discovered my screen. Mind you, Pong wasn't even on the market yet.

There was a cartoonish cowboy moving across my mental/visual screen in a Lite Brite (that toy from the 80's) type format, except with mobility. He was mechanical looking, kind of jerky, and so industrial sounding. I'll never forget that sound. In fact, it was a visually audio experience!

Next a dragon entered stage left, wielding a large, broad blade sword. He grasped the handle with both front claws and swung it overhead in a circular motion that was quite spectacular in mobile Lite Brite-mode. He frightened the little cowboy guy, who exited stage right.

As the dragon sliced the air with his sword in a horizontal propeller-type motion, like a helicopter, I could see the sound whirling, spiraling around my ears. It was a low pitched ringing drone, siren-like but not shrill, very irritating nonetheless. I sat up, agitated by all this activity while my body cried for sleep. When I opened my eyes the dragon and my entire screen for that matter disappeared and the visual audio did too. Whew! What a relief! I laid back down and the moment I closed my eyes my "screen" became luminous again. But now Lite Brite patterns and designs flowed or marched across my screen in rhythm to the ringing, which got louder and louder as it circled my ear.

I was unable to keep my eyes open in an effort to stop all the activity but I did not have to bear the racket for much longer because the sun climbed in the sky and its light prevailed. It out-shined my screen and the sound stopped just as Denny and Victoria got up.

Denny still had hives. This meant that Victoria would

have to work with him at their shop so she could wait on customers while he stayed out of view in the back workshop. This meant that Beth got to baby sit Will. Sitting a three year old with no sleep under the belt and an acid hang-over could have been disastrous but he was a gem all day, like he sensed I needed the mellow cooperation he gave.

So, anyway, I wonder if my aggressive visual thought the other night was a flash-back. I just spent over an hour on this story, so frigging compelled, when I have a jillion other things pressing to be done!

Journal: March 18, 1996

"Monogamy is an idealistic non-reality," I told Jay this evening, in response to the animal magnetism between us. He said, right off, that he'd been thinking about me today. He got me all horned up then sent me home and here I am getting all wet again. What a tease! We're such antagonists with each other.

A little later... I had shut my journal and was moving on to other pressing things to be done but I just flashed on the fact that I haven't mentioned White Zombie with Gary Thursday night at Mercer Arena, a fun time. Afterward we swung into the Off Ramp to see if we'd catch Brainbomb and sure 'nuff we did. In fact, I snagged Jack while he was walking by before their set and said, "Hi." He was psyching, as usual. I might be projecting this but I think not. He seemed a little weird about me being with Gary. None of the guys said hi to me. Hmmm... don't know.

Mark called to say "Sweetwater is at Moe. Maybe see you there?" I got out too late (blabbing with Holly) so didn't bother trying, figuring on a packed house. I went to the Off Ramp instead to grab a Rocket and a brew. Saw nothing of interest listed so went to the Colourbox since it was not listed. Good call. Funny Bunny was playing and what a great set.

The moment the band got on stage I, of course, wanted the cute, tall and lanky guy. And you know what? I did get him. Sammy was an absolute joy to kiss. . . what a great kisser. Whew. His smooth package was nice on my tongue too. Giving him head felt so good and it obviously gave him great pleasure. It was very nice, all of it.

11: Can I Get A Connection?

April 1, 1996 - slid under my kitchen door

I spotted this note on the floor and opened the door to find a little basket of goodies:

Hi there! I know you're working, so I don't want to interrupt. Open your door and then have a Happy Easter or Passover or just a happy day!

Thank you for understanding me enough to be my friend, and also give me the space to be myself. You're too good for words —too good for me— and I'm sorry that I've met you at a time in my life when I'm so mentally and emotionally fucked up! You really are a treasured part of my Seattle Life. You are the only one I know here who understands that like the lake, my waters are always the same, yet changing constantly. Does this make sense? I hope it does.

Spirit of the Goddess Warrior to you!   Holly

P.S.- I still have the BINM interview tape but haven't listened to it yet.

Journal: April 6, 1996

I had a wild hair today and replied to this ad in The Stranger personal section. It was interesting. The guy came over soon after we talked on the phone. I was a tad nervous, for safety reasons, but got he was no axe murderer and home always feels safest. He was cute, quite sweet, and clearly aimed to please. But, he didn't turn my key enough to want an ongoing thing. Wow. Sometimes I amaze myself. What next?

> YOUNGER INSATIABLE GUY looking for an older insatiable woman for a bedwrecking good time. Not looking for my mom or somebody to "teach" me. I'm young, but old enough to be a man

April 8, 1996 - In Zoey's 1996 Bag

Happy Day-after-Easter!

My sweet daughter, I took this box of goodies, the flower essences prescribed in your 1996 astrological projection and a booklet about them, to your Gramma and Grampa's yesterday. I opened the letter to you that's awaiting your arrival to show grandma the astrology page so she'd understand why I wanted you to have the essences. Rosey and Mom both thought it was really neat and thought that you'd love them but both agreed (and, ultimately, I did too) that Eric and Crystal would suspect that it came from me, not Gramma, if you took them home. So, here they go into your 1996 bag-of-stuff waiting for you.

On March 27th I called Becca's house, feeling anxious for you to get to Gramma & Grampa's, both to read my letters and to see Grampa. His pattern of dramatic improvement following each dose of chemotherapy was broken this last time around and I've been concerned that you should spend some time with him. I did not make contact with Becca. First I got the answering machine then someone that wasn't her so I hung up. I was a bit in disbelief that I'd even tried thinking, "WHEW! Stupe, don't do that again!" But, sure enough, I couldn't stand it. I tried again on April 5th and made contact. I hope she very carefully gives you my message and that you get to Gram and Gramps! Love you, Mom

Journal: April 13, 1996

I loved this ad in The Stranger so called just for the hell of it. I got a message machine so decided to script my compatible response. I called again and left it for him. He has not returned my call. Can't say I'm surprised. Oh well, I had a good time composing my reply:

> SEX IS LOVE
> 21yo Aries, red hair, clean cut, musician, poet artist, really? THC, pool, bowling, aliens. 185 lbs., passion, honesty, kids, marriage, REM, friendship, intimacy, green, House of Pain, money? Rage Against the Machine car? Movies, Primus, beauty? Fuck.

Older-than-you. Way. Truly Sagittarius, blonde, smooth and clean. Music is love. Born writer. Live sales. Skateboarder-wanna-be. Normalcy? Corrosion of Conformity. Blunt. 140. Lust. Integrity. Marriage? Been there, done that, fuck that. Time is a measure. Collective Soul. Inflatable Soule. Friendship- mmhm. Closeness, openness, touch, trust, purple. Pennywise, money? Dire Straits, car? Videos, Heart, beauty? Is in beholding eyes. Fuck.

> **KISW** 9 9 . 9 F M
> **Cindy Hammond**
> **Music Director**
>
> Beth:
>
> Sorry it took me so long to get this to you. We'll touch base soon.
>
> Cindy

Journal: April 16, 1996, 9:15ish p.m.

I got Cindy on ring 4 tonight. One ring had already gone by when I actually willed her to pick up. It was right at the end of the great set that followed Fresh Jam. The last song was ending as I pulled into a parking place at home. She told me she was swamped and to call back in a few minutes.

The instant I hung up she was on the air. Why would she answer an incoming call just seconds before she was to go on air if it was not because I willed her to? I waited a few minutes then when she'd started another music set I called again. And, again, she picked up on the third ring. I told her thanks a lot for sending the tape of the Ozzy interview, that I very much respected her journalistic integrity in editing out the too personal stuff, as she'd mentioned; but that toward the end it was confusing to hear only Ozzy's answers and not her questions. "Is this a glitch in the tape?" I asked her. Her voice sounded rather sharp as she responded, "Remember I told you at the end of the interview there'd be snippets, short little takes."

"Oh, yeah. I guess I didn't understand what you meant at the time and I wasn't recalling your words as I listened to the interview."

I told her, regarding tonight's Fresh Jam that I liked the instrumentation but that I was not fond of the "blame" lyric, that I'm not big on the blame thing. She expressed agreement.

I asked her if her evening was planned or would she be interested in going out to see a fun band at the Colourbox after work. I told her that if she liked that real heavy sound like the band on Fresh Jam tonight that she'd like Brainbomb. She responded that she'd never heard of them and kind of a *further more* was the fact that she'd already told me her schedule was packed until May. We said a few more things and I signed off.

I probably should not call her again. She'll call me if she ever wants to go for that mocha. I suppose she thinks I'm some kind of weirdo stalker or maybe a lesbian wanting a date. Ha! And I have certainly considered a number of times that perhaps it's her goal to answer each phone call by the third ring. But. . .? Nah.

Calendar - May 3 to 5, 1996

SLAM CITY JAM – North American Skateboarding
   Championships - Vancouver, B.C., Canada

May 8, 1996 - In her 1996 bag

Good Morning My Dear Zoey,

Well, here we go. I've been up since 4AM. Had a bowl of cereal while the coffee was brewing and since then I've drank coffee and smoked and thought and drank, smoked and sipped and thought some more. I'm a terrible rehasher! I keep rethinking all sorts of stuff, replaying conversations with people and different situations, rereading business correspondence wondering if I worded it so it'd be taken the way I meant it. Kind of silly but I do it anyway.

Mom called me last night and mostly I've been going over and over what she said about the conversation she had with you before she called me. She said you sounded great - relaxed and happy. She said you're wondering if I've done anything toward getting into treatment, not the first time I've heard that. This was the first time that I truly understood your concern though. I used to think that you were worried I actually needed treatment and that you might have an attitude of, "Well...I did it. What are you doing about it?" Now, though, I know that you just miss me and want me to go through the program so you can see me. Oh Zoey, I miss you so bad. You can't know how badly. Not a day goes by that I don't think of you. This whole scene is so hurtful beyond belief.

I've been thinking more than writing and now I have to get hopping. Half of my belongings are in this apartment and half of them are in my new place three doors down. I'm moving to a two bedroom because this one bedroom got way too small real fast once my in-home office got set up in the living room. The new place has much more closet and storage space, as well as more living space. I can set up my office in the dining area, have it more removed from the living room and rent out the second bedroom to bring down my overhead. I need to start saving money and start paying down my bills. I hope to be in a position to help you out with college or art school if that's what you want later on. And, of course, that second bedroom is yours when you are eighteen, if you want it. I love living down here by Green Lake, close to the city. As much as I love nature there is clearly a metro side to me too.

I suppose Gramma told you I went up to B.C. for Slam City Jam. That's quite a story I don't have time for right now. She says you are taking up skateboarding. I love it! You are such a kick! God, I miss you.

Also, Sunday night I went to see 7 Year Bitch. There's a story to that too. When I get my office all set up and rolling I'll get on the computer and tell these stories. Until then Sweetie Heart, I love you inside & outside every day, every moment.

alwaysMom

I am full of stories that never made it to paper in ink. This next little story wasn't mentioned in my letter to Zoey nor did I write about it in my journal. But I knew I'd never forget it.

When I told my boss, Evie, I was going to Slam City Jam she told me she badly wanted me to solicit Airwalk, who made skate shoes. She said she was flying up to Seattle that weekend to see friends so she'd get sample caps embroidered with the Airwalk logo for me to gift to them at the event. She wanted me to meet her flight arriving in Seattle at around noon on Friday so she could hand off the hats to me and I could take them with me to B.C.

My mornings were always full of phone, both to make contact with my regular customers and to make cold calls for

130

new ones. That day was no exception. After hanging up on one call, a glance at the clock had me panicked and dashing for the door so to be at SeaTac airport on time. I was driving up 50th toward I-5 when I saw that the gold ring on my hand on the wheel had no jade in it. There was an impulse to slam on my brakes, to go back and look for it, to figure out what had happened, to find the jade. But I knew that I couldn't. If I stood up Evie she would be pissed.

The panic I was feeling over losing the jade out of Mom's ring was making me sick. I met Evie at her arrival gate and we exchanged a quick hug. Next, I held my hand up to her face so she'd see the empty ring setting then explained I'd lost the jade somewhere between my apartment and 50th street. She saw anguish in my face, handed me hats, gave another quick hug and assured me I would find it.

The drive back home seemed to take forever. I had quite a talk with God. I promised that if I could please find the jade never again would I relate the beautiful stone to my two unsuccessful marriages. I promised that I would view the ring as a symbol of a long marriage that had made it through thick and thin and was happy to have done so—the marriage of Mom and Dad. "Please, God, please let me find the jade."

Thankfully, the parking spot I'd vacated on leaving for the airport was still empty. I pulled to the curb just behind that space and left the car running because I was blocking a driveway. I bent down and scoured the parking space, carefully moving each twig, leaf, and occasional scrap of paper. The knot in my stomach tightened as the search yielded nothing. Alright, I said in my head, perhaps it fell out of the setting somewhere in my apartment. I prayed some more and moved my car into the empty space. As I stood on the sidewalk looking blankly at my locked car, still praying, it occurred to me to look around the car parked in front of me. There, in front of the rear wheel snugged up to the curb, sat the jade in plain sight atop a fallen leaf. I dropped to my knees to retrieve it and to give thanks. And, I kept my word with God. From that moment forward I have revered my jade ring, with thanks, as a symbol of love that endured.

May 13, 1996 - In her 1996 bag, Monday 5AM

Good Morning my dear daughter!

I was at your Gramma and Grampa's yesterday, of course, for Mother's Day and Grampa's birthday. I saw the beautiful card you made for Grampa. That was very thoughtful and I appreciate so much that you took the time to do that. The photo was very cool, very artsy. Also, great job on the development and printing. I'm happy you're seriously pursuing your dream!

Mom showed me a photo taken during your visit. You are so beautiful and wow is your hair ever getting long. Gramma and I were trying to figure out where in the gene pool did you come up with such a heavy (thick) head of hair!

Of course, I thought of you and missed you terribly. And, I'm sure you missed me too.

I need to get started on work, peak season you know and lots to do! All my love, Mom

June 9, 1996 - In The Drawer At Gramma's

Zoey, Lovebug of my life,

I, too, am taking up skateboarding. Ever since I went to Board Stiff at the end of March I am determined to take up snowboarding next season. I figure skateboarding will be good prep in that I can get accustomed to the sideways stance before the snow falls next winter. I finally tried it. I borrowed a kid's board at the end of Pier Avenue in Hermosa Beach and loved it, *can do it!* I have been meeting a number of potential skating buddies both for boarding and a couple of old school quad skaters (like me to date).

Another good reason for me to be on a skateboard is that I'm now courting a lot of skateboard manufacturers and other related companies for their embroidered cap business. I've been working on Thrasher magazine for their hat biz so I can have one of their hats in my sample bag as much as for the sales adding to my bottom line. I think it will be a huge help in getting more skate customers if I can pull out a well done example of their super recognizable flame logo and say, "We're running these in our shop." Plus, they're just cool.

The first time I went to see High Speed Productions, the publisher of Thrasher, in their San Francisco office, I told my contact there that I skate and they might as well

132

have a skater running their hats. Well, when I had to admit that I roller skate he chuckled and said, "Oh, you're a girlie skater." At least he didn't call me a fruitbooter, the term for dis-ing rollerbladers.

I was working out of our L.A. office for almost two weeks. There's lots of stuff going on. I keep myself busy so to avoid having much time or space to dwell on how badly I screwed up and missing you horrifically. When my head gets to ripping on "bad mom, *bad* mom!" (as it often does) I get all depressed and that doesn't do either of us any good. I need to stay up, moving forward and accomplishing things toward an end of being far better prepared mentally, emotionally and financially when you come to live with me again. At least I hope you'll want to try it again for a while, until you get going on to the next phase of your life, as *life after high school* begins...

Oh, Zoey, I find myself wondering where your head and heart will be with regard to me at the end of this tunnel. I can't wait to see you and hug you and hug you some more and hear all about how it's all been going with you. . . these last years (as it will be by then). I can't believe it's been nearly a year since we last had contact.

I love you!

Mom

12: Mounting Skaters and My Skate

Journal: June 11, 1996

Wow tst tst! All the skater boys I've met and all the little soap operas and events around, well, particularly the Abacus guys but also other guys who skate. Like Zoey, I am getting a board. Since I first saw vertical skaters on the ramp at Action Sport Retailer in San Diego back in September '89, when Paul and I were exhibiting our Sundogz project the first time I've been a skateboarderwannabe. But, I have continuously lectured myself, "You're too old. You'd look foolish. Stick to your roller skates." Well now I say, "Who says so? Fuck that."

It was last September I first hooked up with Billy at the Fall Action Sport Retailer Trade Expo, or ASR, which is always in San Diego. I walked the show floor and introduced myself to the exhibiting skate and surf companies trying to round up new biz. But back to Billy who is really sweet and rock hard I must say. . .Mm mm hot bod.

The Sunday night that the show was over I met him and Tony hanging at the skate ramp set up for a biggest air competition a few blocks from the convention center. There was also a sound stage and bands played. But we three, plus a few others, arrived long before any of the action started. I'd gotten a VIP pass from a guy that owned one of the clothing companies sponsoring and, perhaps, producing the event. But, I figured they all said VIP and thought I'd better get there early if I wanted to get a good viewpoint. So I sat there, right up front next to the ramp, for the whole thing talking to Billy and a bunch of skaters whose names I can't recall at the moment. It was fun.

After the sun went down the air cooled, I found myself leaning into Billy to stay warm and that started the sexual energy flowing. Way later that night, after he took all the other guys home up to Oceanside, he came back down to San Diego and spent the night with me in my great harbor view room at the Marriott next to the convention center. We talked for a long time and, of course, ultimately had incredible sex. Again, I have to say, it was fun.

In late October, when I was back in southern California on my return trip from Hong Kong and China, Billy and I hooked up again and had a good time. When I went down to Long Beach, in February, for the spring ASR trade show I was looking forward to getting together with Billy; but there was an interesting twist to it this time around. On the night that we figured to get together I had an obligatory dinner in China Town with my employers. When I got back to my hotel room much later than I'd expected there were three voice mail messages from Billy, "Where are you?" I paged him right away. When he called back he told me that he and Tony were getting drunk in celebration of Tony's birthday. I told him to bring the Birthday Boy with him, that I'd smoke 'em both out. He asked if I would do both of them. I asked how that would work. He said he didn't know but assured me that if I was open to it it'd work itself out just fine. I thought what the hell? and told them to come on over.

It didn't take them long to get to my hotel room. They came in grinning and being just a little drunk-silly. I kept my word and smoked them out as we caught up with each other; my new job, lots of new stuff happening with Abacus, etcetera. We determined we needed to make a beer and condom run. That worked out well as there was so much nervous-type tension in the room a diversion was welcome. We went down to my rental car and proceeded to get lost driving around Long Beach in search of a convenience store. By the time we found one it was too late to buy beer but thank God there's no curfew on condoms.

Back in my hotel room the lights from the fountain and the garden area below cast such a soft and sensual luminance through my open window that we opted to add no more light. We took up the same seating arrangement we'd left, me and Billy on the bed, sitting up, leaning against the headboard and Tony in the armchair at the foot of the bed with feet up on the ottoman. I told the guys I'd deal with Evie later if she complained about my hotel bill and pulled a seven dollar beer out of the room bar fridge for each of us.

Once comfortably settled in I think we had exchanged two sentences when Billy leaned over and started kissing my neck. I whispered in his ear, "Shouldn't the Birthday Boy be first?"

He sat straight up and with a smile said, "Hey, Tony, Beth thinks the Birthday Boy should be first!"

Billy and Tony traded places as a cloud cover blew past the moon outside my window and light beamed in from above now also, adding such an erotic visibility. Any shyness and inhibition passed away with the clouds and with our clothes as, piece by piece, between kissing and touching, they fell to the floor. The intensity of Tony's kiss was so just-the-way-I-like-it that I climaxed mildly with his kiss in my mouth and his hands on my breasts. I rolled him over onto his back and got to my knees. From my new place, kneeling on the bed beside Tony, I saw Billy's silhouette against the moonlight. I didn't know for sure but guessed that he had himself in hand, so I asked if he was enjoying the view. His breathy 'yeah' told me I was right and turned me on all the more.

I kissed Tony on the mouth, down his neck, then licked and sucked his nipples until they were hard and excited. As I inched my kisses down his body I could feel him grow tenser, waiting for my mouth to reach. . . I pressed my tongue to the base, taking one broad stroke up to the head as he flinched and moaned. I lowered my mouth down over the head, sucking him in a little at a time, teasingly, until my lips were wrapped around the base. I proceeded to give Tony head that he'll be remembering on his ninety-second birthday and every birthday in between.

While inching my kisses down Tony's body my knees had found their way to the edge of the bed. Apparently my accessibility was more than Billy could take. It wasn't long before he stood behind me, sliding in and out of my wet readiness. His hands grasped me at the bend between my hips and the tops of my thighs. He slowly pushed me away then pulled me back to him hard, again and again.

Tony warned he was about to come. I pulled my mouth away just in time for his enormous load to explode all over my hand. He pecked me on the head with a little smooch and slid off the bed. He took a quick trip to the bathroom then took over the chair Billy had just vacated and settled in to watch.

In the mean time, Billy had scooted me over to the middle of the king size bed. While he repositioned me for re-entry I pulled open the bed covers at the far side and wiped Tony's sticky gratitude on the sheet. I was not wanting to get up and risk breaking the oh-so-hot rhythm of the moment. Billy and I reveled in our usual gymnastic form, moving from position to position smoothly, each change bringing new sensation and heightened pleasure.

I maneuvered Billy onto his back and straddled him with my feet planted firmly on the mattress, tucked up next to his hips. My legs may not be much to look at but they work real well. I worked Billy from my froggy stance, then, without missing a beat, dropped to my knees laughing and telling Billy, "You are so spoiled!" He smiled his response as I turned toward Tony's silhouette asking, "Don't you think he looks spoiled?"

The funny thing about this, of course, is the fact that I had just positioned myself for my only known ticket to the stars and I spoiled myself by taking the trip. Feeling him rock hard deep inside me, I closed my eyes, massaged my own pleasure and rocked Billy hard until the two inner and outer sensations merged, becoming the only fuel for that second-stage-rocket-booster that releases all my tension, causing my body to shudder while the white light of shooting stars goes off in my brain like fireworks behind closed eyes. Wow, I'm getting wet remembering it as I write!

I was surprised at how comfortable I felt in that scenario. It was so relaxed and open and so very erotic, even when the spell was broken by lamp light as they scrambled for clothes and dressed to leave. I told them I had enjoyed that, reiterated my Happy Birthday wish to Tony, hugged and smooched them both lightly and wished them safe passage back to their hotel with, "See ya later today!" We'd all go back to work at the trade show just a couple hours from parting.

Journal: June 13, 1996

I finally did it. After work today I went to a skate shop down at the south end of Lake Washington because, after much calling around, the man who answered the phone at that shop told me he had Kryptonic wheels in stock. I hate the small hard wheels the guys skate on. Cushy, forgiving Kryptos on my board will help make for an easier transition from my roller skates.

At the store, I also learned he had a good starter board for me. It's either a long short-board or a short long-board depending on one's perspective I guess. He suggested to me that it will be more stable than a short board and more maneuverable than a long one. It's made by a company called Generation and has a cool relevant graphic. I've never heard of the brand but bought it anyway. I now own a skateboard.

All the way home my excitement to get on it inflated. But, by the time I was in my apartment to drop off stuff from the car, drink a beer, go to the bathroom and get a bong rip, my enthusiasm transformed to an equally intense fear. Or, I may simply have been struck with a lick of common sense. I'm not sure. I skipped the bong rip and tanked up on water instead of my usual pre-skate half beer.

I walked across the street to the parking lot for the Lower Woodland Park Playfields, the long strip beside Green Lake Way, with my skateboard under my arm. Nicely, there were few parked cars so a long run available for my momentous inaugural skate. I set the board down, stepped onto it with my left foot in a regular stance, felt beyond awkward, and crashed to my tailbone after the board shot forward from under my foot.

Whoa, my God! Even if I wanted to describe the pain, I couldn't because up came the mental block. I'm not sure if I voiced this or if I was talking in my head but I do recall wagging my finger at the board with, "NO! You will not intimidate me." My right foot wanted to try and stepped up. As I gave my first little push with my left foot, my head analogized getting right back on the horse that just bucked me off lest I never mount again. I pushed a second time. Foot by foot (to say inch by inch would be understating) I proceeded down to the end of the open parking lot, stopped, got off the board, picked it up, turned it around, and stepped back on with my right foot again. This time I dared to push a little harder, then harder and I picked up a wee bit o' speed.

My apartment window came into view and I was ready to go in for that beer and bowl. The sun had dropped behind Woodland Park shading the parking lot so visibility diminished and my ass was killing me. I hobbled inside as the throb grew.

I sure am glad I got back on the board. Tomorrow is Saturday so I'll have all day to get my speed up. Oh! I should add that I buried my roller skates at the back of my bedroom closet. I do not intend to ride them again any time soon.

my favorite anti-hill

13: Deke, Dragons, and What Is That?

<u>June 16, 1996 - In her 1996 bag</u>

Dearest Zoey,

Yesterday was such a magical day. You would have loved it. It was a beautiful blue-sky, sunshiny warm day—you know, the kind that fortifies hope in we Seattleites who grapple with gray gloom oppression. Katie, my new room-mate, and I, flying high with the sunbeams, decided to enjoy the surefire revelry at the Fremont Street Fair. Undaunted by the stiff traffic competition, we circled around acres of residential blocks until we came up on a parked car that was leaving. I pulled into the vacated slot; we thanked the Parking Goddess and torched a bowl, creating the perfect hum for such an occasion.

We locked up the car and walked downhill to the main intersection in Fremont where a parade was in progress, The Freakmont Parade as reputation has it. A float with a Calypso band was approaching the corner where we stood. People in costumes and people in regular street clothes were all in the street dancing to the music and following along with the float. I asked Katie, "Want to dance?"

She squinched up her face and shook her head saying, "You go ahead though..."

"Nah, we'll have a hell of a time meeting up again. You don't want to walk home," I told her; not a good idea, pissing off my new roomie.

As the float turned the corner, arriving in front of us, Katie turned to me with a grin and "Come on." We squeezed past the crowd of observers, wandered off the curb into the street and paraded along with all the uninhibited dancers. Perfect!

We had danced along for a couple of blocks when I remembered the goodies that were stashed in Katie's back-

140

pack. You guessed it, Zo. Bubbles! We blew bubbles and danced along with this float and throng of "freaks" all the way to where the parade ended. I was laughing, saying to Katie, "Who'd have thought when we got up this morning that this would be the day we'd dance in a parade?" I guess there is a first time for everything. In fact, I experienced three Firsts on this day, Zoey.

We bought sustenance and thirst quench from one of the vendors, found an open sidewalk area in the sun and settled in. Once the edge was off our hunger, Katie recalled what other goodies were in her pack; Sidewalk Chalk, my second First for the day. She pulled out the box of many colors and we hunkered down on doodling sidewalk graphics. I printed, in broad swooping strokes "Happy Day!" then got into all sorts of colorful outlining and embellishments. I don't recall exactly what it was that Katie had to say but she found a way to humorously connect it to what I had going. When we'd been at it for a bit a darling mop-haired black girl with an angel's smile, probably about nine years old, asked if she could join us. She contributed some great splashy designs and when we all called it done, our collaborative art had cheerily pasteled about thirty square feet of concrete.

With creative bent satisfied, Katie and I browsed along, checking out all of the wares for sale in the booths. I had plenty of cash with me as I was looking for something special to give to Dad for Father's Day, much preferring this venue for shopping over going to a mall. You know me and malls, yuck. While Katie engaged in pursuit of the perfect purse and chatted it up with a bag vendor, I came upon a booth that had crystals and other cosmic wonders. Here I found not only the perfect gift for Dad, but for you too, and even one for me.

I have to confess the first item insisting, "Buy me!" was, of course, a polar bear. He's a little guy, only about one inch high by two inches long, cast in pewter. Nose pointed downward as if trailing a scent, he trudges along on an ice floe crafted from an unusual crystal that's been cut and polished smooth. It has deep blue at the center surrounded by a ring of clear to frosty white crystal. He'll look great in my polar bear collection. I love him.

Once that was decided, I started noticing all of the different kinds of dragons, wizards and faeries on the shelves. I spotted the perfect present for your Grampa. It had all the right elements and I could actually afford it. After I selected Dad's gift I latched onto yours, last but certainly not least. The dragons I chose for you, one ferocious (on blue crystal like my polar bear, so male energy me thinks) and one goofy (on pink crystal, surely fun female energy), replicate the dragons I've worn around my neck since I learned of their power.

In Hong Kong last fall at the jewelry shop where I bought the gold ring that Gramma and Grampa gave you for Christmas (on my behalf, did you guess?) I bought for myself a gold dragon medallion to wear on the gold chain that your Uncle Josh gave me for Christmas many years ago. When I told the man in the shop of my love for dragons he informed me the Chinese believe that the dragon protects one's personal power. Since it has been a pattern with me to all too easily give my power away, I now wear him religiously to protect myself from myself as well as extraneous forces.

This spring, on a Saturday morning at Pike Place Market I spotted a goofy little pewter dragon grinning and holding a rose quartz orb in the crook of his tail. I bought it and a silver chain so I could wear this dragon to protect my sense of humor when I'm away from home. When I'm home, most thankfully, the whimsically sweet purple dragon you sculpted for me handles this task.

I wish I could give you your dragons now, but, like the flower essences that could be useful to you in the present, they are going in your 1996 bag. There is actually a difference between the two gifts. The floral essences you must consume to benefit by them. But, I have programmed your dragons to be with you vibrationally performing their magic in the now. You do not know it as I write, but you have a dragon on each shoulder working with your angels to keep you safe and whole and always Zoey. I love you so very much, my dear daughter.

The third First of the day came via your dragons. When I had all of my items for purchase on the table where the lady in charge of the booth sat, with whom I'd discussed each item and its purpose, she tallied it up and gave me the total. I realized my cash would be nearly depleted and didn't want to do that. Knowing there was no true immediacy to your dragons, I asked if she would please put those away for me. I promised to send her a check, to include postage & handling, right away and on receipt she could send them to me. She mulled that over and I begged, "PLE-E-EASE?"

Her response was, "I can tell you are a good person. Go ahead, take them now and send me the check when you get home." How cool! I was floored. Someone trusted me to come through. So, needless to say, the moment I got home I wrote her a check along with a note thanking her for her good faith and dropped it in the mail box in front of my apartment building when I left to go to Mom and Dad's. By then the bright day was melting into a glorious rosy sunset perfect for sailing into on the ferry—the crown on a three Firsts day.

Sunday morning when I woke up early at Mom and Dad's I made a card to go with Dad's gift so he'd understand all of the symbolism involved. I don't recall verbatim what I wrote but it went something like this:

Dad, the amethyst crystal is like a satellite dish drawing in positive energy and life-force. Its purple color is representative of such positive attributes as loyalty, strength, stamina and spirit. The ferocious dragon, atop the dish, is there to protect your personal power while the wizard below him brings you magic and keeps your sense of humor flowing. The clear crystal, perched at the highest point of the dish, is a transmitter. Rub the crystal, between your thumb and index finger, to draw into you all of the positive energy, strength and life-force summoned for you. I love you with all of my heart, Beth.

That was on the inside of the card. On the front, accompanied by glittery star-stickers, I wrote:
HAPPY FATHER'S DAY TO THE BEST DAD IN THE WORLD

He genuinely loved it, Zoey. He set the sculpture on the table next to his chair and rubbed the crystal just as I'd prescribed. That made me super happy because it wasn't just a gift symbolizing all of those magical powers; it was a gift of me as much as from me. He and Mom are getting used to loving me the way I come, dancing along in the rhythm of my own drummer.

I shared part of a story with Dad after he thoroughly checked out his gift, a dragon story. However I'm going to share the whole story with you, The Deke & Dragon Story.

While I was in Los Angeles on business earlier this month, Thursday June 6th to be precise, the night before I left to come home I met Deke. I'd gone to Pier Avenue in Hermosa Beach figuring to dine in one of the eateries there so I'd be handy to The Strand and could skate after dinner. I walked in one place where all the stools at the bar were taken and everyone seated at tables was with someone or a bunch of people. Being alone rarely bothers me but that night I was not in the mood to sit at a table by myself and watch other folks be happy and social. I walked out and meandered up the street looking in every bar and restaurant as I went. Nothing appealed to me menu-wise or it was a scenario similar to the ones I'd just left – couples and groups but no loners like me and no empty stool at the bar.

I got to the corner at Hermosa Avenue and headed south remembering a place with a silly name a couple blocks down that served dynamite hot sandwiches. When I saw the sign, Fat Face Fenner's Falloon, I giggled to myself wondering how I could have forgotten a name like that. I was relieved to find one open stool at the bar. When alone and feeling a desire for company, I prefer sitting at the bar because it's not isolated from other people, whereas sitting alone at a table rather defines one's space or territory. I sat on the one available stool and surveyed my surroundings. To my right at the center of the bar was the waitress station. On the stool to my left there was a guy with his back turned to me as he was conversing with the people to his left.

I was scanning a row of beer bottles on the shelf behind the bar, which I assumed were my menu, when the guy to my left whipped around to flash a big smile at me and exclaim "Hi! How are you tonight?" Based on the fact that there was a stool at the bar for me next to a gregarious good looking guy with a great smile, I quickly concluded I was excellent and made my reply to that affect. He introduced himself as Deke. We volleyed some ever-so-typical small talk and then I asked if there was any particular menu item he would rec-ommend. Quite a discourse ensued leading me to guess the guy either ate every meal there or he worked there. I asked and the latter was the case.

We gabbed and laughed and had a generally good time.

144

Out of the blue he asked if I'd ever heard of Black Happy. "Black Happy? Sure, they're one of my favorite bands to go out and hear live," I told him. He explained he'd picked up a used copy of the Friendly Dog Salad CD, loved it, and with the liner notes being full of Pacific Northwest places figured I might know of them. I asked him if he'd heard any Shoveljerk on the radio.

"No, I rarely listen to the radio," he replied. I explained Black Happy is no longer a band and that Shoveljerk is most of Black Happy without the horn section. Then I asked if he'd heard any BINM songs. He hadn't so I asked if he'd like to come out to my car with me, smoke a bowl and hear a BINM sampling. I was long done with dinner and we'd been talking for over an hour. He beamed at me, "We have herb in common too! Sure! When?"

"How about right now? Then I'd like to get out and skate."

Deke stated he'd ridden his bicycle to work and wanted to know, "Mind if I ride along?"

I told him that would be great but when we got outside the air had cooled and he had no outerwear with him. I'd come prepared for this possibility so we stowed his bike in my trunk and drove a few blocks up the hill to his house to get a sweatshirt. I asked if I could come in to use the bath-room. Deke lives with his brother and his brother's girlfriend. I loved their place as it was totally eclectic—brimming with artsy things to look at, including some beautiful and also some edgy unusual original paintings. Plus, there was the start of a faery collection. I expressed my admiration for one particular painting and Deke said "Thanks. It's mine."

"You mean you painted it?"

"That one and all the others too."

"Wow! Nice!"

"I'm glad you like my work." We talked a bit, covered different points of interest I questioned him on, then went back to the car. As we were getting in I asked him if I'd men-tioned that typically skating is a loner activity for me and it's not skating without my music blaring. He was pleased we shared another commonality and went back up to get his music.

As I headed the car to the beach, I rummaged through my fanny-pack in search of weed. It turned out I had very little left and we blew through it quickly still wanting more. I suggested it would probably be easy to hook up with some by talking to any of the skateboarders hanging at the pier. None were visible when we showed up. I told him about a kid named Chris I had smoked out with a couple nights earlier who hangs out at the end of the pier fishing. (Chris is the one who let me try riding his skateboard.) So we skated and walked-with-bike in that direction. Sure enough, there he was. He didn't have any but his buddy was happy to accommodate if I'd roll it. As you well know, this has never been one of my strong points. I messed with it for quite a while ultimately producing my standard tuna, fat in the middle with pointy ends.

Chris offered, "Here, why don't you empty that into my pipe?"

"You have a pipe? Why didn't you tell me sooner?" I tore open the joint, packed it into the pipe, and we smoked. It was pretty good stuff, got quite the nice glow going.

Chris wandered away, as did his buddy, leaving me to watch their poles while Deke exited into the men's room. There was a commotion at the end of the pier. One guy had a bite that was quite a struggle to reel in. He wrangled with his pole, strained to swing around and then hoisted his catch up over the railing. It went thud onto the pier and immediately began thrashing and flailing about, making it extremely difficult for the guy to hang on to the pole. It was not a fish. It was big and flopping around so fast everyone was shouting, "What is it?" "What the hell is it?"

In a half second space of calm in the calamity, I yelled, *"It's a dragon!"* Deke came up behind me laughing at my outburst. He seemed to be the only one to hear it. But I wasn't trying to be funny. I turned to him and repeated vehemently "It *is* a dragon!"

By then a bunch of folks had surrounded the beast and thrown a towel over it. The king of the catch stood on the towel to either side of the beast, pinning it to the dock. He bent down and warily peeled back the towel to reveal a dragonesque face attached to a large eel. He proclaimed it would make a good dinner and made several attempts to get the hook out of its mouth but to no avail. Chris gladly obliged the man by hacking its head off with the long knife

146

he pulled from the sheath on his belt. YUK! I didn't watch. When I the knife appeared I guessed what was coming next and turned away.

The dragon eel part of the story is what I told your Grampa about. He chuckled fairly heartily so I know he was truly amused because he almost never laughs anymore, as though he doesn't have enough strength for it.

Now, on with the rest of the Deke story. When the excitement wound down around the amazing catch, it hit both Deke and me that the wind had become downright cold. We decided to head out for our skate-and-ride to warm up. On our way back to The Strand we came across Chris' buddy, told him of the event he'd missed and thanked him for the smoke. We talked as we walked. More things about Deke and how he thinks and feels about a variety of issues came up, leading me to feel quite taken with the man. I liked his attitude.

Near where the pier intersects The Strand a haunting sound wafted in the air. Deke and I looked at each other, both asking, "What is that?" A gander over the half wall flanking the emergency vehicle ramp revealed a long-haired young man in hippie garb sitting cross-legged on a small mat laid out on the plaza below. He was blowing into a wooden pipe or pole approximately five feet long. The end of the pole opposite his mouth was snugged into the corner created by the wall that separates the beach sand from the plaza and the ramp it butts up to. We stood watching his cheeks inflate and release into the pole, listening to his music, some terrific rhythms in deep timbre.

He finished a tune and turned to greet us with, "Hello." When we asked what he was playing, he explained that his instruments, a second smaller pipe laid next to him, are native to Australian Aborigines. "They're called didgeridoos."

We visited with the guy for a while then took off for our warm-up. Deke told me as he got on his bike that he thought this was a most wonderful evening; first meeting me, next a dragon, and then an unusual musical experience. I assured him I was in total agreement.

As we skated and biked, Deke stayed behind me for the most part. But he came along side at one point so I took off my headphones to hear, "You don't skate. You dance."

147

"Yes, I dance. Whatever the music is doing is how I skate."
I didn't mention that having been married to two men that
wouldn't dance skating became my dance release. After
riding and dancing up and down the good surface a couple
times, the most recently repaved area that runs a good two
miles or more, I slowed. When Deke came along side me this
time I declared, "Work tomorrow! I've got to get going." He
walked me to my car and we reiterated what a remarkable
evening it had been.

He tossed his arms out into the air and queried with
enthusiasm, "HUG?"

I hugged him hard, probably harder than he expected
or maybe even wanted and said in his ear at a near whisper,
"Hugs are good." As we detached, he asked if I had a pen
and paper in the car so he could give me his address. I pulled
my purse out of the trunk, dug around, and produced tools
for staying in touch. I jotted his address and phone number,
promised to send him a tape with BINM on one side and the
new Stone Temple Pilots on the other, and he rode away.

I liked this guy a lot, Zoey. What a stupid place to let
myself go. He's far younger than me, of course. But, he's
friendly in an open, universal way plus creative and talented.
He's got a great sense of humor and a nice smile. He's not
judgmental, at least not about a number of issues that would
have either your dad or Paul absolutely shredding. He is
relaxed and very easy to be with. In fact, at one point we
determined that we could talk to each other about any and
every thing.

I left The Strand with the kind of butterfly feeling in
my gut that I haven't known since the first time I laid eyes
on Paul in this place nearly ten years ago. I repeat, very silly
place to allow myself to go. He lives in Hermosa and loves
it. I live in Seattle and wouldn't think of moving. And, even
if that were not the case, I've set a new rule for myself, the
Five Year Rule. I got from marriage to Paul that all of life's
learning packed into ten years of experience is too much
of a difference in outlook and attitude. If I ever get serious
about a guy again I can be no more than five years older or
younger than him. But then your dad was only four years
older and treated it like a twenty year wealth of wisdom
he had over me. I don't know -geesh- kind of funny that

I should make a rule when breaking them seems more my specialty.

I got home on Friday night. On Sunday I called Deke to say hi and to tell him that I'd made the tape. I got the answering machine so left a message to call. Monday morning I mailed him the tape with a simple note. He returned my call Thursday and said he hadn't received the tape yet. We had a good chat. Early in the next week I called and left another message interjecting humor based on our last phone chat, the idea that the mailman had intercepted his delivery. As of today, Sunday, he has not called again.

Hmmm, so there you go, silly me. I haven't spent the last two years learning to be nonchalant, totally casual and nearly uncaring in my interactions with men—thereby alleviating the possibility of developing a relationship—for nothing. It suits me fine for now, for indefinitely. I have much strength yet to grow before I can consider a serious relationship, even if the man doesn't appear to have a mean bone in his body. I'm not saying that either your dad or Paul were mean spirited by nature; but, they both managed to dish up some helpings of meanness on my plate. If I ever go for Husband #3 he will have to be just like your Grampa, kind hearted and good humored with a zest for life and a love of dancing. I will settle for nothing less.

Oh boy, Zoey, put me in front of a keyboard and I will surely ramble. I was just going to tell you what a fun evening I had with Deke, the dragon and didgeridoos. I guess the rest of it isn't very appropriate to go on about with my sixteen year old daughter. Of course, you will be eighteen by the time you can read this and then you'll be busy getting on with your own life in the adult world. Well, I'll put it in your 1996 bag, with the rest of my letters, up on my closet shelf. Maybe someday it will be of interest. I love you so much my dear daughter and miss you like you can't possibly know.

YIKES! It's now a little after 5PM and I've been at the computer all day! Gotta go, my love. I promised myself I'd get my bathroom and bedroom truly settled in today. Lonni and Pat will be here from Hawaii in just a couple of weeks. I told them they could stay in the second bedroom for a month while they job and apartment hunt.

So, Sweetie Pie, I'm off and running! Yeah, like the last drop of molasses!

I LOVE YOU!   *always*Mom

P.S. - Sheesh. Yes, Zoey, you will believe it. It's now 9:30PM! Holly was here from 6:30 until 8. She left. Ninety seconds later there was a knock at my door. It was Marcus with Holly, who met up in the parking lot. They came in. Holly left most immediately. Marcus stayed until after nine! Do we think my bed and bath are done? Well, now I finish and on no dinner. I'll live. XO Mom

June 20, 1996 - Sent to Eric with July payment

Results of recent CAT scan prompt oncologist to say Zoey's Grampa is "in remission." Of course, nothing showed on the CAT scan right before surgery either. He is off chemo until August. Zoey should go see him while he's having better days. Of course, her Gramma will pick her up at and return her to the ferry same day - <u>any</u> day.

14: Dad and Dining In China

Journal: July 4, 1996 11-ish AM

I am on the Seattle/Bainbridge Island Ferry waiting to embark on the holiday sojourn to Mom and Dad's where we shall celebrate the independence of our nation and a day off work mid-week with family and friends.

Sometimes I wonder if all people replay conversations in their head and visualize scenarios over and over again; rewind and review clips of consequence, analyzing the footage carefully, clicking into slow-mo on those frames that have strong impact emotionally or otherwise. Surely I'm not the only one, but just how universal is this? Sometimes I feel so silly about it; like I'm being a real doof, like maybe I'm placing *way* too much importance on things. Oh! We're off! We've de-docked and are on our way.

Funny. Funny Bunny. Sammy. Wow after these so very many days of hearing his watch peep. Shoot, we're landing at Bainbridge already. I was thinking more than writing. I vow to complete this entry this weekend before I leave for L.A. on Monday.

It's still the 4th of July and I'm on the 9:10PM ferry leaving from Bainbridge for Seattle right now. This is a first! Immediately following the bassoon-ish rumble of the ferry horn, three people on the far side of the front end salon, where I'm sitting, ripped in to a polka on an accordion and two fiddles. They're being well received with applause after each tune. Now their music is accompanied by two dancers. A two to three year old blonde pony-tailed hop-and-whirl girl, and a baby in coppery curls with sweat pants poofed out over diapers is spinning in place while clapping in time . . . almost.

Journal: July 5, 1996

I love that Thursday was the 4th. Four day weekends

rock. I'm using a vacation day today, but it's worth it, just laying low with my coffee this morning then going for a good skate later. It's supposed to be a beautifully sunny day *ha!* after the classic cool, overcast 4th of July. Funny that summer always starts on July 5th in Seattle, after freezing one's butt off most of June right up through the fireworks. So, no doubt, the path around the lake will be jammed. I'll need to go slow but that's okay. I'm feeling pretty mellow, bordering melancholy actually but I refuse to go there today.

I didn't do fireworks last night having gone over to Mom and Dad's. Josh arrived a while after I did, when the three of us were already settled in at the annual block party at the end of their seniors only cul-de-sac. I get a kick out of hanging with the oldsters as a rule but it felt like a fine mist of sadness was hovering in our air space. All the neighbors are aware of how sick Dad is and, where there was clearly a celebratory holiday mood to the day, that mist wafted in and out. I could tell by his posture Dad was feeling miserable yet his smile was shining and he found plenty to chuckle about watching someone's grand kids' antics and joking with folks, as always.

I was glad when Josh showed up. He said he had to go up to his property and wanted to know if we'd like to join him. So, after we'd all eaten a plate of picnic fare, off we went like a Sunday drive in the old days. The only thing different was that Josh was driving and Mom was in the backseat with me instead of him, well, that and about twenty-five years. I guess Rosey had taken the girls over to her sister's house for the 4th which struck me as odd considering Dad might not have much longer and would enjoy time with his granddaughters. But, he didn't get to see Zoey either so. . .

Man! Josh's spot in the foothills of Blyn is beautiful. And, it was sunny! Being near Sequim and nestled below the Olympics, his acreage shares the benefit of the rain shadow. While he did his thing mowing the broad weed lawn at the center of his forest, I quickly rounded up some of the downed branches ahead of him. There was a fierce wind storm last week. I heaped them in the fire pit and got a blaze going. Mom and Dad sat in lawn chairs by the fire and took in the late afternoon views. No matter how bright and beautiful the day was, once the sun dipped behind the trees and we were in the shade the mountain air was chilly. By the time the fire was reduced to embers Josh had handled his chores and Dad was tired, wanting to get horizontal. We headed back to Port Ludlow.

Josh and I both went in the house just long enough to go to the bathroom, get hugs and say goodbyes. The timing was perfect. I only had to wait about an hour in the ferry line, nothing for a major holiday weekend. By the time I got home I was pooped and ready for bed.

It is hard to watch Dad struggle along. He is so frail, so unlike his robust pre-cancer self, before surgery and chemo. He has no appetite and it's hard on Mom. No matter how hard she works to whip up fabulous meals that he would have scarfed up in the old days he just picks at the food unable to find the old verve for it. No doubt, part of that is in knowing he's likely to toss it up. I don't dare suggest he smoke pot to relieve nausea and to give him the munchies. He would be livid. It'd simply re-spark his ire with me around losing Zoey. Neither he nor Mom wants to call her dad to see if he'll take Zoey down to walk on the ferry, like the old days when they'd wait on the dock to meet her on the peninsula side. They told me it feels too uncomfortable to call, not so much because of Eric but because they fear his wife will answer. The thought of getting her on the phone sickens Dad more than the chemo. That's enough on that.

In looking back over my journal I'm surprised at how little I've written about my trip to Hong Kong and China. I don't recall how it came up in conversation yesterday but by the fire I told Mom and Dad a story about one of my dining experiences in China. So, while it's fresh I'll put it down here for posterity.

We were in the small city where our factory is. I can't recall the name of the place because I never clearly under-stood what I was told. After asking my boss to repeat it a couple of times I gave up. And, since we took a train there from Guangzhou after the trade fair (more on that later) it's not on my flight itinerary. The first night we were there, after working all day with the factory office crew and produc-tion managers on the new program we're putting together tailored to attract the active sport industry, we all went to dinner together. The restaurant was the most upscale building I saw in this place, a huge fancy pagoda type structure—white stucco with some wood, some red, and oodles of shiny gold accenting particular architectural features. It was an eye candy oasis in a dust bowl town.

From the host' podium inside the tall double front door, we were led to a private room with a round table at the center that would easily accommodate all ten of us. This didn't make us special. The entire restaurant was divided into separate dining rooms of various sizes so each party had their own space. At the center of our table was a built-in lazy-susan nearly half the diameter of the table. This was in keeping with all of the restaurants we'd been to in Guangzhou and the few times we dined as a group in Hong Kong. Thankfully, we broke into small groups most evenings in Hong Kong and could venture off on our own. We who were born with American taste buds stuck together on those nights, gravitating toward familiar foods.

On this night, as with all of our group dinners, my boss, David, ordered. No menus were offered. A server came, spoke with David in Chinese, and left. We drank tea and went over the day's accomplishments on into goals for the next day until food began to arrive. A rotation of servers entered our room at a slightly staggered pace, each carried one bowl or platter, placed a small helping on David's plate and set the dish on the lazy-susan in front of him. He then passed the dish along with a slight flick of the wheel.

A platter arrived displaying one large poached fish complete with head and tail. David had the server place the platter directly on the lazy-susan without first being served. Enthusiastically he called out to his sister, seated directly across the large table, "Suzanne, your favorite!" At that he gave the lazy-susan a big push, then braked with his hand landing the platter in front of her plate. She swiftly scooped up the head of the fish, set it on her plate and pushed the wheel gently around to me, seated on her right. I took a small center cut and passed it along.

As servers continued to bring various dishes, the lazy-susan filling with a host of foods alien to me, we all began our meal. Suzanne clutched her fish head firmly between her chopsticks and began to gnaw on it crunching loudly.

My sideways glance was met by a gray glazed eye before it disappeared behind Suzanne's teeth. She smacked her lips while crunching bones and brains, eyeballs and teeth, the whole fucking hoo-ha. I proudly fought and conquered my gag reflex.

Striving to create a diversion for myself, I asked, "What is in this dish, David?"

"Vej - ta - bul," he gave each syllable nearly equal strength in his Chinese accent.

"What kind of vegetable, Dav. . ."

"VEJ – TA – BUL!" He interrupted emphatically.

"Oh. Alright then." I did see something with a leaf-ish appeal swimming among unidentified white stringy stuff in the pale grey/beige sauce so placed a dab on my plate after chasing and capturing the leafy thing. I mulled the predominantly cornstarch flavored glop in my mouth and grappled with swallowing while mentally patting myself on the back for bravery.

At the end of the meal, after all dishes had been removed from the table, a server arrived with a large platter of Fuji apple slices for dessert, fresh tea, and toothpicks. The sigh of relief emitted while sliding several apple slices onto my dessert plate was mistaken as pleasure for the meal apparently. David smiled and queried, "Very good, hah?"

I nodded and smiled back, happy to be honest as I reveled in the familiar flavor of a juicy slice. Suzanne's elbow grazed my arm as she reached for a toothpick. I looked to my left to find her inserting the toothpick in her mouth and cupping her other hand in front to conceal the action, and I do mean action. She worked that pick with conviction under such demure cover. It took tremendous effort to contain myself, to not bust into laughter at the contradiction. I was tempted to ask, "Excuse me, aren't you the woman I just saw gnawing on a fish head, smacking her lips, and wiping eyeball ooze off her chin?"

David settled the tab and we exited out a side door in line with our cars. Adjacent to that side door was the kitchen door. Stacked three and four cages high, running along each side of the door, were rows six to seven cages in length under a lean-to roof, creating a tunnel. There was only one species per cage and, in some cases, only one creature per cage.

There were rats and bats and cats, chickens, snakes, lizards, and furry warm-blooded looking animals I was not familiar with. "Vej-ta-bul" rang out between my ears. Again, I was gastric Gibraltar. Odd I hadn't noticed all this as we walked from our cars up to the front door. But, the tunnel was distant from our entry path. More than ever I wondered what I had actually been consuming on the group outings.

The mention of the caged cats outside the kitchen door brought to mind a dining opportunity earlier on in our trip that I also told Mom and Dad about. In Guangzhou, on a table in our hotel room we found a room service menu—a letter size piece of card stock printed, laminated, and well aged. It was pretty tacky for how graciously the hotel was appointed. On one side of it the limited dinner menu was offered, photos of six plates each with a headline and a description. All was written in Chinese with the exception of an English subtitle below each headline in a smaller typeface. Number 5 in the offering was marinated cat roast. Yup, there was the toasty little kitty carcass curved along the edge of the plate with vej-ta-bul and rice for accompaniment.

I gleaned two things from my dining experiences in China. First, I learned a tremendous respect for how the people of this densely populated region with relatively few natural resources have developed a palate for *delicacies* such as shark fin soup, fish heads, and duck feet. Nothing that can be construed edible is left to waste. I managed the shark fin soup but I'm certain David was insulted by me refusing the duck feet. Regardless of the reputed hefty expense and his resulting irritation, I could not bring myself to try this *treat*. And, second, if I go to China again—damn! It was great getting back to Hong Kong for a Hard Rock Café burger and a Planet Hollywood caesar salad!—the first thing I'll pack is a mini-feast stash of granola bars, dried fruit, and turkey jerky.

15: Sex Goddess and Censorship

Last night I went down to West Seattle to scoop up Jack and bring him home for what was left of the pasta salad I made a couple days ago. He is still as animated as he was last Friday at Pain In The Grass. I like to see him this way.

I had already told Jack about the rare opportunity I had for approaching T. at a Pain In The Grass a couple weeks earlier, about requesting permission to reprint the lyrics from [T. song] in my book, and how he'd referred me to The Management Company for that. So I asked Jack, "Do you know how to get a hold of T.? The Management Company isn't listed like he said they'd be. I looked in the phone book and called directory assistance. They aren't listed."

"Yeah. . . well it's not like they want. . ."

I interrupted, finishing for him ". . . every band in town calling 'em to solicit management."

"Exactly. Why don't you just go up to their offices?"

"That seems so unprofessional going in cold without calling first for an appointment."

"Nah. Just go. They're all nice. It'll be cool. This isn't L.A. Ask For Bonnie."

I finished messing around in the kitchen and carried the pasta salad bowl, two soup bowls, and forks out to the table. Lonni got in the kitchen and whipped up a hot pasta dish. Pat sat out at the table with Jack and me while we munched the salad.

Jack added as an afterthought, "Or you can just go see T. He'll be at Crack Town tonight."

"Where?"

"That's what I call Tune Town these days. He'll be there. He and another guy DJ on Thursday nights."

The conversation wound through a variety of sub-topics

around Jack's new name for Tune Town, and then T.

I asked Jack, "Who is T. married to?"

"Some gorgeous super model in New York."

"She lives in New York?"

"Yeah."

"Well I guess that works for a lot of people, that coast to coast marriage thing."

"Pff! Hyeah."

While Pat, Lonni, and Jack sat at the table eating hot pasta I made dessert, a quick-fix fat free chocolate cake to be loaded up with 28 grams-of-fat-per-serving ice cream and, of course, my home-made sinfully rich deep double dark chocolate sauce. After we'd each eaten all we chose to, we sat and yakked about movies and stuff. I went to the stereo and put on Dishwalla, straight to Counting Blue Cars.

"Jack, have you gotten into the lyric on this song?"

"Yeah. . . about the kid. . ."

". . .and bein' a kid with the kid. . ."

"Yeah. Let me see the sleeve."

"Conversation break!" I proclaimed and cranked the volume up enough to preclude anyone trying to talk over it, explaining, "I love this song. I love the phraseology, very poetic."

Jack complained, "I hate when there's no lyrics. Oh, here's how they get you," pointing to a website address cited "for lyrics, tour dates and other info," then added, "We should get going after this song."

While Counting Blue Cars was playing he pulled out the BINM CD that has [T. song] on it and wordlessly scrutinized the lyrics and notes I'd written on the pages I want to re-print in my book.

I asked Jack if he'd like to smoke a bowl. He told me he's taking a break from smoking and drinking. After months of self-talk about it he finally decided to do it. I suppose this has a lot to do with his level of clarity and present state of upness. I smoked a bowl. We all talked a bit more. I went to the bathroom for a quick primp trip and we split.

As we headed for Capitol Hill to drop Jack off to hang with the new guitarist that Jack's been jammin' with my mind was whirling with thoughts of whether or not I should go to Tune Town. Somehow, I think Jack knew what my head was doing. I pulled the car over when instructed to. Jack leaned over wrapping his left arm around me. I leaned into my friend, pulling him closer with one arm around his neck and squeezing his ribs with the other, and pecked him on the neck.

"I think I pinked you," I told him, remembering that I'd just remoistened my lips with gloss.

"What?"

"I think I pinked you," as I wiped his neck and cheek.

"That's okay."

We exchanged our usual "I-enjoyed-that." I pointed out, as I had many times before, that he could call me too. As always, he smiled and chuckled "Yeah" and got out.

I drove around the block and headed toward downtown. I thought about how silly I'd feel if I went to Tune Town and T. wasn't there or he was and I would make a fool of myself trying to get a chance to talk with him. But I didn't want to go home. I then thought of wanting to talk to Junior about hooking me up with his tattooing buddy and that became my justification for going to Tune Town. What if Junior isn't working? Meanwhile my trusty *6000 STE* had guided me there and had spotted a great parking place a mere half block up and across the street from the club. So! What else could I do but go in?

"Three dollars", the doorman held out his hand.

"Three dollars!?!" I exclaimed with eyes surveying the bar in a sweeping glance. "It's so dead!" I complained. We pattered back and forth. "Is Junior working tonight?"

"He doesn't work here anymore. . ."

"Oh yeah?"

". . .but he is here tonight."

I paid up, walked over to an empty stool next to a couple guys at the bar and sat down. I ordered a Full Sail, sipped on delivery, turned to my right, catching the eye of one of the guys and said "Hello". Talked with them a while. Stood up. Looked around. Spotted Junior seated in a booth across from a short-haired blonde couple. Toyed with it a bit in my head and finally walked toward their booth. Junior glanced up. I saw recognition dawn on his face, "Hey."

"Hey. Scoot over." I sat down and, after he introduced me to his friends, stated, "Junior, I want you to hook me up with your tattoo buddy."

At that moment he got up saying he was running up to Capitol Hill and would be back in twenty minutes. I looked at his friends and asked if they minded if I hung there with them. They unanimously agreed that would be fine.

A guy slid into the booth, seating himself next to me while talking to my new companions. He turned to me and said, "Hi. I'm Chris."

"I'm Beth." I commented how disgusting it is that we slip into auto-bob-of-the-head to such non-music, the fact that I had sat on my butt at my desk for two twelve hour days in a row and could hardly sit still another moment. "I need to skate! This music is not what I had in mind for getting out."

Chris prompted me, "Go get some rock and roll!" He then removed himself and wandered over to lean on the bar side of the rail that separated the booth area from the bar.

No longer able to remain sedentary, I hopped out of the booth and bounced in the groove of the current tune up toward the dance floor and DJ. I pivoted just before reaching the DJ, bounced my way back to the table dancily, then landed on my knees with feet dangling off the edge of the booth seat and bounced some more. Realizing I might be annoying my table mates, I slid my feet around under the table, plopped my butt down and asked, "Are you regretting or wondering how you got stuck with me?" They both laughed and assured me they were fine with me. I was resigning myself to the idea that Jack had given me a bum steer when I saw him.

T. had arrived. My eyes riveted to him as he stood at the end of the bar talking with a couple guys, then tracked him as he made his way to the back most table situated directly under the exit light by the pool table. It irritated me that when he sat he was no longer in my range of vision. I slithered out of the booth, moseyed up to the rail, as if to talk with Chris, and turned to see if I could see T. from there. Yup. Cool. As a matter of fact, it appeared that he was gazing at me as well. I quickly dismissed the thought, telling myself that he could be looking at anything or anybody to my left, my right, behind me, but, no, not me.

Chris apparently took my approach as interest in him.

160

He laid out for me the typical Older Woman come-on. I suckered him a bit, until he got more graphic than I was willing to play with. I looked back to the corner. T. was still there. I speculated he chose hanging near the exit to enable rapid escape in case someone like me might want to invade his space.

When I went back to perch on my knees in the booth, so I could see over the heads of those between me and him, I was alone. Chris abandoned the rail, stood next to the booth and attempted to fondle me. "Hey! BACK. . . BACK . . . BACK!" my voice escalated as I pushed past him to my feet and danced my way toward the DJ again.

He was like "*What?*" I shot a scowl at him and moved on.

I felt like a twitterpated, shy schoolgirl. I fidgeted and hesitated. This nervousness was pissing me off but I couldn't get a grip on it. I knew I may never have this opportunity again, to be in the same club and for him not to be on stage. But I couldn't seem to get any further than standing in the aisle next to the booth. I don't remember what distracted me but I was looking over the rail up toward the bar for a bit and when I turned back around, there he was almost within arm's reach. I nearly stopped breathing. I was like a TNT charge about to detonate! What's up with this?

T. finished talking to the people in the booth next to me and looked up. Our eyes met. He smiled and nodded. I smiled, tossed my head back and to the side a bit, and crooked my finger at him in a wordless "come here." And he did. I just about lost it right there.

He sidled up next to me and I said, "They aren't listed."

"Who?"

"Your management company."

"Oh, yeah? The Management Company?"

"Yeah. Wanna smoke a bowl?"

"Sure. Come on back to the table."

I screamed in my head, "My God, he came to me!" With each step toward the corner I felt to be walking deeper into a dream. And now, as I try to write about it, try to talk about what transpired, it seems more and more surrealistic. I guess my oh so effective self-defense mechanisms are kicking in. No matter how real it was at the time, no matter how undeniably strong the vibe was, no matter how

161

comfortable it felt, my intellect now tells me to ignore it. DO deny it. Forget it. Move on. Don't even write about it. Keep it in your head as a cool memory. Don't let it sneak into your heart. He told you himself, "You don't want to know me. I'm mean and nasty." Take *that* to heart. Maybe he is. Why read something more into it than what it was? A moment in time. . . a hoped for but, nonetheless, chance meeting. BULLSHIT!! There are no coincidences. As I told him then, "Bullshit, like I would believe "mean and nasty" for a moment?" He was so sweet, child-like at times and, yes, with a very alive demon or two, but "mean and nasty"? No. Okay. So, write about it before you convince yourself that it was a dream.

We got to the table under the exit sign and T. resumed his position in the corner facing out to the rest of the room. There was no chair for me so I stood next to him, pulled the pipe and lighter out of my pocket and handed it to him. He told me to crouch down. I did. He leaned down with his head below the table, almost pressed up to my chest. I was so tempted to smooch his neck. He torched the bowl then sat back up and passed the pipe to the guy across the table from him, who took it and repeated T.'s move. He gave it back to T. who, in turn, held it out to me. "No, you go ahead." He hit off the pipe again then handed it to me. "T., I have a lot of questions I'd like to ask you."

"I bet you do", he said smiling, almost laughing.

"I do, but I need to get another beer. Would you mind if I came back and talked with you for a while?"

"No, I'd like that."

"You would? Cool. I'll be back."

When I returned with beer in hand I was still in a chairless state. T. said, "Get a chair." I set my beer on the table and wandered away. I looked at all the nearby tables and found no vacant chair so went back empty handed. "Skip, would you get the lady a chair?"

I turned to T., "I wondered if I should just inform someone that they're now sitting on the floor and yank it out from under them." He laughed. Skip was more successful than me. He brought a chair around to where I was standing and set it down next to T. I thanked him and sat down.

When he got back to his chair across from T. I extended

my hand and said "Hi! I'm Beth".

"I'm Skip."

"Nice to meet you," as we shook. I looked at the guy sitting next to Skip and did the same. He was not as friendly, more just accommodating the circumstances. Consequently I don't remember his name. There was a very pretty lady to his left. Again I extended my hand and said "Hi, I'm Beth."

She had a nice shake and warmly responded, "I'm Liza."

I asked, "Is that short for Elizabeth?" She smiled and nodded yes. We had a bond.

I turned to T., "So, how's it all going in New York?" I asked him a lot of questions about BINM, how their east-bound tour went, and about different things that he's done or said at different shows. Some he answered seemingly straight up, some evasively, some jokingly. I said, "Listen to me! I sound like *The Authoritative BINM Show Chronologist*."

T. responded, "Yeah. I like that."

So, I asked him, "What does [T. song] mean to you?"

He got into talking about the metaphors in the lyric without really relating them to anything in way of explanation. His obvious intent was to be evasive.

When he finished with his non-answer I told him, "To me, it's about addiction."

He seemed a little skitchy about that one, as if I had struck a chord. I think it was in here where he referenced my "book of poetry." I set him straight by explaining it's a work of creative nonfiction, a memoir. I added, "A statement within the book is my belief that addiction is the human commonality. We humans are all addicted to something. I happen to be addicted to caffeine, nicotine, and skating."

The mention of skating led me to tell him, with a lot of my usual animation and arm-talking, the story of my parking garage skating accident in San Diego and the injuries that graced the beginning of my Vacation of the Decade. He laughed and demanded I tell the story to the guy whose name I can't remember (who, Skip told me later, is a member of the band Sweetwater). He didn't seem one iota interested so I gladly told him to never mind, no problem.

At the end of a drink, quite a while later, T. says to me, "I'm going for another drink. When I get back you only get one more question so. . . make it count for something."

While he was gone Liza leaned toward me and asked, "How do you know T.?" I told her I don't really, that we'd just talked one time recently due to my interest in reprinting the lyrics from one of his songs in the book I'm writing. We commented on that briefly and then she said, "Well, he speaks very highly of you."

I was pretty shocked, "He does?" She nodded.

When T. came back to the table I was prepared. I'd decided that I may never get this chance again so I better go for it. "Well?" he queried.

I laid it out, "This is a multiple choice question. Would you like to [A] Come home and smoke another bowl with me since I have no more smoke here? Or, [B] Would you like to come home with me so I can smoke you out and do you like you'll never forget?" He was totally blown away. He looked at me in disbelief, shook his head, then looked again. I guess he wasn't anticipating that one.

T. got up and moved around the table to sit across from me. He threw his left hand on the table and pointed to his ring, "I can't. I'm married! I can't."

I replied, "Okay. It's a multiple choice question."

Whoa SHIT!! I've got to get to bed!! I'm going to have to finish this later—so long as I don't forget—no I couldn't do that no matter how dreamlike it all seems.

Zoey, know I am sending you all my love. Be safe and happy, Baby. Sleep well. God I miss you!

<u>July 23, 1996 - a letter to T.</u>

Dear T.,

The question was "Would you like to come home with me so I can do you like you'll never forget?" It wasn't, "Would you like me to fuck your brains out?" That you can do in an alley or a car seat. I was thinking this one little nook overhanging I-5 in Freeway Park could be cool. But, any of that is much better after you've been done like you'll never forget. Since in this question I present myself as a primary doer, and you as a primary do-ee, you might want to consider the benefit of being in a place where there's fun things to play with, that's warm and feels good, where I can be my best. This would be my home. And, yeah, it could get spiritual. Is that a bad thing? How do you know until you go?

164

I still have so many questions ("like children often do" - Do you like that Dishwalla song?) like: Why did you sign the liner in my copy of your CD "T___?" (copy attached - there is very much a story behind the notes I've written on the page, which is why I want to reprint it "as is" in the book. By the way, that was the night BINM played as Space * * * *sucker at the Off Ramp, like we talked about.) Does she really live in New York? Is it rapture? What is that thing you put in your mouth that makes you look like a singing blowfish? Does it hurt? and so many more...

There will be several references to you in my book. If you'd like to see the manuscript so you know when it shows up in the book that it's real, not stuff I concocted, I'd like that. But you have to come to my house.

The pipe you pocketed is refillable. I usually always have smoke and you are always welcome to come pack the bowl. I've been attracted to you for a little over three years now, since the first time I saw BINM play on the advice of a friend shortly after I moved back to Seattle. It was at the Off Ramp and you were wearing big boots with long johns top and bottom, a spandex mini-skirt (pale pink I think), eyeliner and lipstick. T., I would like to know you. In a way, I feel like I already do, like we're cut from the same thread, not just the same cloth, but the same fiber.

Anyway, most people who know me find me likable. Did I mention that's a refillable bowl? If I were ever to ask for something that's not right for you, all you'd need to do is let me know and I'd let it go. I would not want to do anything to hurt you in any way. Like you, I am no angel, but I am good.

The abstract for my book is also attached.   Beth

This letter went into the sealed envelope discussed in the following letter written to Bonnie at The Management Company which I mailed to their office. Jack told me precisely where to find it. I finally wound up the courage to drop in, introduce myself, and ask for a business card so that I could mail them a query.

July 24, 1996

Dear Bonnie,

I nabbed T. at a Pain In The Grass show a couple weeks ago to ask him if I might obtain permission to reprint the lyrics to [T. song] in the book I am writing. He said that he would like that and for me to be in touch with you regarding this issue. He/we assumed The Management Company would be listed in the phone directory, but of course as you know, you are not. Otherwise, I would not just show up on your doorstep without an appointment. Please excuse the presentation.

Since my first talk with T., we met up in a club one evening and I had a chance to go more in depth on the topic of this potential reprint in my book. It seems he'd thought I was doing a book of poetry. I do feel that the lyric is an outstanding poetic piece and would be appropriately placed as such. But, I had to let him know this was not the case. Beyond imparting that bit of info to him as well as the fact that the topic of addiction is addressed in the book, and making the comment, "We're all addicted to something," I was fairly vague. Ultimately, we parted without me getting your number and without me having a feeling for whether or not he wants his lyric included in this sort of project.

So, attached to this letter is an abstract for my book and a rough copy of how I wish to reprint. I am also entrusting to you an envelope for T. which contains the abstract, copies, and a personal letter to T. I would very much appreciate having delivered to him sealed and the two of you can discuss this matter at his discretion. I look forward to hearing from you. Sincerely,
Beth Rice

Journal: August 4, 1996

I walked salad over to Marcus and Holly's tonight to enjoy with Master Chef Marcus' Oven-baked Garlic Potato Extraordinaire. I was immediately to view the drawing Holly had been working on all day. I viewed it with some sense of shock coming from *the Morality Precept on Sexuality and Human Body Parts* Mom pretty well installed in my consciousness. I quickly got over it. I read, on her computer screen, *The Huntress*, Holly's self-characterizations, her "many people." her alter egos. It was a beautiful read. I told her the Patrick Nagel lady hanging in my bedroom is my alter ego, with her guard up against vulnerability. We yakked. I told her about meeting Robby last night and bringing him home to enjoy because he was so damn sweet.

We had a great spiritually charged discussion which included my discovery or more my acceptance of the fact that I am the *New* Sex Goddess of The Western Hemisphere as we laughed and nodded agreement to the lyric of the song she was playing for me on the stereo, Maggie Estep's famed poem put to music by an all girl punk band. This followed my realization, after all the negativity from Paul which had me sucked into believing that I am not sexy, not desirable—one of the why's of my Sport Fuck Phase, I have been learning that men love my sex, my prowess. I rounded up our discussion by sharing, "I think I can speak for both of us on this when I say that when we're together we each find in ourselves our better self, a truer, higher place." Holly was nodding emphatically as I spoke. Earlier on I had said something so lucidly philosophical that my oratory rambled non-stop right into expressing my amazement that I had just said that. Where did that come from? "*Where does that come from?*" we both asked, all the while knowing.

I comment lightly on my Sport Fuck Phase. It may sound like it's all just totally meaningless sex. But, the fact is each man, each time—even each mental, intellectual, perhaps emotional fuck encounter attraction along the search that never manifested physically—has held great meaning for me and I have loved them all.

Honesty scares quite a lot of people.

Journal August 7, 1996

The Management Company's card sits atop my desk, reminding that I have yet to get a reply from them. So, today I sent a fax to confirm Bonnie has received my mailing. At least, that was my initial intent. But, I got on a roll trying to pitch her, to get her on my side, so to speak. I hope it's not another letter I shouldn't have sent.

Robby came over again last night and we had a great time shooting faeries, then giving back rubs which led to very hot yet comfortable and cozy sex. His girlfriend recently broke off their relationship so he's been used to affection. I enjoyed him sharing it with me ever so nicely. I think he'll come again.

<u>On The Management Company letterhead faxed to me:</u>

August 12, 1996
Re: BINM
Dear Ms. Rice,

In response to your fax dated August 7, 1996, I have decided that it would not be in the best interest of T. or BINM to appear in your book in any way.

Please do not use the lyrics from [T. song] or from any other song written by the band, or any artwork from any of their records, CD's or tapes.

Thank you in advance for your cooperation in this matter.

Regards, Bonnie

August 12, 1996 – my reply via fax

Dear Bonnie,

I am in receipt of your fax, sent today. I will comply with your wishes. Names will be omitted and none of the properties you cited will be quoted or otherwise reproduced.

I find it regrettable that you feel my perception or interpretation of the lyrics to a song could be considered a reflection on the writer or what it may have meant to him; and that expressed sincere admiration for the quality of musicianship in and inspired song writing and performing talents of a band would be construed as "not in their best interest." The only thing I have written about T. that could possibly be taken as a negative is that "I find him to be delightfully abstract." And that is only my perception. Mostly I feel it's unfortunate when honesty is a mistake.

I will respect your decision and I will continue to support the band by going to their shows and buying their CD's. And I do sincerely hope that you get them signed to a label that will promote them better than [their old label] did.

Regards, Beth Rice

Journal: August 12, 1996

It's more than a year since Zoey and I have had contact. I keep thinking that she'll feel like if she was okay without me for that long, for three years, that when this is over, she'll think "What do I need her now for?" It's such a frightening thought. It's a frightening, recurring thought.

16: My Tattoo and T.

Dearest Zoey,

As you may or may not recall I have toyed with the thought of getting a tattoo for several years now. But I've never taken the idea too seriously. When you started talking about having one I was playing it down pretty hard, knowing how Eric and Crystal would freak out. And, I was afraid you'd get something real radical that a little later in life you might not be so happy to have as a permanent fixture on your body.

It's just in these last few months that the concept of permanently marking my body with art has started to press upon me as totally desirable but I've not been clear at all *what*. What would be such a part of me that I would enjoy viewing it each time I dress in front of a mirror. . . and where exactly would I put it?

Well, the *where* became the first concrete vibe for me. I greatly attribute the *where* to a line in the movie "Pulp Fiction," which I think should have won an Oscar for All-time Classic Line. It's the one she says as she's lying on the bed in the motel when he comes back to get her (this is paraphrased as I don't recall it verbatim):

I wish I had a little pot. . . a little pot belly. . . Isn't it funny how that which f e e l s the best, is not always so pleasing to the eye?

I have been on a program of herbal dietary supplements that include natural fat burners and being that it's the season, I've been skating a lot so I'm in pretty good shape. In fact—this is a miracle!—the tops of my thighs are almost completely smooth again! Cellulite away! This is definitely attributable to my skateboard. Boarding works a whole different muscle group from roller skating but I know that no amount of exercise alone would do what it has without being in concert with the herbals. However (I digressed) I still have a little layer of pudge and I just don't care because I'm toned under it. I feel good. After hearing that line it seems unimportant. I had been complaining about this little spare tire that has developed into a tummy I can't seem to get rid of. But after seeing Pulp Fiction I decided to go ahead and wear jeans low on my hips with crop tops and put my worst feature out there. Well, after going out like that on three consecutive weekends the funniest thing happened. Here I am thinking "Well, if someone is going to be attracted to me, it will be knowingly, with pre-acceptance of the fact that I have a little belly (as a negative in my mind). But wouldn't you know that each night I went out belly out, men came right up to me and commented things like "What a great stomach you have" . . . "I love your little belly" Yikes! Was I amazed! So, my point is, I want my tattoo on my belly.

I became clear that I would like a little dragon to sit atop my navel with his tail winding down around it. And a fairy, like the one in that Christiansen poster of mine, would fly up above the dragon sprinkling fairy dust down on him. These visions actually clarified for me over a period of weeks. I can't pinpoint dates or times now but I've been getting more and more excited about it. Then I got real clear that I would have the tattoo applied on your sixteenth birthday, in your honor.

Yesterday I finally got on the phone to some tattoo places looking for an artist with strong female energy that would be into this project. But first I called a guy named George at Rudy's Barber Shop because Jack recommended him saying that he likes to do unusual things. Out of respect for Jack, I was going to give him a shot even though I sensed in my mind that I really needed a woman for the job. It turned out that George is out of town until next week and that is too close to your birthday, not enough time to plan and me feel assured that he has good energy for the project plus leave myself time to explore other avenues if the vibe isn't right.

Next I called a place over on 45th in the U District, where Holly said she had seen a lady artist. A man answered the phone and said to call back Thursday through Monday when I could talk to one or all of three ladies. Mind's Eye Tattoo jumped off the yellow page at me, on University Avenue at about 52nd. I called and was recommended to Viki.

I talked with Viki, explaining that I have no tattoos and I want to be sure that, if I'm going to place something so permanent on my body, I will love it. I told her my thoughts for the art and the energy I'm looking for. I got a good feeling from her. We set a consultation appointment for an hour and a half later. I thought "Cool I can get a skate in first." She said bring in whatever you have that you'd like me to work with.

On that note I sat down to have my ritualistic pre-skate bowl. While smoking I thought of what I should take in to her, obviously the poster. When I talked to her about the importance of a good purple, she expressed a concern for my level of expectation vs. the actual outcome of purple in tattooing, which she said will vary from one skin-type and skin-tone to another but almost always is ashen or muted. So, I thought I should take in some of my purple things so we could measure my expectation up to the likely result, be clear on what I'd be okay with. Naturally, the purple dragon you made for me was the first thing I thought of. Recently, Lonni gave me a whimsical little purple dragon guy who is curled up in a ball, sleeping, with a smile on his face so I thought to take him too. Next I grabbed a bottle of bubbles packaged in the wrong purple, to show her clearly what I don't want. There is a beautiful gradation of purple in the crystal slab that my little wizard stands on. And I love the deep purple in the amethyst crystal rock that Victoria gave me years ago.

I picked my butt up off the couch, leaned to my left and craned my neck so to see the clock hanging next to my desk. Oops, not enough time to skate and assure timeliness on my appointment as I still needed to freshen up before going. I replanted my butt and viewed all of my polar bears on the entertainment center across from me. They are such a part of me I thought I should take a few of them also. I walked over and picked up my little Mexican polar bear that you so thoughtfully brought back for me from your trip. I also selected the small ivory polar bear from Alaska that

Josh gave me and the silver Coca-Cola polar bear coin.

Now, I need a good bag I thought. So I went to the walk-in closet in my bedroom and looked through my bag o' bags for the one Hard Rock bag I knew wasn't in use as your bag o' the year. It wasn't turning up. In my search, I kept pushing past the Christmas gift bag that your Aunt Rosey and the girls made for me this last Christmas until I realized that it was my best candidate size-wise. I thought how goofy I'd look walking in to the tattoo shop with a Rudolph The Red-nosed Reindeer bag and then decided "Fuck that!" I also love Christmas and it is very much a part of me. . . SO! I removed your little dragons from the plastic case I stored them in soon as I got home from the Fremont Fair, wrapped my precious Zoey-dragon in tissue and carefully placed him in the case for safe transport.

As I proceeded to load all of my treasures into the bag I looked at the photos of you and me on my desk and thought I need to take these also. So I tucked three framed photos in the bag, gasped as the clock caught my eye and dashed to the bathroom to brush my teeth and hair. I called Viki to apologize for running late and to say "I'm on my way!" I grabbed the framed poster off the wall, Rudolph and friends, and made my way to the car.

When I got to Mind's Eye Viki was just finishing up with a client. I perused her photo portfolio. I exclaimed a number of times, "YES! . . .YE-E-S-S-S!!" not oblivious to the looks I was getting from others seated in the waiting area but not caring. I loved what I was seeing, faeries and dragons and dancers. Then it was my turn. Viki showed me in to her work room, we sat on the couch/table and I asked her "Do you like bubbles?"

"I love bubbles."

"Oh good. I brought you an offering of bubbles."

Zoey, my mouth opened and those words fell out. I had no idea, prior to that moment, that I'd brought bubbles as an offering. I have never made *an offering* to anyone in my entire life, at least not in those terms. I pulled the purply pink bottle out of the bag and handed it to her. She smiled, accepted it and thanked me. I took each item out of the bag, placing it on the couch/table between us as I explained its significance or why I had brought it. When I brought out my Zoey-dragon, displaying it in the flat of my palm, I told her, "My daughter made this for me."

Viki questioned, "She made that?"

"Yes. She's very talented."

Lastly, I brought out the photographs of us. First was the one of you and I that was taken right after Paul kissed the bride out on Hermosa Pier, the Bride kissing her Maid of Honor.

Next was the photo your Grammy took of us on the couch when I came up for Christmas in your 6th grade year; the one where you're sitting on my lap with your arms around my neck giving me a smooch. You're wearing the darling purple dress Gramma and Grampa had just gifted to you. I'm wearing the purple velvet hat that goes with the dress. I looked at Viki and said, "We like purple and we like to kiss."

Then I showed her the photos taken in the booth at Fred Meyer on Capitol Hill the day we went to Westlake Mall to buy Beastie Boy tickets. An aside: I don't recall if I've mentioned it in any of my writings to you but I did not go to the concert. There was no desire to go without you so I sold the tickets.

OKAY! It was all out there. I looked at Viki with, "This is me, my essence, and this is our energy. This tattoo is in honor of my daughter's sixteenth birthday. Would you like to do my tattoo? Will you do a good job on my tattoo?"

Her voice was sincere when she replied, "Yes. Yes, I think I get what you're looking for." And I knew she did. At that, I suggested we blow a few bubbles to consummate the plan. She laughed but complied and we took turns wielding the wand.

Oh! By the way, I think I forgot to mention that while I was in the bathroom getting ready to go, after packing all my stuff into the Christmas bag, it hit me that I wanted two faeries, for the two of us. This obviously changes the whole dynamic of the tattoo from my original concept. But Viki and I talked it all through and got a good idea of where we're going with it. She told me I should save the dragon for another sitting, that what we were planning would be a long sitting for a first tattoo. I will do the dragon in honor of your seventeenth birthday.

<u>August 14, 1996 – in her bag</u>

Hi Zoey!

After work today I took Katie over to Mind's Eye to meet Viki. She'd already started working on a sketch that was absolutely beautiful and perfectly reflects the feel of what I want. Katie and I were both blown away. Viki and I talked some about the coloration. She had not incorporated your name into the faery dust stars like I had asked. When I mentioned this she said, "I don't want to offend you but. . ." and we said, in different words but unanimously agreed it'll ruin the integrity of the design. Viki added, "That's her right there. You don't need to spell her name."

I concurred. "But you must grant me this one wish. Her birth stone is peridot, a sort of greenish-gold color. Combined with the "50's Refrigerator Blue" that you're talking about using, I think it could be really pretty. I want peridot in the Zoey faery wings."

On the way out the front door, I commented that the gargoyle statuette on the front desk was really neat. Viki said there is a store called Gargoyles right up the street that we should check out. So, we did. It is a very cool store. Katie and I had a cosmic experience there that had us laughing so hard I apologized to the shopkeepers for breaking the rather dark and gloomy ambiance. Zoey, remind me to tell you the story of the tattoo of Max from Where The Wild Things Are. I don't feel like writing it all out right now. I'm telling you the story of my tattoo now.

On the way back to the car I ducked into Mind's Eye to say thanks for turning us on to Gargoyles. Viki, on seeing me, yelped, "I'm so glad you came back! I've got my preliminary all done."

"Cool!" I said to her back as she went to get it. She handed it to me, completely colored in and finished, and I was in love. Yes, this belongs on me. I told her how beautiful, how perfect. I took it to a full length mirror and placed it on my belly trying to position it to fit my original vision. It is considerably larger than I'd thought I wanted but it is so beautiful.

"You know it could go different ways," Viki took the paper and turned it a bit.

"YES! That's it! Right there, just like that." I was so

stoked. Katie was out sitting on the trunk of the car waiting for me. I yelled out the door, "Katie! Com'ere! She's got it all done! You have to see it!"

She expressed amazement at Viki's speed in finishing the drawing and then she saw it. Our gazes locked, eye-in-eye, and we smiled and nodded. . . and nodded and smiled, now shaking our heads in disbelief at *how perfectly Beth.* Yup, obviously Viki and I had connected. She was stoked as I was in realizing she'd gotten it exactly right first time out. We set our appointment. She put me in the book for 2:30PM on your birthday. I can hardly wait.

I told Evie several days ago that I want to take Friday before the holiday off. I told her it will be dead any way and I need to have it off. I didn't leave her with any window to say NO. She knows I have it coming. I've got an appointment to have my hair trimmed at noon on the tattoo day. I called Gail last week to see if she could take time to touch up my blonde and give me the purple stripe I'd discussed with her a while back when I was in for a trim. I told her I'm taking the day off and can wait around for her to do me between others. But, no way. She refuses to do the purple stripe. So I've talked to Katie about whether I should brave it and do it myself. I'll be brave.

So, my dear daughter, in honor of you and our everlasting bond, I am having the image of our energy permanently painted on my physical being for your sixteenth birthday. As a prelude, I'm affixing a purple stripe left of the part in my hair to honor our individuality and uniqueness. I wish you could see it. I wish I could see you. But, I do. . . in my mind's eye.

Love, *always*Mom

P.S. - I almost forgot to mention that today I sold three orders totaling 14,650 caps and $65,000 in sales! HA! I love it! I *am* The HatLady!

<u>August 17, 1996 – in her bag</u>

Zoey, love of my life,

Firstly, I want you to know I moved up the date for the application of my tattoo because of two upcoming major events where I stand to be jostled and jabbed in large crowds: Bumbershoot and Action Sport Retailer Trade Show. Both happen within one week of your birthday. I don't want to risk injuring my freshly healing tattoo.

Second, the key story that the enclosed photo can't tell is what it feels like under the tattoo gun. It's funny because I had never really put any thought to how pigment would become permanently affixed to one's skin. And you'll notice that anyone who has a tattoo doesn't talk about it.

I know now that it's almost like being in a private club and, at that, there are more elitist sectors of the club - the stomach, the elbow, and the underside-of-the-arm tattoo bearers hold the highest prestige because these are some of the most tender areas, the most painful applications. When it was all over and I had a beautiful painting of our energy on my stomach, Viki said to me, "If anyone with a big ol' arm tattoo ever looks at yours and says, "That's nothing." tell 'em you'll talk to 'em about it when they've had one done on their stomach."

I'll be the one to break the credo of the club. I'm going to tell you what it feels like so you will have an idea, my dear, the level of dedication that went into this. When she had done the first two or three little blasts with the outlining tool and I was squirming, Viki told me, "They say the outlining is the worst part. It'll get easier."

After about five minutes I thought of her estimated two hours to complete the tattoo and wondered if I was going to make it. I began to think 'OK outline today, color some other day.' Viki must have picked up on that because she started pep talking me. I don't remember what it was she said exactly but I recall my response was, "So it's a mind over matter thing."

She asked if I'd like her to hang the photo of you that I'd brought where I could see it. "Uh huh." She snagged it off the counter where it sat in front of the Whoppers I had placed in front of the shrine as an offering to the Tattoo Goddess, put a rolled piece of tape on the back, and stuck it on a mirror in my range of vision.

I don't have a graphic description of the pain in the outlining portion of the tattoo other than to say that it hurts like hell. When that part was done we took a little break. I stood outside the back door smoking a cigarette, wishing it was a joint, while Viki reiterated the coloring should be easier. I sat back down in the chair and leaned back, ready for the attack. I think she flat out lied. After several blasts with the coloring tool I said, "Viki, I've figured out exactly what that feels like. It's as if you're working with a fine wire brush shaped in a ball like a nylon net dish scrubber and shrunk to fit the end of your tool."

She replied, "You're not far off." The only way I could hang with it was to remove myself—literally, take my mind out to some other place. It hovered in the corner 'over there.' It was good I found that ability. We can say it was my first out of body experience as I viewed the coloring from the corner at the ceiling, detached from the pain.

Toward the end of the session, Katie and her friend, Hank, stopped back by to see how it was going. They'd first stopped in on their way to a reading at a book store up the street when Viki had just a bit of the outline done. Now, reading over, they were curious to see how I was holding out. I could tell by the look of concern on Katie's face that I must look pretty bad. She asked, "Is this anything like natural childbirth?"

"For pain equivalence I suppose; but, really it's more like labor contractions in reverse cuz you're willfully push-ing out your muscles, tensing up for the pain."

Or, as I came to express the experience later. . .

Getting a tattoo is like roadrash
just that instant
when your flesh tears
as you hit the asphalt
If I were to take all the first seconds of contact
for all of the roadrash I've experienced
in my seventeen years of skating
and multiply it by a thousand lifetimes
that's what it felt like getting my tattoo
So, my dear daughter,
I now bear clear evidence
of an incredibly high pain threshold
that I am one tuff cookie
two and a quarter hours later, there
on my tender belly, near my center

we fly
    free
        to be
           together you & me
in our most magical and beautiful faery form
our offerings of bubbles and faery dust
streams of glitter glory converging at my birth link
where we'll summon
the purple dragon
to join with us to play
and to protect

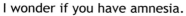

August 22, 1996

If this were a poem I'd call it
    Disappointments &
      What-the-fucks?

Dear Robby,

I wonder if you have amnesia.
Have you forgotten where to go back for your stuff?
Forgotten how warm and good it felt there?
Could it be that was just me?
Did I take off my male emulation just long enough
to remember why I'd taken to wearing it?
I finished the prelude to my book and hoped you'd read it
I now have a beautiful painting tattoo on my belly
and was hoping you'd see it
I was hoping you'd recover your board and we'd skate
Perhaps I'm overly hopeful
If you want to tell me stories please call
I and the faeries await

P.S. - I went to a poetry slam for the first time last night
with my friend, Katie. This, and my recent rediscovery that
I am a writer, could lead to melodramatic prose in lieu of
basic communication.

Hat-head Remnant in Goggles, Chapter Two - Summer 1996

    Poem has dropped in for tea
      or is it me?
    Is it you?
    perhaps tea for two

Because
I am the New Sex Goddess of the Western Hemisphere
there was one before me
but I've now claimed the title for my Self
it's time to take Me down off the shelf
In my PreDenial Period
I just know
there's total acceptance   but
then I'm told where to go
so I forget
jam my round peg
in your square hole
don my costume
read for my role
denial inhibits and it sucks
but somehow I'm all wired up in
your Race for Big Bucks
he who hath the most toys wins
cool car, turbo-prop, big boat
my head fucking spins
I do what's expected
be wife
bear child
when can Me be resurrected?
not now!
be meek
be mild
be obsessed with my addictions
not addicted to my predilections
no time for that
hide in my hat
wear goggles to see
acceptable masks
over who not to be
take up your tasks
work on your goals
your truths become my fears
while hiding Me for so many years
Suppress!
no time for tears
this is the race for big, bigger, best!

but not on a skateboard!
Fuck that !
I open my eyes
I opt to live no more lies
in PostDenial
I offer Poem beers
    IF
if I ever marry again
it will be an anti-wedding
The Church and The Government
will not be invited
    WE
my soulmate and me
will stand naked in the sunlight
      bathing each other with lovelight
          fingers interlocked   hearts entwined
             souls dancing in time
                to the rhythm of our magic
                and the universe
                shall be our witness

August 25, 1996 - In Zoey's 1996 bag

Hello my dear daughter,

    I'm aboard the 2:10 ferry bound for Bainbridge, then on to Gramma and Gramps. I picked up this giant postcard at an Espresso stand at the foot of Mount Index, on Highway 2 to Stevens Pass. There's a little monument there commemorating the filming of Harry & The Hendersons, kind of cute. I was on my way down the mountain trail this morning at about eight o'clock after spending the night under the stars in the woods at a place called Scenic Hot Springs.

    There is a nearly invisible dirt road just past the "59 Mile" marker that leads up to the mountain. I had to park off to the side just a couple hundred yards in, giving us a three and half mile uphill hike remaining to the hot springs. *The ferry just stopped mid-route and announced they were doing this so a family could "pay last respects to a loved one." End aside* People with jeeps and four wheel drive trucks drove in a lot further to cut down the hike. I was envious as we passed by those vehicles parked higher up. But, we were lucky there was a nice bright half moon out because we had no flashlight and it was about 9:30PM when we got out of the car.

The trail was so steep I started huffing and puffing about one hundred steps into it. In my brain, I began chanting, "I am one with the trail and God is in me," then meted my steps to the rhythm of the chant and my breath to my steps. The climb became so easy. I was reminded of that time I got caught in the rip tide at Hermosa and chanting "I am one with the wave and God is in me" literally saved me, brought me to swimming diagonally to shore. So I trusted I'd have help again.

The Hot Springs were so cool. They're on private property owned by two elderly doctors (I guess the story goes) and the four sitting pools, sun/moon deck, and connecting stairs were built by various fans of the spot over the last ten years or. That's some serious dedication. I can't imagine hiking in with lumber, weighty hardware and tools.

Love you! Mom

Journal: August 30, 1996

No, there are no coincidences. People do step in for a purpose. Robby stepped out on his newly-returned-girlfriend to a phone booth and called me Tuesday. Having just gotten his bag-o-stuff and my letter at work (where I left them last week while he was surfing in SoCal, the only way I knew to be in touch) he very kindly dispelled the What-the-fuck? of our brief reconnection. It wasn't just me.

I thank you again for calling, Robby. Lessons come so unpredictably. Thank you for reteaching me to trust The Vibe. As Skip so knowingly put it last Thursday night when I asked him, "Do you know what brought me here tonight?" I pointed to T. with, "Do you wonder how I knew he'd be here?" And Skip shook his head saying matter-of-factly, "A vibe."

Dear Reader,

I feel there is something that needs to be mentioned:

I'm magic

except when I forget

August 30, 1996 - Ode to T. and T. Song

Thursdays are full of you since that night
Yesterday, just like last Thursday, at 6ish p.m.
I got this overwhelming Vibe
You weren't just on my mind,
        but in my head
                throughout my brain
                        surrounding my psyche
til I felt to be in a bubble. . . floating
Were you thinking of me?
Were you willing me to be there?
In the sanctity of that bubble
with thanks to Robby for reteaching me to trust The Vibe
I transcended the Oh-so-commonsensical
Don't-be-silly denial that kept me home last Thursday
and I went
sure as God kisses my breath each morning
by the time I tithed my three dollars at the door
swapped tattoo tales with the man on the stool
and bellied me and my tat up to the bar for a beer
Enter You and your entourage, the guardians of your Child,
that Child my Child would love to love
and wants to play with
wants to know so much better
as you squeezed past me through
the small space between bodies
our eyes met for a half-second
were you looking through me?
or at me through feigned non-recognition?
Skip brought up the rear
his eyes wordlessly holding mine for a moment
as you pressed on through to your corner at the back
by the pool table
as the DJ spun the vinyl that filled the air with beat
our dance began
        with so many questions unanswered
                and so many more unasked
yet undeniably tangled in The Vibe
I went back to the door

182

with my just-in-case left-brain excuse to be there and
asked the man on the stool, with the stamp, taking cash
"Have you seen Junior tonight?"
"Yeah, he's here. At least I haven't seen him leave."
so I maneuvered through the crowd
eyes seeking Junior
heart wanting you
to blow more spit bubbles
that I would cartwheel to this time
if you'd just walk with me to my car again
tongue desiring to be surrounded by your mouth again
one kiss wasn't enough
        right breast remembering your light touch
like at the movies in 8th grade with my boyfriend
        and your question, "Did you like that?"
        "Did you?"
                "Did you?"
                        "Did you??"
                                "Did you??"
"Did you!?!" I demanded, even though you had asked first
"Yeah"
"Me too"
I confessed, wanting to feel your skin
the little hole in your pants by your knee
drawing my touch in
as we hung there on that sliver de la luna
I found myself in your back corner by the pool table
and Junior
"Hey! Wha's'up?" I volleyed to him
feeling you behind me, not daring to turn
not knowing if the woman with you was a friend
or the woman with whom you share a 1040 and
Interesting Couple Media Image
or do you love her?   is it rapture?
having sated my left-brain reason to be there
and with my right-brain in manic panic
somewhere in the middle I wandered away
hoping you'd come toward me again
wishing you'd come with me
wishing you'd come in me
as I fulfilled my promise to do you like you'll never forget

wishing we'd have met between the glass of my windshield
as you laid across the hood and kissed me through it
before you got in Skip's car and
flew away that Thursday night
back in the present again
I half-hear the men next to me admiring my tattoo
and/or craving the body it's on
but I'm gazing at you
in your new spot, bent over the rail
separating the bar from the booths
head to head with Skip, deep in conversation
not knowing if you were meeting me half-way
or if I was being too hopeful
I was half-afraid to slide past you to the dance floor
where my body could gyrate with the pulse
half-loosening my tension
but by the time I half-remembered
to at least half-trust The Vibe
you and Skip had parted and I knew I'd have to cover
the other half-way if we were going to talk
so I took the sophomoric, half-assed route to you
through your friend
as he passed by I tapped him on the shoulder asking
"Do I know you? Have we met?"
"Yeah. You're the lady that's writing the book. . ."
"Skip!"
"Yeah, I met you that night with T. What's your name again?"
"Beth. And I want to buy you a drink. I owe you a couple."
"Yeah, we were just talking about you."
"And I need to talk to T."
I wondered what do you know, T.? what has she told you?
and what were you guys saying talking about me?
later, there you were at the end of the bar
beating Last Call with Skip
I hopped over
"Hey! Isn't that the one I'm s'posed to be buying?" I asked
patting Skip on the arm seeing I was too late
so to you, "Hey, T."
"Hey, Beth."
and we said a bunch of not enough

184

later still, I motioned you to step aside with me
away from your Guardian Friends
and as you complied, again, like that Thursday night
I wondered was politeness hammered into you as a kid too?
like me? or do you like me?
and want to have what I have to give?'
you so obligingly leaned toward me
offering your ear to my voice
and as I brought my lips to your ear
wanting to kiss it
my cheek brushed yours
a bejillion megawatts zapped me and I was melting
were you too? did you feel that?
but I only voiced what I know now
was not the question you wanted to hear
"Did your Keeper give you the envelope I left for you?"
"Uh. . . no."
"Mmm. . . I didn't think so
We had an interesting discourse, she and I."
had I known I'd only get two questions
on this Thursday night as you backed away from me
saying, "Do what you want to do. . ."
I'd have asked better than "Are you in a hurry?"
too late I realized when you answered
"Yeah, I gotta be gettin' home."
I wanted to ask, "Are you ready?"
but you and Skip were half-way to the door
I wanted to yell at your back,
"You know what I want to do! I want to do YOU
like you'll never forget. Are you ready?"
but you left
you left me holding the bag of questions
tied upside down
hanging from the shirttail of the man in the moon
and I wondered as you passed through the door
is your mind's eye looking back at me?
falling just short of denial?
did you want to say "Yes" ?

tu es toujours dans ma coeur et dans ma tete
je pense á toi tous le temps

185

17: The Sixteenth Birthday Bumbershoot Miracle

Journal: August 31, 1996

DEAR God!! ThankyouthankyouTHANKYOU!!!

14 + months later. . . and I saw my baby today!!

OH, Zoey, thank God for Bumbershoot!

Thank God for you!!

I can't believe it! Pat, Lonni, Boundary Girl and I were walking from Memorial Stadium, where we'd just taken in The Presidents of the U.S.of A.'s set - which was great musically but something about that huge stage and them. . . I'm sure glad I saw them at Moe before they went on tour in stardom. Moe was so bouncy and close and hot. Great fun! As I was saying, we were walking toward the fountain to meet up with some other folks. I got distracted by a booth selling cool scarves. I was just starting to look, when there was a voice very close to my right ear saying, "Zoey wants you to know she loves you."

"Is she here?" I yelped as I turned to see who owned the voice. It was not a girl I knew. She nodded. "WHERE?"

"Over there," she said looking back to her right. She turned and started in that direction.

"Are her dad and step-mom here? Her brothers? Anyone?" I asked, following her.

"No, she's just with me and a couple more friends."

She nodded hard in the direction we were going and I took off, straining to see Zoey in the crowd, looking for long golden glints of hair in the sunshine. I was speed walking and scanning as I went, with MY BABY MY BABY MYBABY!!! squealing in my head.

When I got to the crossroads of go straight toward the Stadium or go left down the row of vendor booths, I did my sporadic knee-jerk-left and brought my sights into closer range for higher crowd density in reduced available space.

My heart was pounding and I was nearly hyperventilating when I heard her chuckling, "Mom!" behind me. I whipped around, stopped dead in my tracks and just looked as she pulled the scrunchy off her bun and let her hair down, shaking her head, saying, "I guess you didn't see me." She knew I was looking for her hair! OH Zoey, my baby, I love you so.

I threw my arms around her and pulled her tight to my chest, my cheek brushing hers and I felt the same electricity, the same vibe I'd felt on that very cheek only two nights ago as it had brushed T.'s. I *prrr-eh-s-s-sed* my cheek hard in to hers, holding her other cheek in my palm so no air -NOTHING- could be between us and my other hand was flung around her shoulders, grabbing her tight.

We held in that bliss for several seconds then Zoey started laughing, "Mo-o-om!," and pulling away. I pulled her back to me and held her so close that she quit laughing and I felt her body relax in my embrace. I don't know how long we stood there like that but when I finally let loose and stepped back she was laughing again saying, "I saw that purple hair and those purple socks and said "That must be my mom." We both laughed. We both had known we'd meet up. We both were sending such energy into it, even if unconsciously, that we made it happen.

We were just starting to talk when a voice behind Zoey yelled her name. As Zoey turned to see who it was I could see past her to find that the girl who was calling out was with who I assumed were her parents and a younger brother. And they were walking directly to us. PARENTS! I started twigging. Panic was in every bone of my body. Zoey was tossing comments back and forth with the girl as the whole family approached. I turned on my heels, looked over to one of Zoey's friends saying, "I gotta go now."

I walked away, going back up the row of booths the way we'd just come down. I turned right to duck behind the first building I came upon and hid there, breathing. When I figured enough time had elapsed for them to be gone, I circled around the building and hopped up onto a low cinder block wall. I walked down toward where I'd left Zoey and as I neared the spot I could see that everybody was gone.

I was like a lighthouse beam standing up there scanning the crowd, turning slowly. I looked and looked for a long time, to no avail. Finally, I headed up to the fountain hoping to catch Pat, Lonni, et al knowing all the while that I wouldn't. So, I wandered looking for Zoey everywhere I went.

Some hours later, I was exiting the KISW stage area in one of the rooms up behind the Umbrella Stage, walking into the cool, dark of the evening. A girl was in the distance, walking up a grassy slope toward me. I watched her approach and as she got closer to the light my eyes confirmed what my heart already knew. It was Zoey, alone. We did a quick hug and commenced catch up questions yet talking like no time had elapsed at all.

She had gotten my letters in the drawer at Gramma's and got that we *have* to play by the rules of this game just a limited time and then we'll be free to choose. I showed her my tattoo saying "This is you up here and this is me." I told her I'd done it in honor of her 16th Birthday. She was astounded. I forgot or probably more neglected to ask her what she did on her day. Perhaps I really didn't want to know what I'd missed or what I'd have done differently. I told her about her Year bags, adding that this year's had a gift certificate for a lady tattoo in her birthday card. She chirped, "I don't want a lady tattoo. That'd be lame" or something close to that. I asked how her skateboarding was going. She said it was fine but that snowboarding is great. She told me a little about her boyfriend. We talked and talked and talked. I just touched her occasionally, tapped a knee, an arm, held her hand for a second or two all the while listening enraptly and sharing in between.

Zoey asked, "Do you ever go sit under my tree?" I must have had a questioning look on my face as she quickly added, "...you know, the one at Green Lake." I immediately got a clip of her and a friend sitting under the big tree at the northwest corner of the swimming pool pavilion at the north end of the lake. When I took Zoey and a friend to the lake with me they'd usually hang out by the big tree preferring to observe the scene—others hanging out, bikers, skaters, dogs, various passers-by—over skating a lap with me or walking.

I assumed she meant this tree but to be safe asked, "The one that leans?" I held up my hand with fingers tipped to emulate the tree trunk and chuckled, ". . . at about the angle of an erection?"

Her laughter was accompanied by a horrified face and a "*Mom.*"

With tree confirmed, I answered, "No. I didn't know you thought of it as *your tree* per se. I ride my skateboard by it almost every day so I will now. I do still sometimes put two digits to my neck for your pulse though, like when you were out on the wilderness treks."

Too soon Zoey said she had to meet up with her friends, who she'd lost for a while when I lost Pat and Lonni. I walked with her to the bench outside the west door of the food pavilion where they were to meet at ten. I hugged and smooched her real big, told her how much I love her, entered the pavilion and headed for the ladies' room without looking back. I couldn't bear to.

When I came out she was still sitting on the bench. Our eyes solemnly met. I nodded deeply, nearly bowing in her direction, turned and kept walking.

Bumbershoot is Seattle's Music and Arts Festival held every Labor Day Weekend since 1971 at The Seattle Center. Visit www.bumbershoot.org

18: Kundalini and Me

Teresa Carol has been employed full-time as a Psychic Consultant since 1985. During an emotional trauma, Teresa became aware of her psychic gifts. After a period of training she found that she was able to go into a trance at will to obtain many types of valuable information with exceptional accuracy. Teresa is a Registered Counselor in the State of Washington; a member of Tacoma/Pierce County Chamber of Commerce, and Minister at the Universal Life Church. She is an Instructor of Psychic Development, Investigator of Paranormal Events, and Speaker & Fund-raiser for Public Service Organizations. Teresa has worked with numerous police departments assisting in Missing Persons and other cases; and was listed in the 1993 Oxford University Who's Who of Extraordinary People.

At the recommendation of Denny and Victoria, my first session with Teresa Carol was in 1992 over the phone from me in Torrance, California to her in Tacoma, Washington. Prior to that reading we had only spoken briefly over the phone to set the appointment. We had never met in person.

The following was transcribed and excerpted from the tape recording of my sixth session with Teresa Carol which was in person at her office in the Tacoma area on September 3, 1996. . .

Me: Teresa, I am wondering very much ... if ... what kind of ... hmm ... I feel a really strong connection to a person named T____ ____ ... and I'm wondering what you see with him and me.

Teresa: Well, my sense is that. . . this is really strange. . . I see that ... um... I'm seeing part of the Civil War and I'm seeing that you were a slave and you were an illegitimate child. . . of. . . I believe his father. It's almost like you were a young

190

girl and you were half white and half black. And T_____
was either. . . it doesn't. . . I feel like a stepson to the man
that fathered you. It was like he called this man father but
it wasn't his father. And he. . . you were very fair and very
beautiful and he was very enamored with you. He was having
a hard time it seems, to be down in the south, because he really
believed the slaves should be freed but he was a Southern
gentleman. So he was pulled into the army and he was really
going through a real battle because he didn't want to fight
for the South but he was very Southern. . . you know, the
loyalty thing and just a lot of issues for him. Any way. . . uh.
. . he ended up taking you up North to free you and during
the journey up he was killed by his own people for being. . .
uh. . . a traitor. But you escaped any way. So there's a sense
. . .there's a couple of things. First of all, there was a romance
that started to blossom and went nowhere. And, secondly,
there's a sense of almost indebtedness - that you owe him
something.

Me: In the here and now, we ...huh, that is so wild because
if I could have picked anyone that would be less accessible
to be totally attracted to, it would be surprising. He and
I have. . . I have admired him from afar for three years.
Never thought it would be possible to even connect with
the man except that I felt connected to him all along. And,
I had the opportunity to actually meet him on a couple of
occasions within the last couple of months but there is a
very major roadblock between us. I don't really know how
to access him. I don't have his phone number. I don't know
where he lives. If I happen to run into him out and about
that is my access. Or I can go watch him on stage, which is
what I've done for the last three years. And... um... I have
asked his management company for permission to reprint
the lyrics to one of the songs he has written in the book I'm
writing. .... They said 'No', that they did not want me to do
that. And I feel like we've got this roadblock between us.

Teresa: Yeah. It will stay there for a while too. And, you know,
it's a lot of the same dynamics as when you were a slave, that
there was that class. . . you know, you could not transcend

those boundaries. So, there may be some old karma playing off here.

Me: Boy, I guess!

Teresa: I wouldn't put any expectations on this right now but there will be more involvement with him later but not at this point. So, you know, do what you need to do but recognize that the timing's not right at this point.

Me: Do you think the timing will be right in this lifetime?

Teresa: Yes, but it's going to be after you've accomplished something on your own and that he seeks you out because of what you've accomplished. It's almost like he has to see you as. . . I can't say superior but above him and somebody that he would like to learn or gain from.

Me: Oh, that makes so much sense. Like when my book gets published.

Teresa: Yeah.

Me: Yeah. K.

Teresa: So in the mean time, it's almost like. . . um. . . you're just going to have to accept that this is where it is and enjoy him as an actor.

Me: Yeah, exactly, as I have. And really, I've almost fairly well resolved myself to doing that and, it's so funny because what you say, it really kind of fits with what has been in my mind. It's that when the book is complete and he can read it, there will be a difference.

Teresa: Yeah. You might even dedicate the book to him or send him the first edition signed or something.

Me: You know, I would love to, the only thing is -it's like I say- the only way I can directly access him is through his management company but I firmly felt that I would give her a copy of it too just to show her that I did abide by her request. . .

Teresa: Yeah. And I feel like you don't have to work around her. Your need is to just be able to pass whatever you want to on to him.

Me: Yeah, communicate. That's always good.

Teresa: . . .I think that the bottom line here, Beth, is that you are more in touch with what's going on with you than you're giving yourself credit for. Basically, because you don't have the education to see the process, you know. Einstein says we all have 20/20 hindsight. It's not 'til we've gone through something that we can truly perceive what we've been through. It's not in the moment that we ever look at something and know it. It's after we've been through it. So, it's like you need to honor this process, but you need to minimize any of the trauma or the stress that can be catalyzed.

A lot of people who start developing spiritually, like you're doing, awakening the Kundalini . . . the Kundalini is very highly explosive sexual energy. Now, the monks and the nuns knew this and that's why they chose abstinence, so that they could put this energy into incredible creative works and works devoted to God. Now, you're not a nun or a monk so that's not required of you. But be aware that there's gonna be a lot of people out there that'll suddenly find you . . . and you may find that women too may try to get you into sexual relationships so don't be surprised if it happens but be kind of aware that you may begin to draw a lot of people who are interested in you sexually. Where it's flattering, it isn't meeting your needs. . . . Do you *know* what Kundalini is?

Me: I've heard the term but I'm not real familiar.

Teresa: Well, it's the creative energy which. . . creative energy creates life, which is part of sexuality. And the Kundalini, as it awakens and arises, brings you to new spiritual awareness and perceptions. But, people that aren't used to it or don't know how to master it, because it feels like a bad case of the hornies, that's all they want to do. But, if you're aware that it's the awakening of the spiritual energy and you begin to work with it and see how you can guide it into your art, your writing, into other areas—it doesn't have to be exclusive— what you'll find is that you'll do incredible work at this point. But if you just put it all into sexuality that's all you'll get. It's kind of like having electricity and the only thing you hook into is the vacuum cleaner. If you realized you could plug in a clock, a microwave and everything else then you'd get a lot accomplished. Right? But if you just think that's only there for the vacuum cleaner, well, you get a lot of vacuuming done! Just really be aware. I normally don't tell people what to do but I would really suggest for you that you stay out of. . . um Click. END OF TAPE

Calendar: September 6 - 9, 1996
Leave for San Diego - Action Sport Retailer Trade Show

Journal: September 11, 1996

Wow. Ha! This trip was a kick. I can add Jim Sage and Mike White to my. . . my what? Repertoire? How about a list called: Skaterboys I Have Done? I know, I'll start notching my skateboard! I want Teddy Avare next. Based on shit we were tossing back and forth at each other about the real-ness of my tits versus his dick, my command, "Show me!" and his final comment, "Not here" indicates he might be wanting some of the Hatlady's (famous?) head. That would be cool, help it come together smoothly. Or maybe if I'm in total fuck 'em! mode, I'll do that guy that was so unfucking-believably rude to me at the Abacus party on Sunday night following the close of the Trade Show.

We were celebrating Jim's Championship win on Satur-day night at the ESPN Extreme Games and Abacus' overall success at the Show. Yikes! Never has anyone been that rude to me in my entire life. He was so way fucked up. Amazing what can come out at times like that. Like what? . . .times of extreme horniness? All I can figure was that Mike White, or maybe it was Mac Bunn that spilled a story about Mike and me getting it on in their hotel room right before head-ing north to the party.

After Mike and I played—o! I have to interject—Mike asked me how old I am and when I told him his reaction was "Cool, I made a real woman cum!" Makes me laugh and wonder what he'd been doing up until then. But, after that, I was in the bathroom on the head when Mac came back to the room to grab his stuff because everybody he'd been down in the bar drinking with (while Mike and I were

194

playing) was leaving for the party. He popped right into the bathroom to grab things off the counter and he was kind of mumbling apologies and eyeballing me at the same time and all I could do was stare and follow his motions. I don't think I said a word. Pretty soon he was out, shutting the door behind him. No doubt Mike had already given him the score sign before Mac came in the bathroom.

Well, anyway, about the rude guy, all I can guess is that he really wanted some too. What throws me is that he would think his methodology would get him anywhere! I highly doubt Jim said anything about Saturday night. Ha! When I woke up he was on the floor, because I'd been snoring too loud! Shit. And that Davy guy, from Australia, damn he was cute. He was a combination of my Paul and my favorite funny bunny. Whew! I wanted him! But, I wanted to do Jim too. It just didn't seem right that he should win over the long standing World Champion and not get his brains fucked out! So I took them both back to my hotel.

I was right about the vibe on Tony's birthday not being easy to duplicate. It was a bit awkward. PLUS we had no condoms and no car so these boys just got head. That was fine because I do love to give head—thanks to Paul helping me hone my technique for his pleasure. I've since learned the power I wield with good head skills, which brings me pleasure in knowing I'm good and powerful and giving joy.

Davy either pretended to or did actually fall asleep soon after we got to my room. So, Jim won first place twice. In the morning, Davy woke up shortly after I did and found me behind the shower curtain. He just gazed at me while I bathed and it didn't bother me. I am getting pretty brash these days! He asked me what he had missed and I told him, "Just some incredible head." When I came out of the bathroom with a towel around me he asked if he could have some now. So. . .

It just occurs to me that Billy and Mike White are the only two that have actually been inside me. But I figure if I made them cum, I did them. So that would also include Rick, even though we never touched each other! Ha! Five notches! I can't count Davy for six because he's not with Abacus. Actually, I think he might be with Galaxy because that's whose suite we went to immediately following the vert competition. We went from there to my room. They gave me a cool pair of deck shoes.

Sometimes when I think about it it's hard to believe that the New Sex Goddess of the Western Hemisphere has been lurking in the Beth who was pretty shy about her body and physical presentation, the Beth who has always been so super monogamous. But I'm enjoying the title and the duties that go with it. When the tiara no longer fits I'll proudly pass it to the next New Sex Goddess.

SO! There we have it for "Beth's News In Skate" update!

19: Closures and Poetry Percolating

September 14, 1996

In the very early morning before the sun rose on
the first day the air smelled of Autumn this year
my father, in the autumn of his life,
rose above earthly pain
while the sky wept and we slept
he crept silently away
I awoke and found on his bed
only his empty Earth Suit laying
as it'd been just an hour or so ago
with breath yet crossing his lips
as leaves turn to red, yellow and gold
my mind has in hold
you are my hero
when crossing the water to be by your side
a most brilliant rainbow arced far above the tide
it shone the most regal rainbow purple stripe
ever I've seen
Dad, you know what that means
loyalty, strength, bravery
you are all these things
my love for you abounds
as we place but a whisper of you to ground
with Merlin and magic
the love of Jesus
and your humor
all blessings from God
as the warm yellow sun cuts through
the cool blue September sky

we wonder not why to sing loud choruses
wrapped in cheer as you would only have it
in the Autumn of this year
you called yourself Dan, Dan the Tank Car Man,
The Meanest Man In Town
Dad, I know you were just trying to disguise
The Sweetest Man To Be Found
You were so many of my favorite people
Party Sing-Along Leader
Home-Made Ice Cream Feeder
Santa, sage, Easter Bunny, mentor,
Tooth Fairy and all the rest
like your song says,
"Parties make the world go 'round"
and you were the best!

September 16, 1996 - Fax to Dad's Oncologist

From: Beth Rice, daughter of your patient

Dear Dr. Oncologist,

I haven't had the pleasure of making your acquaintance personally, but my parents have spoken very highly of you. I'm writing to thank you and your staff for the marvelous care and warm regard with which you have all treated my father and mother.

I assume that you have heard my father passed on very early Saturday morning. I found his empty EarthSuit at 4AM and it was quite apparent that he passed as peacefully as could be possible.

I have been with my folks every step of the way and have heard in great detail the result of each office visit. I have often thought that you have perhaps known or surmised more than you have shared with my folks but the manner in which you shared information and suggestions with them was always perfect for each stage I now realize in retrospect. I thank you for the wisdom and care with which you treated my father's illness as I feel that you, in concert with the tremendous love and care administered by my mother, allowed my father several months of life and opportunity that I did not even dare to have hope for in December of 1995.

God bless you, Beth Rice

Journal: September 22, 1996

Like the poem says, we buried Dad's ashes yesterday along with the wizard and dragon perched on the amethyst piece I gave him for Fathers Day. Mom seemed puzzled that I didn't want to keep it as a memento. But, I felt it should stay with what he has left here on earth. All morning long, even as we drove to the cemetery where we held his grave side service, the sky was nearly black and pouring rain. But, thank heaven, as we drove up the little gravel road to his plot, it stopped. Shortly after we parked Zoey and her dad arrived. I felt nervous walking over to their car, unsure how I'd be received with well over a year having passed since Eric and I had last seen one another.

Zoey was barely out of the car and standing straight when I threw my arms around her, pressing my heart to hers. Eric wordlessly watched, then ambled around the car to stand before me. He looked into my eyes and succinctly offered condolences. It was so wonderful to see Zoey again even if the circumstances were sad. She commented on my gold dragon pendant. I immediately began fumbling with the clasp wanting to put it on her but stopped, looked to her dad questioningly and he nodded approval. As I drew the chain around Zoey's neck and hooked the clasp under her long silky blond hair, I told her about buying it in Hong Kong and what the man had told me about the Chinese belief that the dragon protects one's personal power. I asked her to please wear it always.

It wasn't long before all the people we were expecting had arrived and arranged themselves in a circle around the urn-sized opening in the earth Josh had dug earlier in the morning, despite the deluge. We got on with the service.

Josh read the words on death I'd selected from *The Prophet* by Kahlil Gibran; then typed, and printed for him as he was at a loss on how to participate.

Thankfully, Eric had complied with Mom's request in asking Zoey to please share in the service. She read the lyrics from a song, for her Grampa after this eulogy:

My Grampa was a wonderful, wonderful person; a Father, a Grampa, as the many roles he played in so many people's lives. I remember his laugh, his smile, the birthdays he shared with me - mine and his own; making the holidays special, and the barbecues and ice cream that he loved and that he was so good at making.

From picking blackberries and watching trains go by in the gazebo at the old house across the Sound; to The Farm here on the Peninsula and fishing in the pond and playing with the goats; to watching the new house in Port Ludlow get settled, I've seen some of the changes through the years. Even now that he's moved on, I'm sure there will still be more changes, and therefore memories made.

While he was extensively in and out of the hospital, there was a song that I listened to that made me feel good about the goings-on, a song that is calming and also reassuring that all will be as it should—good and well. The name of it is "Angel" written by Jimi Hendrix, and I'm going to read the lyrics..."

Then, when Zoey had finished, an astounding thing happened as I read the poem I wrote for Dad. At the line, "as the warm yellow sun cuts through. . ." IT DID! The sun pushed through the clouds to shine down on us. Fucking amazing.

<u>September 26, 1996 – a letter to. . .</u>

Hey T. - Did you see the eclipse tonight? It was pretty cool from the south end of Green Lake. Also, tonight the moon is in its fullest, largest state of being for the whole year. There's a *need- to-know*.

I have wanted to talk to you for such a long time but it's looking unlikely if things continue as they have thus far. I'm too slow getting my brain to connect with my mouth when in the presence of someone I'm awed by and you would be one. I think you are brilliant. You do what you do so well. I love your voice. And what you do with it.

Recently I learned why I'm so fucking attracted to you, why every time I see or hear that you'll be playing in town I have to come watch you. If you believe in karma I have the story and I'd be happy to share it with you. If you're not in- terested or not ready, I am disappointed, but I understand. I need for you to know of the things written on the enclosed pages.

I wish all the best for you always

       lots of fun and love and peace of mind

        Beth

On a Post-it note attached to a copy of Ode to T. & T. Song

T. - You may or may not like what this piece is saying but in either case I think you'll appreciate the quality of the writing. It was well received the one time I read it "Open Mike" at The OK Hotel. I'd like to read it in the Slam but promised myself I wouldn't unless you were there. If you'd like to come see me on stage, as I have so many times to see you, just about any Wednesday night at The OK Hotel (after 10/2) I'll be there and I'd love to read it to you. It rocks when I read it. Sign up for reading slots is at 8:30.

September 29, 1996 - Sunday night

Hey T.

There is a bunch of stuff bouncing around in my head and, as much as I'd hate to be too rangy, I'm just going to drop it out here and see where it goes.

If I were to rub my coffee pot tomorrow morning before putting it on the warmer to catch the drip and a magic Genie were to wisp out, granting me one wish to be true in exchange for his freedom, I'd wish that you would want to come to my place some night and just hang with me -one on one- and have fun. We could do anything that we wanted to. One of my favorite pass-times to share with friends is faery-shooting games. This is not with guns. The faeries have shooters and they fly. It can be for any stakes you can imagine, not just guzzles of beer or hits off the bowl. . . or? And the coolest thing is that it is always a new game with new dynamics because we make the rules.

Every time I've had occasion to meet up with you, you're in a hurry because I've caught you somewhere in the middle of your trip. You must just hang out some time. My wish would be that some time you would want it to be with me. T., my physical attraction to you and the desire that I've openly expressed to you (by way of the question that was supposed to "count for something") is very real and very unlikely to just go away. It is a karmic unrequited vibe. I think you know this to be true. But, I will ever so gladly put it way to the back burner if that would make you more comfortable. I'd love to just talk with you, in slow mode. I still have a jillion questions but I also have many things to tell you.

I hope that my directness does not make you uncomfortable. I know you know you are magic but I wonder if you have yet remembered the full potential of your magic. I think not.

I was so bummed at missing *T. Quick* Friday. What did you decide to do at the last minute? Did you do a solo acoustic set? Were you jamming with other musician friends? Is this an Official Side Project? What? I knew you'd be at Moe on Friday but I didn't get that you'd be on. I'd have been there sooner. I love to watch and hear you perform. I didn't expect for you to be immediately in my face. That kind of threw me. I was SO down on not getting Part 3 to you. . . like that would be my only chance in the world to do so! But today I realized why I had left it in the car and felt better about it.

I'd like to know if you like to kiss, if you liked my kiss.

I went to Tune Town Thursday night full on knowing you would not be there but, questioning my natural knowing, I had to go any way. I'm just learning to trust it.

Do you like ALL kinds of bubbles? I also do a pretty fine round-off with the Official Olympic finish! (reference *Ode to T. & T. Song*, enclosed)

If you ever need to get taped again I'd love to help. Fact is I was so distracted by wishing I could have taped your pants that night at the Fenix that I went home alone, walking away from a couple of damn fine, interesting offers! How silly! You're just doing what you do and unbeknownst to you, you're ruining my sex life!

I talked to your mom one night at RKCNDY, the night the record people were there according to her. (I thought it sucked that you'd pack the Off Ramp to the rafters on the gig before and the gig following -or maybe one of those was Sit N Spin- BUT the night the record people were there you'd get the smallest, deadest crowd I could never imagine to be at one of your shows.) Your mom was nice. I confessed to her, "silly as it may seem, what with me probably being closer to you in age than to him" that I'd wanted to take you home for a long time. That didn't seem to phase her. I thought that was cool. But when I asked her if that was your girlfriend you were leaving with she did say "I hope not. He's married." I'm not sure why I feel compelled to share that with you.

So the key notes here are:
The bowl is refillable. I'd love to make up a faery game with you. I'd love to show you what my book is about and what I plan to do to keep all of my writing intact without going back on my word to Bonnie (enclosed). You will not get any more from me than what you would want. If you don't quite know what to do with any of this -me- or don't choose to do anything with it at this time, I understand. Just <u>know </u>that I will welcome hearing from you any time you're ready—next week, next year, next decade—hopefully this time around.

Your all time fan,
Beth   [phone #]

October 1, 1996 - Attached to my Dad poem

T. - I am including this poem because I like it and because ARGH! How to pull these thoughts together!? I just finished a segment of my book that discusses the car-wreck-brush-with-death I had at age 19 and how it caused me to start taking risks. My dad died September 14, last month (after a long battle with cancer), and I wrote this poem about that, and him, to read at his service. I think it is this recent look at our mortality that reminds me to take risks.

> And that is how / why
> I am able / feel the need to
> give you this envelope.   B.

I carried *this envelope* around with me from the time of writing until October 21st assuming I'd run into T. sooner or later and could deliver it directly. However the contents changed several times. Initially I'd intended to copy him on the correspondence between me and Bonnie at The Management Company so he would be informed of that which she'd supposedly held back from him. But, ultimately, I decided to pull out anything having to do with the book because at this point it was not about reprinting lyrics. It was about connectedness, my feelings, an unrequited desire and karmic release.

I'm not certain what writings made the final cut but I believe it came down to the two September letters; the letter from July which Bonnie did not forward to him as requested;

a copy of *Ode to T. & T. Song* and my Dad poem (each with the little notes above attached); a copy of the first page of the transcript of Theresa's September 3rd reading; and, the following handwritten cover letter (of sorts):

October 18, 1996

    T. -

    This letter might wait eons til it meets up with you because I'm certainly not leaving it *in care of* anyone again. Obviously, some interesting stuff has come down since my letter of September 29th, which follows this cover—becoming friends with Rena, who happens to be involved with Keith, who happens to be one of your roommates, ALL of whom happen to be practically my neighbors!

    The couple times I've hung out at your house have been thoroughly enjoyable -kicked back- except the night you happened to be downstairs and I froze like a statue -idiot- unable to deal with it. There is a good vibe in your house and I'd like to think I'd be okay to come by once in a while just to be friendly. I know you're tied in with someone and that's all cool. My point here is a number of my many questions have been answered very recently. There is nothing I would say to attempt to invalidate anything I've written on the following pages, even with the new info. It is what is.

    The contents of this envelope have changed since that night at Moe, when you told me to "go get it (the third part of your present). . . I'll be here." A couple things have been deleted and others added. The bottom line is I have to get this off my chest or I might implode. I hope you will read it all. I am done with it now; until some/such time that you might want to look into it. If that time comes, I'll be here.

Beth

    PS - I like the new material BINM did both that last night at RKCNDY and at Moe recently. And, I'm sorry I didn't know about your side project playing last night or I'd have been there to check it out. Hope you had a good time with it!

By Sunday, October 20th, this envelope weighed like an anvil in my bag and like a wet blanket on my brain. On the 23rd I was leaving for Ohio on business and I'd decided it was absolutely necessary for me to get this off my chest and out of my bag before I left so that I could focus on the task at hand, selling hats. I came to this conclusion while baking banana bread and cookies Sunday night.

So, on Monday morning I packed up a bag of goodies for all the house mates to share— T., Skip, and Keith—and attached a little note. In the case that I didn't find T. at home it seemed best to have a reason to be knocking on their door. I drove the few blocks between our homes, parked on a side street and climbed the many steps up to the front door, as though mounting Kilimanjaro, and rang the bell.

What little breath remained with me as the door opened disappeared when I saw T. standing just arm's length away. He looked surprised to see me and quickly, yet politely, made it known that he was just on his way out to the studio. I was surprised to hear my voice coordinate with the opening of my mouth in telling him that I'd brought "goodies for you guys, and I have something for you, T."

He accepted the bag, expressing thanks, and watched with interest while I rummaged through my little purple velvet back-pack, as he had that night at Moe a month or so ago - leaning into me with his face just inches from mine. But, this day he maintained a distance. I pulled out the very thick envelope and handed it to him.

At this point the puppy belonging to him and his new-ish girlfriend (I'd heard he was planning to get a divorce) bounced out the door, down the steps and around the corner of the house. I said I'd get him. T. told me not to bother. I said, "He might go out in the street. I'll get him."

So, I followed the pup, rounded him up, and herded him back up the stairs where, at the top, the door stood open. T. was no longer in sight. I stood at the foot of the stairs gazing at the door as the pup dashed through it, wishing I could too. But, I turned and headed back to my car.

I was going to get on with preparations for the trip and leave with a freed consciousness, as I'd promised myself I would. I had put it all out to him to the best of my human ability. It was now his decision whether to go beyond the physical and remember, whether to explore the dimensions of this karmic bond or not.

October 17, 1996 - No, no ... Thank You

I'm in the home stretch
rounding off my morning pilgrimage
with Honey Bear Bakery Triple Ginger Coffee Cake,
two packs of Dave's Lights and that cool free duct tape
riding in the passenger seat
when out of the corner of my eye
I see a neat hat at the bus stop
riding atop a cute person
OH! . . .it's you, my dear friend Katie
you don't see me
you're entrenched in a book
it's too late to honk and catch your look
so I just wish you a good day
on my way back to work in my home office
as I am unlocking the door
still vibrating with good stuff that came my way
last night at the Slam
thinking warm thoughts of. . .
and how badly I'll miss
you when you make your pilgrimage
to the City by the Bay
on your way to meet Destiny
I get to my desk and there on my screen
is a pretty purple Post-It that says:
"Beth- In all this time I've been so wrapped up
in my stuff that I've never said thank you for
all you've given me. Love you! K- "
My mind's eye sees you in that luscious hat at the stop
and I drop into my chair thinking
K-, you've given me the key to me
you were there when poem stopped by for tea
you reminded me that I CAN
write my own book
how ever can I thank you, my eternal friend
for making me look
at what's been in me all along

pushing me to give voice to my unsung song
go get your MFA
I'll look forward to the day
when you come back to stay
and we can again play
leaving our mark in sidewalk chalk murals
and a rainbow of bubbles over Elliott Bay
I love you too! B-

October 1996 -

Truth in Bones

The skeletons in my closet
are knocking loud upon the door
they're rattling the door knob
shouting "We won't live here anymore"

There's at least one skeleton in one closet
in each and every household across the U.S.
due to the manner in which our civility
and social mores have evolved and progressed

They say some two thousand years ago
Moses descended the mountain
with a stone tabloid in his hand
etched upon its smooth, hard surface
were God's Ten Rules
set forth for the welfare of man

Two hundred and twenty years have passed
since the founding fathers of our land
scribed an expanded discourse called Law
on paper crafted from one of
God's greatest gifts to man

So began a new nation of peoples
who came here to escape oppression
but along the way man twisted God's Rules
and Rightness became retrogression

For only after slaughtering most
and corralling those who remained
of the people who were first their host
did they feel their Rightness ingrained

Those Native people were true to Spirit
they knew the rightness of hemp
to be inherent in the Law of Nature
to change this only fools would attempt

And fools they are who've made new Rules
that not only honor legal tender and greed
but berate our spiritual essence on Earth
the sewing of Human seed

Yes, God gave us sex for procreation
but if that was Her only intent
why does it feel like re-creation
when my pent-up passion is spent?

Goddess gave us joy with our sexuality
and the Church of Man takes it away
with conception as the only reality
all else being Satan at play

God gave us the Law of Nature
and she gave us the Law of Love
Man created irrelevant deviations
that weren't handed down from above

All of our blessed spirit plants
in Man-made Law have fallen from grace
and the playground of pure lustful sex
Man-made Church calls a filthy place

Here we are, all laden with guilt
we all have broken the Rules
each deed we dare not speak of a bone
hung on our skeleton with Man-made tools

I say open the closet door
let the skeletons into the light
let's call the sacrum Inhibition
and the cranium Wrong-From-Right
the vertebra we'll call Fear
the metatarsus will be known as Hate
let's label each bone with a Human pain
then pile them outside Heaven's gate
where we'll dance around a huge bone-fire
and before God our guilt dissipate

20: Your Tree, Haiku, and Hearts

I had a long chat with Mom last night. She told me Zoey called to check in on her and that they had a nice visit. Mom said Zoey sounds happy, like all is going well. I'm so glad they touched base.

November 3, 1996

Love Light

I sat under your tree today
on my skateboard
with arms stretched out behind me
hugging the tree to my back
my head laid on the trunk
and I hid behind very dark sunglasses
so none of the passers-by would see me as
I felt quiet thoughts of you
the sun fell through the leaves
leaving leopard spots over goosepimples
on my wind-blown, bare legs
and where the light warmed my flesh
pores opened oozing love and warm wishes
which I sent to you on faery wings
as the faeries took flight
out over the lake before me
they tossed magical dust into the wind
it shimmered on the water and glittered in my heart
lighting my soul
as I knew
that all is well with you

Journal: November 11, 1996

Today was Veteran's Day. I found that a lot more companies beside the banks take this day off. Of course, I was supposed to be working and our shop in L.A. was working but I was in the mood to bake cookies. I had a huge hankering for gingersnaps. What with my office being next to my kitchen I could afford to bake and did. My phone only rang twice; once was a customer checking on an order and the other was Evie checking in on me at the end of the day. I was honest with her and told her I had baked cookies after making many unanswered phone calls. She was not happy with me. I came up with a good alibi. Having already dunked at least a dozen of those gingersnaps in milk and crunched them down I was struck with guilt for adding them to my thighs. I told Evie I had baked the cookies to send to the Abacus guys as a thank you for their business. Sometimes I amaze myself. She liked the idea but shot me down on using the company's account for Airborne Express overnight delivery with, "Too expensive. Send Second Day service."

THE HATLADY'S FAX COVER SHEET

DATE: 11/20/96   FROM: Beth Rice
TO: my only skaters east of the Rockies FAX:
ATTN: friendly contact

Hi! I wonder what kind of thoughts my poem evoked. The question is: Did you get a visual? Here it is in hard copy, the double Haiku O' The Day:

Seattle rained snow
The HatLady and the elves
lunched well on haiku

north sides snow hammered
ball park lamps across the street
they are all North Poles

Are you shooting for The Road Warrior Extraordinaire award? Yikes! Gotta pick up a few Atlantic waves to carry you over to the Pacific? Here's a rhyme for the Road Warrior:

On the road,
there are three G's to do:
gas. . . grub. . . and go
Never stop for less than two !

My motto when in *gotta get there* mode. Talk to you soon.   Beth

Journal: December 8, 1996

OH MY GOD! Lonni just called to let me know that she has a letter to me from Zoey! She said that during Silver-chair's set last night at the Deck The Hall Ball she was zoning, thinking about her and Pat's upcoming wedding and wondering how to get an invitation to Zoey, when she saw a girl that looked like Zoey standing down on the floor in front of the section of seats on the side where she and Pat sat. She said that as she leaned forward to focus on the girl, the girl turned to leave and sure enough *it was her*! Lonni said she got up and moved down the stairs to the floor as quickly as she could and was able to tag Zoey's arm just before she disappeared out into the crowded hallway. Lonni said they hugged and talked and then Zoey sat down along the wall, pulled a little pad out of her backpack and proceeded to write me a letter for Lonni to deliver to me. I cannot wait for lunch-time tomorrow so I can run up to Lonni's work and pick it up! She said Zoey looked real good, seemed relaxed and self-confident. That is such good news. Zoey told Lonni that she misses me re-e-e-eal bad. Oh God, please make the time fly!

The night of Deck The Hall Ball, Rena and I went to Moe. We were hanging out down in the band room for a while. She wanted to introduce me to a friend who used to go with her sister back in PA years ago. Now he lives here in Seattle and has been a nice touch-base for Rena, a familiar face so far from home. I guess he used to play for Sky Cries Mary and also The Posies so, a bit of a celeb. He seemed like a nice and an interesting guy. Hmmm someone close to my age. And this is kind of funny, but, while we were down there visiting, Jason Finn, the drummer for The President's of the United States of America, popped in and Rena introduced me to him like they're old friends. Rena is a kick! I told him their set had sounded real good over the radio. The End, who sponsored Deck The Hall, broadcast the whole show. He humbly said thanks. He seems like a real nice guy. I spoke to him very briefly one other night at Moe, the night he got up and kicked out a song with The Fastbacks.

Well, guess I better get on with the day. . . GO! HatLady!

December 7, 1996 - 14 pages on a 3 ½" X 4 ½" note pad:

Mom — Hi, I'm at this concert tonight and I saw Lonni in

the hall and I actually got to meet her infamous Pat! I thought about you so much on your birthday. I can't believe how weird it is sometimes. I gave Lonni my boyfriend's phone number. He's hella cool and he's kind of one of those All-American preppy Tommy Hilfiger-type boys, but he's the only boy that's made as much of an impact on me as John. (Well, maybe not as much, but the closest to it.) He's really good to me. I've been with him for three months or so. I can honestly say I love him and mean it even though I'm not in love with him. He's fabulous, he's sweet (he buys me things – not that that's important). My parents are absolutely in love with him and trust me completely when I'm with him, and they trust him, too, which is a very good thing.

Interjectory Note: Zoey has referred to Eric and Crystal as her "parents" for years. I am Mom—the only Mom—but they are her parents. It took me a long time to get a grip on that, but its a fact. I have to add another thought: I learned that Zoey's boyfriend lives with his parents in the biggest house on one of the "best" streets in one of the nicest neighborhoods. In fact, tell me if this isn't ironic, its the same street my folks lived on when Eric was prematurely taking claim to their estate. Ha! I find that so funny, in a twisted sort of way. Anyway, I suppose, aside from the kid having a preppy appeal, that's a good part of being so enthralled with him—the boy's family lives in a worthy neighborhood.

His parents love me too. I'll find some way to get you a recent picture of me and one of both of us together too. You'll be amazed because he's just not my "type" at all. But, somehow we get along better than any boy I've ever been with and he respects me for who I am even if he doesn't necessarily like it (my dress, etc).

School is going very well cuz my teachers all love me, and I'm getting good grades. The last progress report came out two weeks ago, and here ya go!

per. 1 = Photography - A
per. 2 = German - C+
per. 3 = English – B
per. 4 = American Studies – B

per. 5 = Geometry — C-
per. 6 = C.L.I.P. - A

Total GPA = 3.2 ! ! ! Yay! Bravo! Yep. My folks actually are letting me catch up through C.L.I.P.! Cool, huh? The shitty thing is, even though I'm getting a 3-point now, I don't think Eric is gonna let me take drivers ed. Shitty deal. Oh well, I should be used to it now. My boy drives me anywhere I say anyhow, and does basically what I tell him. I don't abuse his generosity though, so that's good. I do his chores all the time. It's good to do nice things for people you care about in return for the things they do for you.

As far as drugs and alcohol go for me, well, I hardly ever smoke out anymore. It just makes me tired and hungry and gives me cottonmouth and bad breath. Yuck. No fun included. I don't even do any other things. Alcohol, that's what I do some-times. I seem to have grown a liking for the ol' Southern Comfort. Good stuff there, cuz I know my limits and can come home and the folks know not. They've been really cool, though. They even found a letter in my room when I wasn't home and read about my plans to get a fifth and a quarter ounce with a few friends. They just talked to me and grounded me for two days. I could even talk on the phone. I just explained that I hardly ever do anything and that we're all juniors and seniors in High School. What can they really expect? Like they never did stuff? They know I don't have a problem anymore, and they're still proud of what I've done and what I'm doing and what I want to do, and are starting to learn that they can't change my thoughts and/or plans for my future.

Everybody misses you a lot. They tell me so. Even last night, I was talking with Gene Wall (Do you remember him? He was a Senior when I was a Frosh). He was saying how he misses the old days when me and him were really good friends, and how he was sorry that things got so fucked and misconstrued. Everyone still thinks so highly of you and wish they could talk to you.

Me and brothers are all like best friends now. My parents are actually aware that I have sex and are about as cool about it as I'd expect them to be. They know I will whether they say so or no, so they don't really fight me about it. Skating season is out (suck), but I got a snowboard and boots and shit. My boyfriend gave me pants so I'm stoked. I'm actually going up tomorrow. (Cool!)

I really miss you. I talk to my cat about it all the time and I wear your necklace 24-7 except for concerts for fear of it being yanked off or lost. I have my pictures of you on my vanity mirror, even though they're old. Oh well. Better than not. I love you and I miss you. On the night that it turns from me being 17 to 18 you'd better not be in China or wherever the fuck you might end up going cuz otherwise I'll be staying the night on your front porch wondering if I'm even at the right house, condo, or apartment or whatever. But anyhow, I'm coming looking for you. Me and a friend or two probably if that'll be okay.

I hope you're doing well because, for the most part, I am. My curfew is even 12:00 midnight. Yay. I hear your work is treating you well. I hope you're starting to see just a little bit older guys so one day you don't accidentally pick up on one of my friends or something. I'd love you any way but it's just healthier, ya know. I don't go out with little fetuses or people yet-to-be-conceived, you see? I'm just kidding. (Half way) But it's cool. I love you. I gotta go meet my brother and I gotta call my boyfriend. ♥ Me!

Journal: December 18, 1996

Billy at Abacus called me today to ask, "What's up with the cookies?" They had just received the chocolate chip cookies I sent them Monday. I asked him if he wanted me to not send cookies, being a little baffled by the response. He said, "Hell no. They're great. They're already gone. Everybody loved 'em. I'm just wondering. . ."

I broke in with, "Cookies are love, don't you know? I love working with you guys and I love to bake." I didn't add that with Zoey not here to help me eat them I needed to send them out so not to wear all the calories on my thighs or butt.

Journal: December 22, 1996

I just now, at this moment, Sunday 8:50AM, have consciously

accepted that the core of my being has held the belief that I am unlovable. My experience with those who "love" me, by my perception of their actions, has told me this. This has been a message to me repeatedly since the day I was born. The woman who carried me in her womb for nine months and gave entry to this life of opportunity gave me away— with reason, no doubt, but as an infant in the earliest and. . .? Would that be the most intense state of non-remembrance? I only got that she gave me away. I've known this forever as my folks told me and Josh that we were adopted from the git-go. But I didn't know what it meant until I was about five years old when the neighbor girls informed me, in a heated moment of disagreement over who knows what while playing in their yard one day, that my mom was not my real mom.

I remember running home. I see it all, a very clear clip. I was crying when I ran in the kitchen door. Mom was right there and asked, "What's wrong?" When she heard my story she sank onto a kitchen chair and pulled me to her lap. She said to me "Remember we have always told you you're adopted?" I nodded yes. "Well," she continued, "that means that your dad and I wanted you so bad that we waited and waited until we could hand pick you to come home with us. You are very special."

From that moment forward, I viewed and communicated being adopted as something I was very proud of. But prior to that, my deep down subconscious knew I'd been given away twice in fairly rapid succession. First by my birth mother; and three months later by the foster mother mandated by The Children's Home Society. It was the policy at the time, as the agency attempted to assure the adoptive parents a healthy "normal" baby, to place the infant in a three month probationary foster home setting for observation before finalizing the adoption. At least, this is what I've been told. Mom also told me, after Zoey was born, she hated that policy and told the agency so with, "I wouldn't be guaranteed a perfect baby if giving birth myself."

Another practice at that time was to *seal* the original Birth Certificate. I don't know if it was by federal or state law but it was the case in Minnesota. The only Birth Certificate I've ever seen bears my adoptive name and no time of birth.

I stopped here to go to my room and masturbate.

216

Whoo! Good one! Quick, too. I'm back. I wonder if I had no name or a temporary name for those three months. Maybe I was "Baby X" or numbered for my date of birth. I just tried calling Zoey's boyfriend. She wrote it on a separate, dedicated slip which she included with her note to me via Lonni from the Deck the Hall Ball. I got an answering machine and hung up before the beep I think. This is the only attempt I've made. Every relationship along the way WOW! I just went to the bathroom to relieve myself. On my way back I glanced in my room and noticed the blind was still closed and my vibrator was still atop my night stand. Ooo! I don't know what's up with this but that made five great intense ones! As I was saying, it seems all the relationships I've had lacked longevity or have known times of isolation or separation. The latter would be the case with Mom and Dad. I know they both love me but I don't think Mom liked me a lot of the time. And, Dad chose to work overseas all those years. There was Eric, my next "Beth is unlovable" message. Then, Paul; and, most recently the many who passed through the revolving door of my sport fuck phase. Some got caught in the door for various reasons and numbers of revolutions—which makes me think of Jay's "There is no middle ground between submission and revolution"—but it wasn't for love.

So it goes my spirit guides have assured me how well I am loved. I do know God loves me. However, I'm not certain what the message is. What's the lesson?

Zoey's Christmas card - In her 1996 bag

When the heart speaks, its whisper can be heard across time and distance.	Zoey, I love you and wish we were together again.

I miss you so bad, my love. After this one, only one more Christmas without you. Then we're back to making lefse and doing our usual stuff. I love the note you sent to me via Lonni from the Deck the Hall Ball. Thank you. I felt your thoughts and love on my birthday. I hope 1997 is a great year for you and a fast one for us both.

XOXOXOXO *always*Mom

217

21: Lust, Laws, and Lost

> WARNING: The Surgeon General has determined that doing anything, anytime, anywhere, with anyone may be hazardous to your health.

This was on the front of my New Year's card for Zoey. The inside read simply: Have a nice day. But I added *And a Happy New Year!* with a tiny heart acting as dot on the exclamation point. Then I wrote a note that wraps all the way around the outside edge of the inside of the card:

Zoey, thank God/dess for Bumbershoot, for your dad's efforts on getting you to your Grampa's service, and for the Deck the Hall Ball. Thank you for being you, Zoey! I love you. And I miss you something fierce. We're almost half way there. I pray this is the last fucking countdown we ever do again EVER. Thank you for the beautiful shared remembrance of your Grampa. I am so proud of you! Thanks for the great improvement in your grades. Thank you for your love. I'm really looking forward to seeing a bunch of your photography. I'm glad you're doing so well in it but what else would I expect from one so brilliantly creative as you? Hmmm? Thanks for knowing that I'm learning too. You're the best Zoey!

I hope 1997 is the best year yet. 1998 will be the best year EVER! All my love, *always*Mom

I signed it precisely as I have signed most all of my correspondence to Zoey since she was six years old, including the heart shaped smiley face balloon floating atop the string flowing from the last *m*.

I got a fun card for Mom too. It was hard to discern if it was a man or woman on the front of the card. It could go either way so good marketing by the card company. The individual was wearing the most ultra-gaudy pseudo-cowboy outfit one could ever imagine. The inside said:

Don't Drink and Dress!

I added: Happy New Year, Mom! I know this comes a little late but I laughed so hard when I saw this and thought you'd get a kick out of it. Here's hoping 1997 finds each of us well entrenched in a personal mission of value and growing in God's light and love. I love you, Mom!
Your favorite daughter,
Beth 1-1-97

I signed her card consist with what had become a running joke between the two of us since the time I'd queried, "Is this my favorite Mom?" which was in reply to her, "Hello?" on answering my phone call one day. Her retort had been, "I'm your only Mom!" I laughed and told her, "Yeah, so, you can still be my favorite Mom too."

Journal: January 1, 1997

After I finished writing Mom's and Zoey's Happy New Year cards it occurred to me that its twenty-five years since I turned eighteen, a birthday that I had most anxiously awaited since my fifteenth. And now, I anxiously await Zoey's eighteenth birthday. There is something ironic about this.

I paged Jack. I pretty well figure he won't call back, but he's also been known to surprise me. I'd like to tell him that I'd rather be giving him some great head right now. I'd love to recreate the awesome feeling sex we had on the couch, mid-movie Saturday night. Whew... YEAH! He was here from Saturday night through Monday morning. I took him home at lunch time. It felt so good to have him here. I actually prepared and we ate three full meals. Imagine that! I cooked scrambled eggs with onion, ham, and cheese for breakfast and ate some! Yikes! I ate better and slept more than I have in a long time. God, I love that guy. The dynamics of our relationship are so damn weird. But I guess if on any level its working for both of us. . . what the hell, huh? I wonder how many other women friends he has like me.

Katie called from Hank's house. Staying at his home has been a real eye-opener for her and she is so grateful to have had this time with him before heading off on her journey to meet destiny. She and her friend from school days, Marty, have had a couple good talks since his arrival last night. I'm looking forward to meeting Marty.

Yesterday I had quite a number of T. thoughts, wistful like. Rena and Keith got tickets for the three of us to go to the show and private party at RKCNDY. I ended up telling them to go without me and leave my ticket at the door. It took me forfuckingever to get ready. Granted I had way too many things to do in the allotted time, going for the Retro Diva feel for the evening, and not wanting to go into the New Year with a faded out, old purple stripe in my hair. But it wasn't too long after my arrival that, in chatting with Rena, I learned why I just absolutely couldn't get there any faster than I did, at eleven. T. and his girlfriend had been there for Julie Brown's band's set. Teresa's words came back to me: *Just know that the timing isn't right at this time.* Manta Ray's set was just starting. I went over and said hi to Steve Gardner, from KISW, who manages these guys. He recognized me right off and greeted me with a warm smile. I really enjoyed their set.

When it was time to make a move out into the night and some new destination Keith said he wanted to go home and asked if I wanted to come hang out with him and Rena. I sensed without question that he was looking at the three of us playing. Rena and I had talked about this several nights prior, that it is his fantasy and whether or not each of us would be into it—and, if so, whether we thought it would be a good idea or not. It seems we concluded that it would probably be safest for the friendship (to remain intact) if we abstained. When I said, "No", to Keith's invitation Rena looked at me with him and also queried, "No???" But, her eyes told me I did not want to open up that potential can-of-worms. I pleaded kiddingly with Keith for a rain-check, adding I was a little too wired to not stay out. However, when I got in my car I put it on auto-navigate and headed immediately home alone. My mind kept saying "I have too many things to do tomorrow to stay out and get wasted."

January 1, 1997

14 or The Poem Made Me Do It

I have the kundalini edge
or I'm over the edge
I'm not sure
I just had 14 Count 'em!
14 cums in a row!

This is either where my creative energy
and sexual energy merge
or it's where I practice creative avoidance
around getting any writing done
by completely giving in to the urge
to go to my room and masturbate

I was cumming
up on fucking 7 in a row
thinking Yeah! Lucky 7! Is this Heaven?
but when 7 had cum
and gone I thought
fate says 8, open the gate!
One more for the dragon! O-o-o-h, God!

But, as 8 was a Minor, I thought
Go for it! up to a Major
break your record
This rager is all mine!
Take it. . . Number 9!

This poem is running through my head
laying on my back
atop my bed
Why stop now?
round out '96
with a round of hot sex
here I cum again! *HYE E E A A AH!*

I feel my body
feeling ready for more
remove the vibration

What else is in store?
fingers implore
for me please
all on my own
here I cum with a grrro o o ooan

So, why stop at 11?
an even dozen must be Heaven
but on my way to 12
I'm laughing
my love of asymmetry
wanting a Baker's Dozen!
Okayokayokay *OKaaaaay* whoo! DEAR GOD! OK!

What? number 14 is on the way
one more
for good measure
reveling in self pleasure
what a way
to spend the first day of
The New Year
with poetry doing
sex praising God playing sex thanking God having sex
in a poem

Once my poem had been put to paper and my kundalini edge sheathed, I became a researcher for the balance of New Years Day. I'd been looking forward to isolating time for this project.

At my request for photocopies of the pages in his 'Book of Laws' pertaining to Controlled Substances, Dick Carville, my attorney, provided me with computer printouts of those Washington State laws. For the sake of brevity I present only sections pertaining to my case. Further, I cite the titles of the specific laws; then, excerpt, condense and/or paraphrase for readability sake.

But, first, what is a narcotic? According to the definitions in my three dictionaries, the word narcotic seems to be a catch-all for any substances which induce in the consumer "sleep, lethargy, reduction of pain, dullness." Opiates are specifically referenced. It is also stated that narcotics can be and often are addictive; and, when taken in excessive doses cause stupor, coma and even death. In two dictionaries, the "*3)*" definition takes it all the way out to "*anything* that makes one dulled, sleepy, drowsy or lethargic." In those terms television is a narcotic.

Marijuana is defined in one of my dictionaries as a plant having   leaves and flowers that are smoked to create a euphoric feeling. Another says that it is hemp and that a poisonous drug is made from the leaves and flowers. According to Hemp Initiative Projects of Washington State, "Intoxicating hemp [marijuana] has no known overdoses, or deaths, in over 10,000 years of use."

What is a hallucinogen? All my dictionaries state its a drug or substance that produces hallucinations. How does the dictionary define hallucination? "...a perception of sights, sounds, etcetera that are not actually there; or the imaginary object apparently seen or heard; or an illusion." In one case, the word delusion is offered as a synonym.

The word delusion brings to mind the word delirium; and then, delirium tremens. I recall learning that in conjunction with alcoholism. The term was explained in one of the family counseling sessions I attended while Dad took up his one month residency in a treatment program for alcoholism. The counselor explained to us that our loved one[s] spent their first week in treatment as patients, heavily dosed with drugs (barbiturates and relaxants I think, some kind of downer at any rate) so to avoid the possible discomfort of delirium tremens, which are commonly associated with alcohol withdrawal. The dictionary tells me delirium tremens is a state of "violent delirium resulting chiefly from excessive drinking of alcoholic liquor and characterized by sweating, trembling, anxiety, and frightening hallucinations."

Alcoholic beverages, when consumed in excess, are known to cause hallucinations, stupor, coma, even death. I question why alcohol, or liquor, is not considered a narcotic or a hallucinogenic in the eyes of the law, as prescribed by the State of Washington, and listed on Schedule I. My dictionary says of alcohol, "classed as a depressant drug." But not in the state of Washington.

You'll see "marihuana" listed as a hallucinogenic on Schedule I;

but, again, not alcohol. This strikes me as a horrendous double standard within the applicable laws of Washington state.

As all statistics tell us, many millions of Americans have at least tried smoking marijuana. You, dear Reader, no doubt, know someone who has tried marijuana. In fact, whether you know it or not, you probably are acquainted with someone who smokes it regularly but not to excess. I have met and smoked marijuana with successful business owners, attorneys, published writers; even presidents and vice presidents of multi-million dollar companies, as well as other active, productive, law abiding citizens—given the exception of this one law. Some enjoy smoking marijuana on a regular basis, others on an occasional basis as the opportunity presents itself.

Ask anyone you know who has smoked marijuana about the hallucinations they've experienced. I believe laughter will be a primary response. But, someone might be inclined to tell about how marijuana intensifies all the senses—how a nice touch or sight, and good sounds, smells and flavors all become amazingly fantastic. Most folks like this feature. There is a flip side of the intensifying coin, however. If one is in an introspective mood or feeling sad before smoking, those feelings are likely to also be intensified, not such a popular feature. In any case, if hallucinations, they're not of a dangerous ilk.

I must give kudos to Mrs. M., my eighth and ninth grade Sunday School teacher, who always advocated "self-investigation of the truth." You might be interested to find out how your state defines alcohol/liquor, marijuana, hallucinogenic, and narcotic, and how these substances are treated under the law in your locale. My purpose in this discourse is to underscore the inequity in the laws of the State of Washington (and likely most other states) regarding penalties for offenses involving these substances.

The answer to my question regarding why is alcohol not listed on Schedule 1 is, of course, simple: it's legal. Alcohol Prohibition began in 1920 in the United States; and was then ended in 1933. During those thirteen years organized crime took control of the distribution of bootleg alcohol. Ultimately the Suffragette women of the 30's undid the work of their predecessors who fought to enact Prohibition in 1920. They learned that prohibition did not cure any ills but, in fact, only made matters worse.

RCW 69. 50. 204   Schedule I.

. . .(a) Any of the following opiates. . .

(b) Opium derivatives. . . *Several of the numerous chemicals listed have codeine or morphine in the names:* (5) Codeine-N-Oxide; (13) Heroin; (19) Morphine-N-Oxide; (21) Nicocodeine ; (22) Nicomorphine . . .

(c)   Hallucinogenic substances. . . *Of the many chemicals listed several refer to forms of amphetamines. Some are complex chemical names that also show "Some trade or other names" which I assume are pharmaceutical designations because the hallucinogenics most popular for recreational use or abuse do not list common 'street' trade names. I list these cited substances with common [street] names:*

(13) Lysergic acid diethylamide; *[a chemical a.k.a. LSD or Acid]*

(14) Marihuana or marijuana; *[a plant a.k.a. Pot, Herb, Weed]*

(15) Mescaline; *[a plant derivative a.k.a. Mescaline "on the street"]*

(17) Peyote; *[a plant derivative a.k.a. Peyote "on the street"]*

(20) Psilocybin; *[a plant a.k.a. Magic Mushrooms, Shrooms]*

(22) Tetrahydrocannabinols. . .*[plant derivatives a.k.a. THC]*

(i) Delta 1 - cis. - or trans tetrahydrocannabinol, and their optical isomers, excluding tetrahydrocannabinol in sesame oil and encapsulated in a soft gelatin capsule in a drug product approved by the United States Food and Drug Administration;

(d) Depressants *(the last of the four Schedule I categories)*

So, the chemical inherent in the marijuana plant, Tetrahydrocannabinol or THC, is not legal for the general consumer in its natural plant form or otherwise. However, pharmaceutical companies are allowed to extract THC from the plant, mix it with sesame oil, put it in a capsule and sell it.

RCW 69. 50. 401   Prohibited acts: A—Penalties

(1) . . .it is unlawful for any person to manufacture, deliver, or possess with intent to manufacture or deliver, a controlled substance.

(2) Any person who violates this subsection with respect to: (a) a controlled substance classified in Schedule I or II which is a narcotic drug. . . is guilty of a class B felony and upon conviction may be imprisoned for not more than ten years, or (i) fined not more than twenty-five thousand dollars if the crime involved less than two kilograms of the drug, or both such imprisonment and fine; . . .

RCW 69. 50. 406 Distribution to persons under age eighteen.

(a) Any person eighteen years of age or over who violates RCW 69.50.401 by distributing a controlled substance listed in Schedules I or II which is a narcotic drug or methamphetamine . . . to a person under eighteen years of age is guilty of a class A felony punishable by the fine authorized by RCW 69.50.401 . . . [*$25,000*]. . . by a term of imprisonment of up to *twice* that authorized by RCW 69.50.401. . . [*twenty years*]. . . or by both.

Note: The copies Dick Carville provided to me in 1996 did confirm what he had told me in his office during my first appointment with him in 1995: up to fifteen years/$20,000 fine. The last two paragraphs above reflect how the law reads as of 2011, as found at this State of Washington website.:
http://apps.leg.wa.gov/rcw/

"The Revised Code of Washington (RCW) is the compilation of all permanent laws now in force."

RCW 66. 44. 270 Furnishing Liquor To Minors

(1) It is unlawful for any person to sell, give, or otherwise supply liquor to a person under the age of twenty-one years or to permit any person under that age to consume liquor on his or premises or on any premises under his or her control. . . .(3) This section does not apply to liquor given or permitted to be given to a person under the age of twenty-one years by a parent or guardian and consumed in the presence of the parent or guardian; (4) . . . given for medicinal purposes . . . by a parent, guardian, physician, or dentist; (5) . . . when such liquor is being used in connection with religious services and the amount consumed is the minimal amount necessary for the religious service.

Classification: Misdemeanor on the first offense and a Gross Misdemeanor on the second or subsequent offense.

Maximum Penalty:

First Offense: Two months in jail and a $500 fine.

Second offense: Six months in jail and a $500 fine.

Third and Subsequent Offense: One year in jail and a $500 fine.

This was the law in 1996. Like the controlled substances RCW's concerning Schedule I drugs, the above RCW has since been revised. Regarding the penalty structure, in 2011 it reads as follows:

Every person convicted of a gross misdemeanor defined in Title 9A RCW shall be punished by imprisonment in the county jail for a maximum term fixed by the court of not more than one year, or by a fine in an amount fixed by the court of not more than five thousand dollars, or by both such imprisonment and fine.

It is mind boggling to me that marijuana has for decades been on the same schedule that lists heroin; and, now includes methamphetamine. The inconsistency of values in the laws as they apply to Marijuana and to Alcohol is as criminal as the offenses in my opinion.

I want to reiterate that a parent can give their "person under the age of twenty-one years" alcohol with no repercussions if it is consumed while the parent is present. But a parent smoking marijuana with their "person under the age of twenty-one years" will be punished the same as if not the parent, as a Class A felon. I am not an advocate for drinking alcohol or smoking pot with one's children or teenagers. I am merely pointing out that the differences in the laws pertaining to the two substances are horrific. It is not a rarity for a good person to make a wrong choice. Is twenty years in prison congruous with this act? How does this serve anyone involved?

<u>January 8, 1997, Haiku O' The Day (outgoing phone message)</u>:

> Beth is at the store
> Needing a caffeine fix bad
> Please tell her you called

January 27, 1997, Monday, 9:35PM Mountain, in her 1997 bag

Zoey -

You have been on my mind all day. Each time I'm focusing on packing, airport, gate, flight # and time you are
on my mind and I'm just about melting as I write this. I
LOVE YOU SO MUCH! It was so-o-o-o wondermous hearing
your voice last night. When Gramma told you I was "in the
other room" she didn't realize I'd gone to her bedroom and
picked up the phone so I could hear your voice.

I'm sitting in seat 19F (window, right side) on flight
1458 at Denver International on my way to Dallas. Remember when I went to Dallas back in '95? Well, same trade
show. This is my third time now. I love you and miss you so
much. God your voice. . . you sounded so good.

Lonni told me what you said about Silver Chair at the
Deck the Hall Ball, "They play what they play well but I like
girl bands." We just got towed away from the gate and the
engines revved up and I felt like my vibes were soaring to
you. I was listening to "The Road Home" CD by Heart while
waiting to take off and now I'm anxiously awaiting being in
the air for ten minutes so I can turn them back on again. I
like girl music too. Ya know, oops! That was a pretty sketchy
"w"! Ha ha ha HA HA! I miss your laughter and can't wait til
this is OVER! I have loved Heart for a long time, since 1974
or so. I saw Heart's Wilson sisters at Moe a while back at the
"Home Alive" CD release party. It ran two nights and I went
to both. Love you, *always*Mom

February 2, 1997, in her bag, on Best Western Dallas North letter paper

Hi Sweetie Love!

They just made the announcement Seattle is about two
hundred miles away and we are beginning our descent. The
Dallas Show was pretty good. I think I'll see a few new customers and an increase in business from some existing ones.

I just reread the note I scribbled to you on the flight
to Dallas. Ha! Sometimes I become so overwhelmed with
feelings of you. You are always with me – every day – everywhere. . . but sometimes it's like I'm about to explode. I
wonder if you get these vibes too.

Once again I'm seeing a new guy. His name is Demitri. I
think it was the weekend following New Years that we met.

He is twenty-eight, sporting long blonde hair (again), but he is sweet, very kind to me, a good lover, silly, we laugh and have fun together. *And*, what else? He plays guitar, of course. Time for tray table up. . . more soon   XOXOXO

February 15, 1997

Lost

feeling disconnected
only a cobweb tie to God
just memories of Dad
and an invisible link to you
faith finds me wanting
I touch reality on my board
cruising to the north shore
I can feel wheels connecting asphalt to earth
rubber souls sending vibrations
of every twig and stone up my legs
to meet the February sunshine
that pounds on my head
and the cool air
that blasts my lungs
in the pit of my stomach
that seems vast
bottomless
unfillable
unreachable
as I cling to the chain link fence
that separates me from your tree
my hope of grounding dashed to the dirt
as I gaze at the trunk
only imagining the warmth
of the texture
of the bark
on my back
and not a single faery to be found
where is my magic?

February 16, 1997 – In her bag

My dearest Zoey,

I wrote this bad poem today but felt it yesterday. I felt it so bad that I called your boyfriend. Fortunately he answered the phone. I told him a fence has been up around your tree (as the path is being repaved, a major project) and asked him if he would please give you a big hug from me. I told him thanks for getting you over to see Gramma. I miss you so bad and I miss Dad and I'm feeling lost. I called Mom before I called your boyfriend and she tried to cheer me up but. . .

I've been pretty sick about four out of the last five weeks, first that bronchial-been-hit-by-a-truck flu, then a good week, then laryngitis for two weeks and in the second week of that I also started bleeding (about a quart a day!) ten days before my cycle was due! I'm all fucked up, still bleeding but almost over it just in time for when I'm really supposed to start! What the hell? AND in these last three weeks I've done one week in Dallas at a major trade show (with no voice); a week in L.A. holding down the fort while my boss was in Hong Kong for Chinese New Year's; and then the Action Sport Retailer Trade Show in Long Beach too - with little to zero voice and losing way too much blood daily! So I guess that could explain why I'm having a little trouble bouncing back.

I'm now running some logos for Thrasher and Slap magazines and Abacus! One of Abacus' riders beat Tony Hawk on the vert ramp at the ESPN Extreme Sports in San Diego last September while I was there for ASR. Because they're my customers and buddies I went to their big celebration party Sunday night following the contest and trade show. What a gas! It really gave me some credibility at ASR - having Thrasher and Abacus for customers I mean. I think I'll be getting quite a few new customers out of it this time! If not I know Evie (my boss) won't let me go again. I had to talk pretty fast to get her to send me this time - by reminding her that the ASR leads I got last September were all wasted due to the fact that Dad died the very next weekend after I got back from that show. I know I seemed pretty together at his service that day but then I spent 'til New Year's '97 in a daze most of the time, missing him. January I started to bounce back and then all this fucking sickness! Well, I'm going to lay *very* low now until I get to feeling like my usual self.

Believe it or not! Jay called me on Feb 4th. Yes, I marked it on the calendar. Pretty weird. It'd been about ten months since the last time we'd had contact. I asked him, "Why are you calling me now?" He just wanted to say hi. But as the conversation unwound it got a bit more interesting. We truly are connected, as much as ever. What he really wanted was to ask if I ever think about him. I said "Yes. You'll always have a place in me and I will always care about you but I had to get past the passion, Jay." He said he understood. I told him he is welcome to call and say hi anytime and that I'd welcome a chance to get together with him to catch up and see how it's all going with him. But I also told him that I don't want to know his pager number and if we do get together it will be a whole new thing. And that was pretty much it. I don't know if I gave him what he was looking for. I suspect not but nonetheless I won't be surprised if I hear from him again in a year or so.

Well, love of my life, I've been at this computer for the whole damn day it seems. I was having trouble with my e-mail. It took a long time to get it up and running again and then I had to spend a long time answering it all because most of it was customers' stuff. It's now three in the afternoon and I'm not much feeling like it's been a Sunday. So, Lovebug, now I have to get unpacked, do laundry, clean house and, by the time I'm done, go to bed. Oh Boy.

One last thing, I have a new roommate. And, somehow, I seem to have inherited her boyfriend as a roommate also. Plus, after being gone for a week I came home to a quarter inch of grit on the floor. It's time to lay down a few rules. I need this like a hole in the head. Katie, who was a great roommate, has moved to San Francisco to go back to school for her MFA, Master of Fine Arts. She is also an e-mail buddy. I guess I've not yet mentioned that I did finally talk Evie into buying a great new computer for the Seattle Office, which is me.

I hope all is well with you, my Love.
*always*Mom

22: Hugs and Hope

Prison

tree jail and jail free
all the same to me
no hugs can be
hadtohadtohadto skate today
sun almost fell down
before HatLady's phone did
cheated, board in passenger seat
to north shore
hustled down my favorite anti-hill
rounded the corner only to find
your tree is still
incarcerated
only worse
chain link still intact
but it will be gone soon
leaving your tree
encased in concrete curb
tidy dirt in a box
gone is the thinning grass
over balding soilskin
of earth and element
ha! if I got looks before
imagine the buzz brought on by the woman
in the purple hair sitting in the flower box
I'll fit in the box about as well as your tree
whowhat belongs in a box?

March 1997

On Being Human

addiction is the human commonality
we are so addicted to our humanness
and so addicted in our humanness
that in addicted so, our humanness
if we lessen our obsession with obsession

power * keeping-up-with-the-Jones's * career ladder
* dress-for-success * fashion * image * watching television
* watching The Market The NBA The NFL The Track
The Lotto * keno roulette blackjack slot machines *
machine guns hand guns hunting rifles * war games *
video games * head games * extreme games * love games
* on-line junkies * judging * jogging bowling boating flying
skydiving scuba-diving tennis golf fishing skiing
skating * hating * SkinHeads PinHeads PotHeads
HotHeads PartyHeads Pollers Rock'n'Rollers Leaders
GoodDeeders * greed * gluttony anorexia bulimia * pain
* fire * high wire * tattoos * nicotine caffeine sugar
alcohol amphetamines heroine LSD Cocaine Procaine
Prozac Ritalin Valium Librium Demerol Seconal *
SafeSex PlayfulSex Pornography * Play By The Rules
* religion * rightness correctness refinement
confinement conformity * anarchy * abuse * control

my addiction's only a minor affliction
compared to his * hers * theirs
we see what we want to see
we hear what we want to hear

and move on to passion
for the lesson in love
for our humanness
will find release

233

Journal: March 27, 1997

When I think about forgiveness for parents, wanting it to come my way from Zoey, I now realize that I want it to go Eric and Crystal's way also. I said early on that I didn't believe I would be able to let go of the anger at Eric for his actions until he offered up an apology. I am now changing my perception of this whole story. I am beginning to be able to view it differently.

We all are just a bunch of multi-dimensional entities, as Seth would say, choosing to be lost in our Humanness: creating our dramas, floundering around in search of truth and/or a better way, tapping into our spirituality and the wholeness of our being at varying rates. What is right? Who is wrong? It's the very same song. If I carry concern for being judged then why or how can I possibly make judgment?

Last night while I ate dinner I started Chapter Six of Seth Speaks and I am, again, reminded to keep humor with me at all times, to relax and move forward in the process without taking it all so seriously. I hope I will soon be able to discipline myself to sit quietly on a regular basis, silencing my brain's intellectual ego chatter long enough to be open to my whole being, my many dimensions.

I remembered a little bit of a dream I had last night. That always makes me happy, makes me feel like I'm not really all fucked up. The ninety-eight percent block in front of conscious memory of my dream activity that's been in place since I was eighteen years old has, all these years, left me feeling that there is truly something wrong with me. (There's that word again!)

Gotta get to work! I'm running over into HatLady time!

Thank you, God/Goddess/God-in-me, for my many blessings and for this new day: a new opportunity to live and learn and love and teach. Thank you, Zoey, for finding me and entrusting to me all of this opportunity to learn and grow. You are my LoveLight. Be safe and happy. Only one Earth year, five months, and four days to go.

April 2, 1997

Shadow Hugs

Riding in from the north
passed right by your tree today
pretending not to see
arced left
cut up the edge of the basketball court
rounded up the side, coming full circle
to sneak up on
your tree
is still imprisoned
so I stand on
my skateboard
clinging to the chain links
waiting while my shadow hugs
your tree
in the gold dust air
that blows past my body
as the sun settles
on my back
I waited so long
a man asked, "What do you see?"
my reply, "A poem falling out of me."
I turned and imaged the bark of
your tree
on my back
while faeries danced
in the beams glowing low over the water
on my board, up the path
it arcs left and left
and left
again
tangled in my headphones
entwined in your faery's spell
one hug wasn't enough
shadow and senses hug

your tree and you
it hits me
the no longer balding soilskin
lost to tidy dirt
has a new 'do
a cool punky style
anorexic unruly vines
your tree has gone city
she's a city tree
all right by me
changing
with the tide
it'll only be
one earth year
    four months
        twenty-eight days
'til I'm by your side
I ride
for java in green, star$$$
ebony mocha to the scene
outdoor table with tray
to catch the ashes
as a skinny roll
of paper catches
the poem falling
out of me
into the twilit gold
violet catching ebony

Journal: April 2, 1997

Going to the Poetry Slam with Katie unlocked the poet in me. It seems for the last twenty years or so I'd forgotten I write poetry. Making connection with Zoey through her tree brought on my muse only to frustrate it and me with that gawdawful fence! Now poetry wells up in me and I have to find something to write on before the inspiration is lost. In the case of Shadow Hugs I walked over to Starbucks at the top end of the lake and asked if by chance they had a piece of paper and pen I could borrow for a bit. The girl at the counter was super nice and wanted to help but all she could offer was a cash register roll for paper. It worked. Once I got the poem typed up I rolled it around the roll of paper containing the original hand-written version and put it in her bag.

I was just closing up here when a scribble inside the front cover caught my eye and made me laugh: *M R R M E* I recall coming up with an idea for a great organization to benefit humanity, kind of like M.A.D.D. We'd say it *'murmy'* Moms for Rape Reduction thru Masturbation Education It seems like a viable idea but I won't be the founder and spearheading it.

April 3, 1997 – a letter to. . .

Hi May!

Thanks so much for the sweet card and the photo of your baby. Cam is *beautiful*! Congratulations! I wish the two of you all the best, Little Mama.

I've gone to my mom's one day out of each of the last two weekends and have accomplished next to nothing on my book and I'm feeling so fucking pressed to forge on and get to the next print phase so I can get it out in search of a good agent or a publisher and just be the writer I am and stop with the HatLady stuff. I love being the HatLady for a day job but that's all it is. My boss is really getting to me. And now it's full on fucking hat season and twelve hours a day is barely enough to feel like I've finished all that's on the HatLady's desk each day.

Last night after work it was too gorgeous not to skate and the fourth in the Your Tree series of poems fell out: Shadow Hugs. I like it a lot. When I saw Zoey at Bumbershoot on Labor Day weekend, she asked me "Do you ever go sit by my tree?" I knew which one she meant but I didn't know until then that to her it was her tree. Well, after that it became a bit of a grounding place for me and the source of four poems so far. It is the big, old tree outside the swimming pool pavilion at the north end of Green Lake, at the southwest corner of the north parking lot (which is undergoing a re-do in conjunction with the complete re-paving of the two and three quarter mile path that goes around the lake).

I can be such a blubber head with too much on my mind all the time. So, I can't remember if I asked you if you like poetry or if you'd be interested in seeing some of mine but I'm sending you some regardless. The first four of the Your Tree series are enclosed. Now, with Shadow Hugs, I've determined that a series is clearly growing so I've taped a print of each of the four poems to the frame of my all-time favorite piece of Zoey's kid-art, The Longthong, which is hanging on the wall in my hall. I think you might have seen it that time you visited us at The House Of The '90's. If not, May, you're probably asking, "What in the hell is a Longthong?"

When Zoey was four years old, she came to me one morning, rubbing the sleep from her eyes saying, "Momma, I had a funny dream last night." I asked her what the dream was about but the only part of the telling I recall is her saying, ". . .and there was a Longthong sliding down a rainbow." I asked her what the Longthong looked like. She said, "He was kind of like a unicorn because he had a horn on his forehead and he had wings . . . with hearts on them. But he had horns like a deer too; big claws like a dragon and a long tail with a ball on the end." So, a Longthong is a beast who lives in another dimension that Zoey visited one night while her body rested in sleep.

You might wonder how I'm so certain of this. At the time, I was mystified. So, I asked if a story about Longthongs had been read to her day care group. "No", she responded, shaking her head. I asked if she'd seen something about Longthongs on Sesame Street or if her babysitter, Connie, had brought a book with a Longthong story in it. "No," she responded twice.

"Well then," I asked, "who told you about the Longthong?"

Her answer was emphatic, "I saw him in my dr*eee*am!"

I asked her if she could draw the Longthong. While I got ready for work I pondered the phenomenon and she colored me quite a picture. The rainbow and Longthong took up the top half of the paper (letter-size in vertical format) and the lower half was consumed by:

TO MOMMY WOMMY   FROM ZOEY DOEY

X O X O X O X O X O X O X O X O X O X O X O X O X O X

Seriously, May, the Longthong story truly opened my mind to accepting all that I've read on parallel lives and other dimensions beyond the physical plane we consciously live in. It was a major spiritual revelation for me.

Gotta go! Talk to you soon. Love you big!   Beth

April 5, 1997

Glowing

OOOooo that boy!
so well worth waiting for a he who
I know feels so good
love that kiss
still Sammy
funny bunny
thanks for planting
all over me
so-o-o glad I rode out
my wave of shyness
and just said NO
to missed opportunity

morning sun beams brightly
kissing your back lightly
becomes thunder in my bed
I joy to take in your rain
ever so glad you came
I board my land ark
alien with rainbow
clinging to my chest
a masthead as I boat
around the lake
sailing the course
weaving through
the waves of people
smiling Good Morning!

Music in my ears
riding in from the north
sun glows on
the faeries on deck
rounding the northeast bend
I see your tree
is at last FREE

I cannot express
the overwhelmedness
of the joy emanating
from me
to meet sun glow
surrounding
your tree
in sweet caress

She - beautiful City Tree-
stands proud, Lady of the Lake
Guardian of Love
I feel your warmth and offer up
thanks for this day
we're on our way
to freedom

April 6, 1997

Sunny Sunday

had to get in the box today
to get free
to feel you
in the bark of your tree
on my back

feet firmly planted
on the south side
I lean back
and look up
at golden sun glow
in closed eyes

home
riding straight to your heart
on a carpet of faery dust
raised up
by wingbeats
in sundance gladness
to the moon and back

Journal: April 27, 1997

On looking back thru my journal I'm surprised to find I've made no mention of my plan for last night and all the ensuing excitement for its arrival. At Bumbershoot last fall Zoey told me her all-time favorite band is Sky Cries Mary. When I heard from Rena that her old friend from PA would be opening an all-ages show for Sky Cries Mary at RKCNDY I called Zoey's boyfriend. Thankfully he answered the phone. He confirmed that if I sent him tickets he would get Zoey to the show. And, he did. I got to hug her in the lobby before she went in to the showroom but her boyfriend wanted to hang back and talk to me.

Between bands Zoey emerged to the lobby to get a drink, to say hi and get a hug then disappeared again. I did not see one minute of the show and consequently not much of Zoey. It seemed more important to finish the rounds of questions her boyfriend and I had for one another. He was curious about our current circumstances and clearly stood in judgment of me, as stated in his, "Yeah, but you were the parent, the adult in the scenario."

I looked him in the eyes and responded, "What? You think adults and parents never fuck up? They can and do. I'm living proof. If I had it again to do differently. . . but I don't."

When the show was over, Zoey and the girlfriend who came with them found me and her boyfriend in the lobby. We chatted only briefly. Zoey thanked me for sending the tickets. I told her that Lonni and Pat were getting married and would love to see her at the wedding. Her boyfriend told me to call him with details and he would get her there. I got one last long hug and they left so Zoey would be home before curfew. The evening did not go as I had pictured it in my head while waiting for the day to arrive. I felt let down on one hand but all the grilling from her boyfriend was well worth the Zoey hugs in between and the hope that I'd see her again soon.

23: Can I Find A Peace?

May 12, 1997, for Thrasher Magazine: unpublished

Skateress, Your HatLady

Back in my 20's, when I was young
I was really a hell of a lot older
I find now every passing year
makes me grow a little bit bolder
in my 30's the likes of Metallica, Def Lepard and Scorps
began consuming much more space
in my audio pleasure collection
light yuppie jazz falling from grace
when I coupled rock-in-a-Walkman
with my after-work-skate more and more
I became a rollerskating junkie
a hard ass old school addict to the core
at the ripe old age of 35,
in the Fall of '89 at ASR in SD*
I scoped vertical skating for the first time
instant skateboarder wannabe
I watched with awe
as those skaters so fine
fearlessly caught huge air, spinning big tricks
landing perfect every time
for years I was trapped in denial
telling myself you're too old. . . you'll look silly. . .
what will people say?
at age 41, after a great many life lessons
I decided FUCK THAT!
and became the skateboarder I am, a hella happy day
now I'm 42 going on 22, a pretty unusual lady

I cruise my home lake on forgiving gushy wheels
attached to my 36 inch long board
aaaaahh! This is how flying free feels!
I storm the street with a phat purple stripe in my hair
no doubt the cause of many judgmental talks
but ask me if I care cuz few in the know will dispute
that your HatLady rocks!

à la Thrasher: Live to skate ⚡ Skate or die

*Action Sport Retailer Trade Show in San Diego, California

Calendar: May 20, 1997
Metallica and Corrosion of Conformity at Key Arena, 7PM

May 26, 1997 – in her bag
Hi Zoey –

Pat and Lonni's wedding was Saturday and I was so hoping you'd be there. When I talked to your boyfriend a couple weeks ago I erroneously told him it was the coming Saturday (the 16th - a week early) and he said you two would be there. When I figured out my mistake I was still hoping you would make it and was so very bummed when you didn't. But, Sunday it hit me that being Memorial Day weekend you were probably out on your dad's boat or something. It was such a nice service. I think you would really have enjoyed it. The garden it was in was so beautiful.

Even though you weren't there physically you were there in spirit. I know this because I brought you. Remember at Bumbershoot when you gave me the key to our apartment and told me to keep it always? Well, it is still on the same safety pin and I have pinned it to the handle of a candlestick holder that sits on my bedside altar/table. Because there was no shower for Lonni and since I was the Maid of Honor, I figured it was my responsibility to be sure the bride was wearing something old, something new, something borrowed, and something blue.

For something old I gave her a hat pin with a pink heart shaped crystal on the end that Mom had given to me years ago and had been laying at the bottom of my jewelry box. For something new I gave her a pretty pair of blue stretch lace panties from Victoria's Secret. (You know she's about five months pregnant. I figured they'd fit for the day.) For

243

something borrowed she pinned our apartment key inside of her top. She and I talked about the significance of the key and we hoped you'd be there but somehow we both seemed to know you'd be with us in spirit only. For something blue I taped a note in the bottom of the box that said "Refer to something new." We laughed. Fortunately, her mom had given her a set of new rhinestone earrings and a necklace so she was truly covered on all points.

We all left for home at about 5:30PM. I took a nap and ate. At 10PM I met everyone—fourteen of us including the friends of Pat and Lonni visiting from California, Montana, and Colorado—in Pioneer Square at the Old Timer's Café. There was a good blues band playing. Poor Lonni was so pooped. She'd been up since early, had such a big day and no nap because of everyone staying at their apartment. She was starting to talk about going home and I said "Wait a minute! You can't go home until you have your Wedding Dance. You aren't even married until you have your Wedding Dance!!"

Lonni said, "Okay but it's got to be to Mustang Sally." When the band went on break I asked them if they could please play it. They said they didn't know if they remembered it but they'd try. After they came off break they were starting the third song when at least eight of us yelled in unison, "MUSTANG SALLY!!!"

The lead guy said, "Yeah, we'll butcher that one at the end of this set."

I thought, no. This is not good enough for my friends. I told everyone, "You know, I have a gut feeling that if we walk down to Larry's Greenfront whatever band is playing there they will know Mustang Sally and play it with gusto. Let's go." So they all followed my lead the block and a half down to Larry's. I told the guy at the door that the only way we could enter his establishment would be if the band would play Mustang Sally. He told me to ask the band. They were just finishing a song so I popped my head around the corner (the stage is in the front window) and asked the bass player.

"Sure," he replied, "Come on in." As the last of us wove our way in to the packed club the band lit up Lonni and Pat's song. We all boogied down—squealing, high-fiving the bride and groom and each other and generally making a spectacle of ourselves. It was great fun!

Everybody was quite amazed at the accuracy of my gut feeling. And it is truly amazing how the more I come to trust my natural knowing the more accurate it is. Every day I find that I am more and more psychic. Remember when Teresa read you she said the same of you? I hope you are coming to trust your natural knowing too, my dear.

For Pat and Lonni's wedding present I went to Gargoyles in the U District wanting to get them a wizard of some sort. Wow, I found the perfect wedding gift for them. It's a ceramic tea pot so it's a domestic-type item. The pot is a beautiful gnarly dragon. His tail is the handle. His neck and face form the spout so the tea pours out of his mouth. The lid is a wizard sitting cross-legged. It's glazed in mottled fiery red and golden tones with accents of moss green, too cool! I made a little gift card and tied it to the handle of the pot. It read:

Lonni & Pat – As you partake an evening tea together from this vessel know that you renew the power of the dragon that protects both your union and each your personal power as the wizard maintains your magic.

Much love to you two, Beth

I also made their wedding card. Here's the verse I wrote:

Today, as you step together
onto the path you have chosen
I pray that your journey
always will be blessed with
the warmth of sunshine
the sweet newness of freesia-scented Spring
the clarity of a star-filled sky
the constancy of the moon's cycle
the power of the ocean's wave pounding the shore
and the smooth, roundness of the stone on the beach
that has withstood the turns of the tide
and all tests of time

I love you, Zoey!
Mom

245

<u>Calendar: June 10, 1997</u>

Space****sucker at Moe's Café, 10PM

Ode To T. 2

relieved a myriad of tension
in thoughts of you today
five silver platters in the deck
one song each picked to play
alone I play out my wish
while Anne, with Heart, belts out
"All I want to do is make love to you"
me too still
I wish to do you
like you'll never forget
What do you think that means?
I'm misunderstood it seems
I wish to pleasure you
make you feel
so good
relaxed
real
warm
builds to hot
touching and kissing every spot
that's wanting more
quickening at an unhurried pace
whisking you to a place not seen before
an indulgence not a lifestyle
at peace for a while
for a moment in space
in that place beyond the moon and the stars
squeezing through the bars of time
between us
Kevin lights every Candle in the Box
"cover me" sings he
your shelter I'll be
a warm place to come
along the way
a friend
your option
to go

or come
along
LIVE soars through my brain, "turn my head"
again and again you do
wish you could remember
"It is written in the stars above
You'll be. . . right next to me",
Depeche Mode croons in a groove above the beat
I'm really dreaming now
turn up the heat
and I'm coming again
as Pearls Jam and Eddie's world "turns to black"
wondering how to be the sun in your sky
for a day
don't ask why
it just is
and will be
til you set me free
to thank you like you'll never forget
if only you could remember
magic
if only my magic
wouldn't flee
each time I find you in front of me
skittering away like a timid child
wishing I could just say
come play with me for a while
are you ready?
to delve into my bag of questions
to pull them out one by one
are you ready?
to pack the refillable bowl
unwind in the smoke
talk soul to soul
are you ready?
to succumb to my faery's spell
drop into the bucket
slide down my wishing well
are you ready?
should I offer red wine next time?

July 3, 1997 – in her bag

Hi Sweetie Heart!

You, as always, have been very much on my mind. Well, that's a daily thing. I guess I more mean that I've wanted to write you a note. On Sunday June 15th I went to the 100th Fremont Sunday Market thinking it was going to be the Fremont Fair. I had it in the back of my mind (the hope) that I might run into you. Well, it turned out that the Fair was the next weekend. So I quit hoping for seeing you and just wandered through the market.

At the Flea Market area I bought you a cool $2 ceramic dragon that I'll enjoy until you get it. It's too big for your bag so might as well have it out to enjoy. I also picked up this pair of silver and peridot earrings for you. Since I knew I'd be in L.A. during the actual Fair I thought I'd make Sunday your gift buying day.

Saturday, the 21st of June, the day of the Summer Soltice, I went to the Third Street Promenade in Santa Monica where a party was taking place for the occasion. They had two or three sound stages set up with bands playing, food booths, etcetera. I picked up the (also enclosed) cool little pen at a booth there. FYI, it takes Bic refills.

I miss you so bad, Zoey. Now we have but one year, one month and twenty-seven days. I can't believe this whole thing sometimes. I feel so sickened by it all. And "all" covers a lot of territory. They say (whoever all of *they* are) that we need to forgive ourselves our errors and move on having at least learned from them, not to repeat them. Well, Zoey, you only have one childhood so I can't possibly blow it twice! I have blown the one shot I had. I know if I'm to stay sane and live productively and have something to offer or give to the world I have to let go of the anger at myself, bear the pain without too much anesthesia (pot and alcohol) and get on with it. But, this is not an easy task. Frankly, I'm a fucking basket case a good deal of the time. I manage to hold it together on the outside, like I'm having great success in my day job being the HatLady. And, I have managed to maintain a few good friends – i.e. Lonni, Pat, Katie. But, I've even kind of started to wear them thin.

So, I've decided I seriously need to get into some counseling. I have a lot of pain I need to deal with, different issues.

I've managed to stuff it all down deep for a long time now, pretending and/or hoping it will just go away. But it jumps out and slaps me in the face at the most inopportune times and it is finally time for me to really drag it all out, look at it, feel it, digest it, and release it—get the baggage off my cart! Teresa told me in one of our more recent readings that I have a lot of grief work to do. I guess this is what she meant.

I told your Gramma that I cut out six ads to call for women's counseling and support groups. She suggested I try Alanon first. It's free and she has heard great things about results people have had in this group. So, I found that there's a Monday night meeting just over in Fremont and I'm going to go next week.

Also, two weeks from this Saturday, I am going for the third time to start my meditation class again. Tuesday nights just weren't getting it for me. Something always came up. So I'm going to get the full shot of instruction in a one day Saturday class. Then I'm going to truly discipline myself to do it! Every day! The few mornings where I started my day with meditation were so great, so much calmer and peaceful. Well love, I'm running out of page and need to get in the shower so 'bye for now.

I love you with all my heart. Every day I pray for my angels and guides to be watching over you and every day I look to the day we can be together. *always*Mom

PS – For some reason I keep flashing on the 4th of July 1994 with you, me, and your friend, Dean. That was one of the first couple of times we smoked together. It all seemed so simple and innocent then. That was such a fun day.

July 4, 1997 – a note card to Mom

Mom, Thanks so much for gathering all those goodies for me: Gramma's life story, the great photos, and the letters. Thanks for my angel pin. And thanks for just being you. I so enjoyed your company Sunday and rock picking on the beach with you. Thanks for loving me the way I am. I know I've been a real trial for you and a disappointment at times; but, that has gone both ways. It feels good to come to a place of peacefulness and acceptance and appreciation for each other in both our likenesses and our differences. I now know you are a special angel who has always been with and for me.   Love, Beth

24: Seattle Hempfest

Hi Zo! Just thinking of how much I love you and where I'll go to at Bumbershoot hoping to see you. I wish you'd get to your Gram's. I hope your boyfriend has offered. An on-line spree to the bank tells me he has cashed the check I sent him so you could buy a birthday gift of choice from me. I hope you have a great birthday. MAYBE I'LL SEE YOU! Can't wait to hug you again! (One year, ten days to go)

Journal: August 26, 1997

I went to Mom's Friday. She took me out for dinner to the Ajax Café, a casual, old and rustic setting with a four star restaurant menu in a tiny dot-on-the-map town called Port Hadlock. Went rock-picking at the beach with her on Saturday, had some great talks.

I got home at about midnight:30 and fifteen minutes later the phone rang. "Who the hell is that?" I thought. None other than that sweetheart from the skate shop on the hill who'd just gotten back from an Oregon surfing expedition and was feeling horny, needing affection. He came over. We watched what he dubbed a cheesy surf movie, played a round of Faery Shooting, ate ice cream with chocolate sauce and went to bed. It was actually very nice, a pleasant unexpected occurrence.

Sunday afternoon I went to the Seattle Hempfest. I had to screw up the courage for it and at first found myself looking over my shoulder a lot. I was afraid of running into Zoey's brothers. The last thing I need would be for them to go home saying they'd seen me in that setting. I also feared seeing any kids from the House Of The '90's as they'd surely want to smoke out with me. Damn, that would have been uncomfortable. Fortunately I saw no one I know.

The event was very informative. I got lots of good

literature and possible connections for finding a deal on hemp paper for my first edition. It was rainy and they were having technical trouble as a result. But people seemed dedicated to hanging with it. After some time passed where nothing was happening on stage musically, they introduced a speaker named Ralph Seeley, an attorney in Seattle who is terminally ill with cancer and sued the state of Washington for the right to use marijuana saying it is his best medicine for warding off the ill effects of chemotherapy.

His talk was inspiring. My eyes were glued to him and I was hanging on every word. He asked us to all please get out and vote to support Initiative 685. At the end of his talk he said the Sunday morning Post Intelligencer ran a story on his loss of the suit and included the discourse of the one dissenting judge, Justice Richard Sanders. I picked up a copy of the PI on my way home and have to say it's hard to believe that only one judge offered this opinion. I applaud him for doing so. These particular paragraphs really grab me:

". . .Let us recall both *Roe* and *Casey*, like the case before us, focus upon an individual's claim that the state lacks sufficient justification to dictate to a woman matters associated with her bodily integrity, specifically abortion. A majority in *Roe* recognized that the state "may properly assert important interests in safeguarding health, in maintaining medical standards, and in protecting potential life." Similarly, a majority in *Casey* recognized these same legitimate interests, yet held that "legitimate interests are not enough."

If the state's interest to regulate abortion in the context of *Casey* and *Roe* is insufficient, the state's asserted interest to criminalize Seeley's ingestion of marijuana to ease the effects of nausea is even less so. *Casey* focused directly on matters "involving the most intimate and personal choices. . . central to personal dignity and autonomy, which are central to the liberty protected by the 14th Amendment," and then states:

At the heart of liberty is the right to define one's own concept of existence, of meaning, of the universe, and of the mystery of human life. Beliefs about these matters could not define the attributes of personhood were they formed under compulsion of the state.

251

Apparently the Supreme Court thought personal choices essential to personal dignity and autonomy are constitutionally privileged even when those choices are at odds with legitimate state interests. . ."

I don't view smoking pot as an attribute of my personhood per se but it certainly should be my personal choice to ingest marijuana rather than a martini to take the edge off of and give perspective to what unfolded in the universe on any given day.

Highlighted in a separate text box is the bold heading "A brief history of marijuana and its regulation." At the bottom, under seven concise paragraphs it states —*From Justice Richard Sanders' dissenting opinion in the case Seeley vs. State.*[1] The facts he presents, which primarily give focus to where marijuana once stood in U.S. pharmacopeia but also touch on hemp usage, jive with the extensive historical information Jack Herer offers in *The Emperor Wears No Clothes.* The last highlighted paragraph, his closing statement in this history says:

"Under Washington law, use of leaf marijuana is illegal for any purpose. Doctors may never prescribe it no matter how efficacious it may be in a given case. In contrast, Washington law allows doctors to prescribe cocaine, PCP angel dust, opium, and morphine."

A while back I made a "Hempy Stuff" file to keep all such related items in so I put the PI article in there as well as all the literature I picked up at various Hempfest booths including a promo poster for Initiative 685. The Initiative is calling for the legalization of marijuana, heroin, LSD and some other Schedule 1 drugs as medicines that doctors can prescribe. Apparently a doctor wrote the Initiative. I tucked the poster inside The Stranger article that ran on the topic back in July. That writer did not see much hope of 685 passing saying that it was worded too broadly to gain popular support. They got enough signatures to bring it to ballot so it'll be interesting to see how it comes out.

Sunday night I went to see Collective Soul, truly an outstanding concert! I love that band. They played their hearts out and obviously were having a great time doing it as they had a super enthusiastic audience to play to. I love it when that positive energy exchange gets going.

This coming weekend is Bumbershoot. I hope the weather has gotten its gray, cool rainy bent spent by then. Great line-up of performances plus I can't wait to go to the book fair, tons of authors to talk to. I hope to run into Zoey on Monday at the stage where Sky Cries Mary is playing. Saturday is her seventeenth birthday, one year four days to go.

One last thought: Approaching the one year anniversary of getting my tattoo I determined I would not add the dragon as originally planned. I couldn't bear the thought of enduring that kind of pain again. Furthermore, I simply didn't feel the need. The fact I didn't call the whole thing off after the first few blasts of the outlining tool tells me that perhaps my tattoo was more about the pain than the tattoo itself. It was a form of penance. After seeing Zoey at Bumbershoot last year I am finding it easier to stop the self-talk in which I kick the Bad Mom self around the block again. Thank God.

August 28, 1997 – in her bag

Haiku 'O The Day: I sat across from
               your tree today in a new
               way across the lake   I love Zoey.

BUMBERSHOOT 1997
3 days of bliss

Journal: September 2, 1997

Zoey gave me her pager number and informed me that 1-4-3 means "I love you." The next day I paged her with 1-4-3-3-6-3 meaning I love you, three hundred sixty-three days to go. I plan to page her every day of the count-down. After a few days she'll get it.

September 26, 1997 – a fax to Billy at Abacus

Hey Billy! I'm glad you enjoyed the cookies and that you think I rock. Thanks. I think you guys rock too. No matter how many skaters I get to do hats for you guys will always be my favorites. My board is so cool. Thanks so much for the new deck. Pretty damn weird that my skateboard was stolen out of the skateboard check at the tradeshow. Kind of kills the point of having it, huh? It sucked having to walk between my hotel and the convention center the next day. I sure appreciate you hooking me up. Have a great weekend!
Beth

[1] *Excerpted from Justice Richard Sanders' significantly condensed history of cannabis in America, presented in his dissenting opinion in the case of Seeley vs. State:*

Historically, cannabis has been used in a variety of ways. The original Declaration of Independence was written on hemp, as was Thomas Paine's "Common Sense." George Washington and Thomas Jefferson grew hemp. Benjamin Franklin used hemp in an early paper mill.

Throughout the 19th century marijuana was used as an anticonvulsant, as an analgesic and in the treatment of rheumatism, epilepsy, and tetanus. In 19th century America marijuana was listed in the "United States Dispensatory" (1854), was generally available in drug stores . . .

However, marijuana was repressed by the federal government in 1937 through a stamp tax so burdensome, both financially and procedurally, that it virtually eliminated any legal use of marijuana and hemp. The purpose of the tax was prohibition, although it was effectuated in the form of a revenue measure because of constitutional limits still enforced against federal lawmaking power.

The elimination of cannabis came from pressures exerted by newly created Federal drug control agencies, cotton and timber interests, and chemical industries. Marijuana was removed from the "United States Pharmacopoeia and National Formulary" in 1941.

Shortly after the Marijuana Tax Act was held unconstitutional in 1969, in a failed attempt to prosecute Dr. Timothy Leary for possession of untaxed marijuana, Congress passed the Controlled Substances Act, placing marijuana in Schedule I and directly criminalizing any use of it. Washington state followed suit in 1971 and adopted an identical regime also placing marijuana in Schedule I.

Justice Richard Sanders well served the citizens of Washington on the bench of the Supreme Court from 1996 to 2011. With particular interest in the state's Constitution, he's known to quote a favorite passage: "All political power is inherent in the people, and governments derive their just powers from the consent of the governed and are established to protect and maintain individual rights." Washington Const. art. I, § 1.

For a more comprehensive history of cannabis in the United States go to www.jackherer.com. Click on Chapter 4 of his book.

25 : HatLady Holidays

Journal: October 2, 1997
Life rolls along quite well, quite quickly. I went to the Buckaroo last night to pinball out a poem. There have been a few rolling around with the marbles in my brain, incomplete but coherent, just not dropping out. Queen of Distraction allowed herself to be so. Fisherman Mac aka Roaming Ricky, who hadn't seen a woman in the flesh for seven months was way too tempting to pass up. So home with me he came and came and me too – whoo! Mac called me from work at lunch to let me know he has to go south for a couple weeks but would it please me to see he again? I look forward to his return for a serious rematch IF we can find the sixth faery. My most current drought has ended with the September rain. Jay called me last night and we really talked, really shared feelings about what was and what might be. Jack I meet tonight at SubZero. Friday night it's the Ballard Firehouse for some good ol' 80's buttrock. Saturday BINM plays Sit'n'Spin. I, of course, will go: like moth to light, magnet to steel, river to the ocean. And, by then, I will have released the poem that lies in me for he. . .
> still
> and I will give it to him
> in hopes that he will
> give to me the chance to give what I have to give
> so at last I can be free
> aaah... life rolls on
> the wheel
> the deal
> on random orificial schpeel

Calendar: October 10, 1997
Mike Watt+Black Gang Crew @ the Crocodile Café, Doors 9PM

November 3, 1997 – a fax to Abacus

Billy, I got your message. I swear! Sometimes I am too much of a girl to deal well with you guys! You'd drive me nuts if I had time for that sort of thing! But I don't. I'll be in your office on Thursday or Friday of this week. I'll be in north San Diego and south Orange counties for both days but have a number of people I need to see. So, maybe it would be best to meet up after 5PM on one of those days. Let me know.
Beth

Journal: November 5, 1997

As The Stranger projected, Initiative 685 failed to pass. Tim Killian, the doctor that wrote the Initiative, plans to get another one going for the November 1998 ballot. Maybe I should volunteer to get signatures or something. When? When do I have time?

November 14, 1997

Roadtrippin' and Signs I Believe

I'm just a pusher
big ol' wheels give
more roll
for the push
I'm a cruiser
no trickster
no vertical flyer
I just cruise
I skate

I'm cruisin now
behind the wheel
on my way
with hopes of being
HatLady-of-choice
to more skaters
Left Santa Monica
in buckets falling
from the low ceiling
of flannel gray
rounding the bend

through Ventura
the blanket lifts
and sun smacks the day

Hot damn
my spirit soars
with the ocean
wide open
to sun glint kisses
crowning the waves
I see the curve
of our Mother
Earth

I leave Santa Barbara
a happy HatLady
torch a bowl
on the roll
I'm cruisin to Santa Cruz
though it's now night
the sky is bright
I trust the wheel to the road
look over my shoulder
to the right
out the back window
the full moon glows
behind the slit
in puffy cloud lids
an eye on the night
My breath catches
on such splendor
I marvel at my spot
as just a dot
in the universe
and offer thanks
for my guide

I'm cruisin
behind the wheel
I feel the moon

watching over me
can't help but look again
the clouds shifted
to show me
the sign of peace
silhouetted in the light
of night

Eyes on the road
mind racing
through thoughts
that appreciate
moon signs

Have you ever seen a five point star in the sky?
You know, you've seen two or three
by the name of a mediocre restaurant
or an old B movie in the guides
or one in print symbol
for Texas as Lone Star State
but have you ever seen
a five point star twinkling
in the sky at night?
I have
blinked
IblinkIblinkIblink
I think
my contacts are fuckin with me
but   NO
I know
I have now seen
a miracle
in the night
on high
in the sky
over my left shoulder
I believe

Is the moon still with me?
yup, back-light on donut cloud

mystical moon glow
in deep tunnel of donut hole
I'm on a roll

I'm cruisin
a fuckin five point star
in the sky is following me
while moon eye
to peace sign
to donut hole
becomes moonshine
behind a laughing bird

I laugh intoxicatedly
how can that be
I check to see
is the five point star still with me?
Oh, dear God!
this one's new
now there's two
I think of you
my dear daughter. . . and me
two true stars wink
and I know

Green is my daughter's
favorite color
the town of Greenfield
celebrates broccoli
on her birthday
while Castroville is
The Artichoke Capitol of The World
signs in the center of town tell me so

Signs in the sky
I thank you
and I'm cruisin
I just cruise
so glad
I'm just a pusher
I skate

November 20, 1997 – a note for Zoey's bag

on a cute greeting card then continued onto a second...

Zoey – I'm sitting at the bar, smoking a cigarette and sipping on a black coffee with whiskey in it (to soothe my very sore throat) discussing 'not much of a drinker' which the bartender and I have in common. I got to thinking I haven't paged you yet today and since I'm not at my desk looking at my wall calendar where I've clipped the polaroid of you and me taken at Bumbershoot and keep track of the countdown, it occurred to me I should recount because there are many days this month that I've been away from my desk.

This month, November 1997, I have paged you from Encinitas, Carlsbad, Carson, Santa Monica, Santa Cruz, San Francisco (all in California) and from the Toledo, Ohio area last night. Today I'll page you twice – once from the Detroit airport (where the bartender is now topping off my mug with coffee for the third time) and then again from Denver if there's time.

In September I paged you from Lansing, Michigan; San Diego, and Torrance, California.

I so love you and miss you Zoey.

Second card: So, like I said, here I am at the Detroit airport. I went in the gift shop thinking to get you something for your bag for later. Your boyfriend pretty well chewed me out when I told him I'd started a shot glass collection for you. So I explained it's like a spoon collection except most airports don't have spoons any more. I told him I fully intend to tell you that I'm not advocating their use. They're just for fun for pete's sake, something to collect. Regardless, I didn't get you a new one. I looked at tee shirts and various trinkets then decided I like these cards best of all, *and* a chance to write to you since I haven't for a long time. But – oh, Zo! – you can't begin to guess how much I think of you my dear daughter.

Love, *always*Mom

November 25, 1997, 5AM, to put in her bag

My dear Zoey,

I am writing to you from my bed by the window in room 1665 of the Virginia Mason Hospital on Capitol Hill.

It's just a few days after I picked up those cards for you in the Detroit airport. I didn't and haven't mentioned anything to you about suffering my winter nasal/bronchial syndrome because it has become such a typical way of life for me since I returned to Seattle. Of course, smoking is the root of the syndrome; but, it was not this bad in L.A. Any way, I think this is going to change. It is my goal to change this.

I had a frightening experience on Sunday. Late Thursday night I got home from a two day trip to see my big corporate client in Ohio (via Detroit and Denver, I can't believe the ridiculous flights Evie books for me in order to save a freaking buck!). Friday morning I went to see my doctor. He gave me three prescriptions: the antibiotic Amoxicillin, a decongestant, and a cough syrup with codeine and expectorant (helps to cough up crap).

I worked at my desk the balance of the day. Then at 4PM I went for a skate on Green Lake. I bundled up good for my skate but didn't wear a hat and it was crispy cold out. I just had to skate. When I got back I was feeling pretty spacey so grabbed a brew and a bowl and sat on the couch watching the sun set behind the trees of Woodland Park out my front window. I've been on a hectic schedule all month and figured just gelling for a bit was a good thing. I was thinking to go rent a couple videos and just lay low because I wanted to go out Saturday night to hear a band I like, Numantra, which has a lead sitar instead of guitar – pretty cool.

I ended up staying in because I wrote a new poem that had started for me on Thursday night of the week before as I drove from Santa Barbara to Santa Cruz (cool trip – need to tell you about this later). The moon was out real bright and doing trippy things so I finally pulled over to the shoulder and made notes of all that I'd seen that seemed to belong in a poem. Well, Friday night I wrote the piece they belonged in.

Saturday morning I keyboarded it and did a bunch of HatLady stuff at my desk. I really can't remember much of Saturday other than I wasn't feeling very well. Oh! I napped a long three hours or so on the couch. So I braved leaving the house long enough to go rent videos. Sunday I still had one movie left to watch. I was not feeling right! I was taking the medication given to me but it didn't seem to be doing much. In fact, my breath kept getting shorter and shorter, to the point that by 3PM I called the Urgent Care desk at Group Health on Capitol Hill. I wasn't panicky yet so followed the nurse's suggestion to drink hot tea and give it an hour to calm down.

Four o'clock rolled around and it had leveled a bit but by 4:45 or so my breath got shorter and shorter faster and faster. I called the Urgent Care number again to confirm that if I got in there they'd have equipment to help me breathe. I was afraid to drive given thoughts of passing out behind the wheel or having a heart attack or God knows what. So I called Josh and Rosey. They weren't home. I called Marty who has no car but Hank and Katie were just leaving for Tacoma so dropped Marty at my place and he drove me down in my car.

He left me at the door in the Emergency drive-thru and went to park. I dashed inside, up to the desk and all I could gasp out was, "I need to breathe." They flew around the desk, yanked me into a room in back, slapped an oxygen mask on my face, slipped an IV in my arm. . . boom, I could breathe. Alright! I got up to leave saying, "Thanks!" The doctor entering the room at that moment told me to sit back down and said I was going nowhere.

They took an x-ray and it showed pneumonia on the lung area around my heart and, so, here I am in the hospital. They're giving me heavy-duty antibiotics by IV and a bronchial dilator. They've also got me huffing three different inhalers. I hope to talk them into letting me go home today since they're no longer running me through the gamut of breathing tests several times per day. The nurse tells me the IV antibiotic is really the only reason for me to stay now so I'm going to suggest that they can leave the little receiver tube in my wrist, send me home and I can drive back to the clinic when I'm due for antibiotics. We'll see what they say.

Okay! It's all confirmed. Rosey's going to be here to pick me up at 11AM and I'm going home. The doctor has assured me that if I go home and start smoking again I will unquestionably land right back in the hospital again. So! Needless to say I've got some serious thinking and *doing* to do.

I love you, dear Zoey, and want to be here to enjoy you!
All my love, *always*Mom

263

Journal: November 26, 1997

Something I didn't mention to Zoey in my letter was my True Addict Adventure. One night I was jonesing so bad for a cigarette that I got out of bed, put on my slippers, grabbed my IV pole and wheeled it to the door. I looked up and down the hall – not a soul in sight. I got my coat out of the little closet and proceeded to the elevator with my IV pole in tow. No one was around to watch me hop in and travel to ground floor.

I went out the nearest EXIT door and landed on a sidewalk butted up to a circular drive-thru. It was freakin' freezing but I stood there trembling and waited for a human being with tobacco to come by. It didn't take long to realize this was not a frequently used entry and was about to hang it up when a guy came sauntering up the walk. I hung on his every step in my direction. When he got within range the first words out of my mouth were, of course, "Have you got a cigarette by chance?" Thank God and my angels for bringing that guy my way. He handed me a cigarette, lit it for me, and made no notice of my attire or equipment. I actually got back to my room without crossing paths with anyone. What the fuck? Is this a hospital?

Yes, I do have to take some serious action on my smoking. I know I'm not going to quit so I have to change how I do it. I'm going to start rolling my own. And, I will no longer smoke at my desk. When I must have a smoke I'll walk away from the desk and go roll one; then pay attention to smoking it. Breathing smoke second-hand off the end sitting in the ashtray while I type is a waste of money and my lungs. Plus, it doesn't scratch the smoking urge itch. It seems every time I think to take another puff it's time to put it out so I just light another one to set down in the ashtray after the first drag again. Talk about a really stupid cycle.

I'm going to track on my calendar how many cigs I smoke each day for a few days then calculate a daily reduction plan to post. These are the new rules.

Speaking of rules, I broke a few in Ohio on this visit. I've been working with a number of the buyers for this company since late '95. They were my biggest account with the little hat company in Everett, before Evie split for L.A. and started her new company. I cold-called them one day and got lucky as they were looking for a low ball price on a huge hat order they had in house. It was quite a piece of work to get them on board with Evie's new company but they did come with me and are still my largest account and growing.

However, they have a lot of buyers that aren't using our services yet. So I suggested to Evie that we have an in-house luncheon catered in one of their conference rooms. We'd invite all the buyers in for lunch so they could meet me, their rep, and view samples of our offerings. Evie thought it was a great idea so with the help of a couple of my favorite buyers all the arrangements were made in advance.

On the big day I found the room was set up with school-room type desks, the kind one slides into from the side that has an attached arm holding a smallish tray to write on or put a plate on as was the case that day. I placed my business card and a pricing guide on each of the twenty or so desks that were arranged in a semi-circle facing the large table where I was able to lay out my samples. At the back of the room the lunch buffet had been set up. People came filing in. Those that I already work with came up to say hi and I hugged each of them. Everyone filled their plates and took a seat.

I introduced myself as the sales rep for Evie's company; mentioned the names of the buyers who already know me, stated that I looked forward to meeting the rest of them individually while on this two-day visit, and let them know I hoped to work with each of them as their hat and embroidery needs arose. Then I dealt them a surprise. I said that the folks who already work with me are familiar with my passion for the color purple and each of them chuckled. However, perhaps the rest of them might wonder about the purple stripe in my hair so, while they ate lunch and before I got into talking about product and services I was going to read them a poem I'd written about the color purple in hopes of offering an understanding and assurance that I'm not as weird as it might make me seem. A few had been eyeing me rather skeptically.

In the beginning it was tough
being purple and finding my own
Dad is blue and Mom is red
I'm the result of a seed they've sown

they've been very influential
since they both are a part of me
but they both have two sides
making for complexity
I got loyalty from my Dad
Mom gave me romance
he gave sad
she gave rage
the balance of all this was an intricate dance
until I blended
now I'm magic
I took all that red and blue gave me
then softened it down
now I fly on faery wings
I am the wizard's gown
I am love and passion
I am peace with power
I am nobility in grace
I am the petal of a flower
yes, it was tough in the beginning
but by patiently blending my gifts I've grown
into the beautiful hue I am
I am purple standing strong on my own

I recall the day I wrote that poem. I was feeling real colorful, downright rainbowish, and wrote a second poem I call God is a Color Carnival. I found it in my poetry folder, still in scribble format, while I searched for the Purple poem before I left on my trip and will staple it to this page when I'm done with the rule breaking story.

I definitely learned who I want to work with after reading the poem. Some made it clear they had no intentions of ever working with me by leaving the room as soon as they finished eating; saying sorry they couldn't stay for my product presentation as they were swamped at their desks but thanks for lunch. Others came up, after I discussed all my samples and the services we offer, made a point of introducing themselves, handed me their cards and said they hoped I would get by to their desks to see them and the jobs they're working on. They also commented that I was the first sales rep to ever read poetry to them and they loved it. It was super cool.

That night a handful of the folks I've been fond of for some time now went out to dinner with me. We all had a good laugh over the response to my poem and they let me know they weren't surprised by who ran out as fast as possible. We all agreed I likely wouldn't enjoy working with them any way.

After dinner we went to the only club in their suburban town that had music and I bought us all a round of drinks. A drink or two later a couple folks said they had to go. Shortly after they left one of the vice presidents of the company they all work for came to our table, said hello to me upon being introduced, then whispered in one of my companion's ears and walked away. When he was gone his confidante leaned across the table toward me with a big grin and asked if I had any weed on me because the veep was looking for some. My friend knows me well enough to think I might have some with me. I was absolutely amazed but said I did. Two got up, left the table, and soon returned with the veep in tow. He was now thoroughly delighted to have made my acquaintance. We few who remained went out to the parking lot and got in his SUV. I rolled a joint and we passed it around. I am still totally blown away by the whole thing. Whodathunk, huh? Rules schmools.

God is a Color Carnival

It is said
white is the presence of all color
spin the chromatic wheel and what do I see?
all hues blurring into one white light
the omnipotence of spectrum reigns over me
black is the absence of all color
black is the dark of despair
hope is in the rainbow
to reach the peace in white light
take a spin through the Color Fair

doo doo doodle oodle OO doo doo OO doo doo

calliope!
it's a carnival!
a prismatic cornucopia!

267

but watch out
they do it with mirrors
some colors have two sides
blue is closest to black
bummed out   broken hearted
true blue bumper car takes a beating
leaving me bruised
ah! purple
sad leaves for sovereign
majestically the magician waves his wand with passion
bordered next to the rage in red
rollercoastering to romantic and warm
Wild card!
Orange is the free ride!
I'm a coward when it comes to the ferris wheel
yellow and my bucket's swinging on the sunny side!
Caution! I'm green at the gills
envying those with their feet on the ground
I'm spinning – I want to get down!
I'm spinning & spinning & spinning & spinning
How can I get up if I haven't been down?
I'm spinning & spinning & spinning & spinning & spinning
WHITE & spinning & spinning & spinning & spinning
into the white light ... whew! ... Thank God!

November 28, 1997 – the day after Thanksgiving, in her bag

Hi Sweetie Heart – I thought of you all day yesterday.
I gave thanks that you are my daughter and that the day
when we'll be free to enjoy each other again draws nearer.
I am thankful that you are doing well (or at least as well as
can be) and that you're enjoying your senior year and making plans for (or at least thinking about) your future. I am
so <u>SO</u> VERY PROUD OF YOU! As always, I believe you are a
most beautiful soul.

I know that purple is not particularly your thing but
this little jewel is a symbol that I hope you will wear always.
It is now an earring, of course, but we can make it into a
ring or a pendant if you prefer. The thing is it is one of a
matched set and we each have one.

When I came back from Kauai and showed you how I had traded in the heart-shaped diamond in my wedding ring for a heart-shaped amethyst I think I told you my story or philosophy about that change but I will now repeat it. I don't know if this goes for the just the army or all military services or what but I do know that the Purple Heart is a medal given to those who have been wounded in action (perhaps during a particularly brave or heroic mission or. . . ? whatever). If one is alive to receive this medal, obviously this person has survived. We have in a very strong sense been wounded in action and survived. I hope you will wear this proudly, as I will mine, a symbol of your strength and beauty. We are survivors my dear Zoey.

You are in my heart forever and always
Your mom, your sister, your friend

Journal: Monday December 8, 1997, 8AM

a 7/5/7 Reverse Haiku of the day:

> I'm not just goofy-footed
> I'm just plain goofy
> And I quite like it that way

The other day I learned from my contact at Thrasher that the way I skate, using my left foot to push, is called goofy-footed. I told him the bunion on my left foot is on fire after a lap on the lake. He asked why. When I said that's my push foot he replied, "Oh, you're goofy." I retorted I didn't think I was all that goofy, that it's the only way my skateboard feels right to me. He laughed with, "No. I mean goofy-footed. That's what your style is called."

Journal: Sunday December 14, 1997

My Christmas cards are ready to mail tomorrow. I think my skate customers will enjoy the humor. My big front window is all dressed up for Christmas in a fun silly way. It's what inspired me to make the cards. I shot pictures of it, picked the best one, and then had reprints made. I got some Christmas-y stationery which I folded in half such that the card would open from the bottom up. On the front it reads:

Here's hoping this holiday season brings
more bare butts and buns swinging your way!
Wait – make that. . .

Then at the top of the inside:

> *. . .four bear butts, two bunnies with buttons,*
> *and two buddy boards below!*

On the bottom half of the paper I glued the photo:

Hoping 1998 is your best year yet,

Beth

and my window at Christmas time

Photo: courtesy of The HatLady

Journal: Sunday December 14, 1997 - continued

Haiku o' the day:

> People don't get me
> It's more rule than exception
> God bless exceptions

Part 3: Anger, Action, Joy, Fear

"...There's a lot of intellect around you. You're a very deep thinker; but you don't always share your thoughts. You're a very emotional person and will often let people see what you're feeling before you let them know what you're thinking... It's a time for you, I feel, of just really being clear on what hurts, what needs to change and getting your balance back; then recommitting or re-involving yourself..."

Excerpted from a transcription of the tape recording made during my first session with Teresa Carol, Spring 1992

26: Your Tree Comes To Life

Resolution Brings Conclusion

New Years Eve I came out to watch you play
knowing I could not continue this way
one last shot before mind over matter
hopeful this night the barrier would shatter
while your songs lingered in the air
I kissed your cheek on my own double-dare
and beckoned "Want to go shoot faeries?"

Your eyes widened in shock
I tripped into double-time talk
"Come on! it's a fun game!
sure it sounds wild but I'm fairly tame"
how is it that one so delightfully abstract
doesn't get your essence would surely attract
one of like mind? or see we're two of a kind?

Still you didn't feel the metaphor
once again you headed for the door
just one hour into the new year
I watched as your crew loaded your gear
you hopped into the get-away van
leaving me to wish you'd understand
you play so beautifully, why not with me?

Waiting for a cab in the pounding rain
I convinced myself there was nothing to gain
by allowing my mind
to give you more time
I resolved to no longer obsess
in the hope you'd one day bless
me and my gifts with your presence

273

CLIPS & CONSEQUENCES   PART 3: ANGER, ACTION, JOY, FEAR

Journal: January 1, 1998

I am done. No more. BINM was playing down in Pioneer Square last night. And, well, the poem says it all. I had a couple of my Christmas cards left and thought it would be a perfect way of explaining what it was I'd asked of him, "I have a bunch of un-inaugurated seasonal targets. Want to come shoot faeries?" So I pointed out the targets on the card adding, "Four bear and one bunny butts." Then half way down alongside the photo I drew a little arrow with, "Those are faery-shooters in front of the purple boa."

By my signature, on the top half, I wrote, "I hope you have huge success with the new CD. I'll look forward to having it and to coming out to see BINM when you're all unapproachably famous playing a big arena!" And, below the photo:

"T. – I'm sorry if I've given you cause to fear fans and/or have regrets around publishing T. Song. It was never my intent to bug you but then I never planned to put together a book of poetry either. Funny how things work sometimes."

I've made a couple trial versions of my poetry chapbook, "Your Tree & Collected Poems for Personal Freedom" - more on this later. I put T.'s Christmas card in a large envelope with one of the rough drafts of *Your Tree*. It will be in the mail tomorrow. I need to stroll by and get the numbers off his house. A walk is a great way to start the New Year.

I never did write "more on this later" as I was busy getting my poetry book out, making it happen. And, I continued to read at the poetry Slam and other open mike venues, going out to hear music, riding my skate board, and, of course, being The HatLady. Zoey was on my mind and in my heart every day, as always. And, I stayed in the rhythm of paging her daily with 1-4-3 and how many days to go.

274

January 8, 1998

Pulse

Where the lake once was
just yesterday
twilight faeries with wings aflutter
glissade slippity on 3-ply mylar
color: blue haze/amber/smoke
reflecting horizon in sky
pinprick accents bright
I fall in stride with the faeries
skate glide skate slide skate

Your tree shivers in scant lacy slip
black filigreed silhouette on
hazy mylar stellar ribbons
juxtapose streaming boa clouds

Legs akimbo, my butt settles on
the nose of my skateboard
longjohn layered back and hatted head
cozy into the bark of your tree
through thin slits
I see the lake is back
golden twinklies surfing the ripples

My heart feels a pulse echo
back to me
from your tree
two digits at the pulse
near my throat
assure me it's you

YOUR TREE

&

COLLECTED POEMS
FOR
PERSONAL FREEDOM

! LEGALIZE IT !

SIGN THE PETITION

VOTE

PROCEEDS TO BENEFIT THE WAR ON THE WAR ON POT

Purple
Stripe
Publishing

Our mission . . .
is to provide support to activist
groups from coast to coast who
are dedicated to the tasks of:

- exposing the misinformation and untruths which have rendered one of God's greatest gifts to mankind an evil, illegal plant

- educating citizens of the United States of America on the topic of hemp/cannabis/marijuana in the belief truth will eradicate fear

- ending prohibition, thereby ending the War on Drugs, which has become a frightening war on people

Support to activist groups will be both monetary via sharing profits on sales and by publishing pertinent and vital information to meet these ends.

This is a TREE - FREE book
40% hemp ▶ 40% flax ▶ 20% cotton
VIRGIN NON-WOOD FIBERS

When **HEMP** is grown in the USA again:

♥ this book & a multitude of environmentally friendly products will be more affordably priced

♥ lives of oxygen-giving trees will no longer need to be sacrificed for paper or building materials

♥ dependency on fossil fuels will be ended

♥ there will be countless new jobs

♥ U.S. citizens will benefit greatly by the medicinal & nutritional uses of this miracle plant

When **MARIJUANA** is legalized & regulated for adult use

★ users will create a new Tax Base

★ state & federal tax dollars can be allocated to schools & health care rather than more prisons for non-violent users & growers

★ incarceration can be reserved for real criminals

"Humankind has not woven the web of life. We are but one strand within it. Anything we do to the web we do to ourselves. All things are bound together. All things connect." **Chief Seattle**

YOUR TREE is an 8 poem chronology depicting one mother's means of abiding the loss of her right to parent her daughter due to the wrongful laws imposed on **marijuana** - 12 poems for personal freedom follow.

I dedicate
this book
to the most beautiful soul
I have the joy of knowing,
my daughter, Zoey
with hope that the people
of this great country
will wake up!
speak out!
and
lead the way
for all our children
and their children
to live in what can again be
the Land of the Free
and
the Home of the Brave

Please, be brave. . .

The Cause
   In my human condition,
   balancing on the tight rope of freedom of spirit
   drawn over the chasm of my broken
   mainstream middle-American family
   having danced far too long to the adversarial tune played
   by the father and step-mother of my child
   in concert with The Laws of The State of Washington
   in their treatment of Marihuana as an illegal substance,
   making criminals of those who choose to use it,
   I am enduring an imposed separation from my, now,
   seventeen-year-old daughter.

Now, well over two years into this imposed separation, I wish to offer a collection of my poetry, including the series entitled Your Tree, and other selected poems, for the benefit of humankind by donating 50% of all profits from the sale of this book to Washington Hemp Education Network (or 20% to W.H.E.N. and 30% to the activist group in the state where purchased) in the hope that through education, hence empathy, and applied efforts we can reverse the widespread effects of specific corporate and governmental brainwashing, ending this criminal injustice against the citizens of the United States of America known as Hemp Prohibition; allowing for a healthier, a more economically sound, a more ecologically safe, a more sane, a more peaceful, loving, and freer nation.

PLEASE buy several copies of *YOUR TREE*. . . give them as Christmas, Birthday, Ground Hog Day, No Occasion, Any Occasion, and *especially* simple I Love You gifts.

PLEASE read *The Emperor Wears No Clothes* by Jack Herer. Prohibition of Hemp Marihuana *does* affect your life daily. Educate yourself and pass the word with your gift.

PLEASE be aware! Know that we all must work together —*quickly*—with faith that the power of our collective energy and efforts can divert the path that is presently leading us to a police state. Your vote *does* count. Use this privilege, your right, and, as important, use your voice.

It is my hope that any one poem, or even line, in this book touches you in such a way—whether with humor or with heart—so as to spark you into action, to get involved.

Sincerely yours,
Beth Myrle Rice
advocating personal responsibility and use, not abuse

January 23, 1998
Attn: Sticker Guy
From: Beth Rice / Purple Stripe Publishing

Be a soldier in the

✌ **peaceful revolution**

Suggested Retail
$7.95
That may seem steep for this
little homegrown book but it
illustrates our whole point:
We want to grow at home!
Legalize it!
The cost of FREEDOM
has never been cheap!

- The dotted line denotes the overall size of the label
- PLEASE be sure to make adhesive REMOVABLE
- Ink is PMS #349 Green onto Clear mylar
- Size has been reduced to approx. 4 ¾" X 2 ½"
- Quantity ordered = 1,000 labels

Thanks!   Beth

When informed the label company's minimum order was one thousand pieces I was hopefully naive in thinking that not only could I sell so many books but I'd be reordering stickers soon. After roaming through many of the indy book stores around Seattle to see how other poets published their chapbooks I determined I'd do it differently. Most chapbooks were in rough shape with curled corners on the covers and often with tattered edge pages. I found clear plastic envelopes the perfect size for holding my books. They also had resealable flaps. That feature was my cause for ordering the labels. I planned that when delivering inventory to each book store, I'd bring one store sample for customers to peruse and all the others would be protected in the clear envelopes. Where I ordered removable labels, for ease of handling once purchased, I figured the appeal would deter people from opening the envelopes, particularly when a sample book was readily available.

<u>February 2, 1998</u>
From: Beth Rice
To: Book Editor @ The Stranger
Re: Your Tree & Collected Poems for Personal Freedom
    (book enclosed)

Dear Editor,

On January 30th I emailed you in response to the ad for The Rendezvous Reading Series and today I am following up on that with a mailing to the snail-mail address shown in that ad. This submission to you, at The Stranger, may be redundant but, if so, only to the degree I am seeking every possible means to gaining exposure for my book.

It is my hope that you'll read my enclosed book of poetry and offer a review of it in your column. I think of most of my poetry as accessible, written with a clear message that most can relate to or at least understand. My goal with the pieces selected for this book is to reach and touch the mainstream populace. Where the cover of the book is not likely to attract that buyer it hopefully will catch the attention of the hempster who can forward the message, the book, along to one or more of the "brainwashed" (critics of the movement to legalize and regulate the use and sale of marijuana) in their sphere of influence.

Last year when Ralph Seeley addressed the attendees at Hempfest he commented something to the affect, 'Here I am preaching to the choir again." It's time for the choir to sing louder, not just "in church" but to all that will listen to reason.

My "little homegrown book" has just become retail ready. This is a very grassroots effort to open the minds of the general populace to education on the topic of Legalization of Hemp/Cannabis/Marijuana, in all its forms and all that it has to offer the human race and the environment we live in. It is my goal to place it in a number of independent book stores, music stores and hemp-goods stores not only around Seattle and the state of Washington but as far-reaching as I can get with it via telemarketing and mail. Sales and marketing is my specialty.

Additionally, W.H.E.N., Washington Hemp Education Network, has agreed to run a link from their website to mine-yet-to-be-established in hopes of promoting direct

mail-order sales. I will be contacting other pro-legalization groups with web-sites for the same purpose. Also on my agenda is a call to the display ad department at The Stranger as I believe that an advertisement featuring the product with the tag line "Available at:" will be attractive to the stores I hope to place it in, especially if you also review the book. I have applied to read at the Seattle Poetry Festival and will also apply to read at Bumbershoot. And, as much as time allows while burning my candle at three ends, I am reading at Open Mikes and seeking featured reader slots (The Globe 3/3/98) around town to promote both my book and W.H.E.N. Thank you for your time and consideration.
Sincerely,
Beth Rice
Purple Stripe Publishing

I don't know why I was compelled to detail my marketing plan for the book reviewer. I think perhaps I was hoping he was on my side, so to speak, that he was in agreement with the goal of legalization—I mean, after all, he worked for The Stranger. And, no doubt, I thought dangling potential ad revenues would be a point in my favor.

I did indeed place a number of ads in The Stranger, not just to promote book sales but also in hope of drawing people to the First Monday of Every Month March[s] planned by W.H.E.N. I loved the prospect of legitimately writing off the advertising expense while simultaneously promoting an event not sanctioned by the IRS due to the purposeful goal of changing public policy. No review of *Your Tree* ever graced the pages of The Stranger; nor were any of my applications to the cited readings accepted, excepting The Globe.

Journal: February 25, 1998, Wednesday

Haiku o' th' day: I get in the box
step gingerly to your tree
over gangly vines

Saw an angel butt
one cheek white and one cheek black
sun in blue spot sky

Journal: March 3, 1998
"Featured Reader" debut at The Globe:
       Homeland by Salon Productions
Reading: The Cause, Truth In Bones, Your Tree: 1 to 6

I had the joy of reading a lot of poetry tonight to a full house. I feel I was well received. Josh came to video tape me so I could use it to work on my performance. We got there early to have a bite to eat. He had something stupid to say about every person who came in The Globe. He was commenting on their hair, their tattoos, but especially their piercings. With his, "I've never seen so many holes in so many faces" I told him to be quiet, quit being rude.

I asked him to please do a test run on the camera to make sure it was working. He wouldn't, said it was under control. When it was over and we were headed home he confessed the realization, "There's a lot of intelligence behind those holes." And, I learned that there was no video for me. The film still had that clip on it, the one it comes packaged with to hold the reels static. Since I was actively reading by the time he figured it out he didn't want to be monkeying with it making noise. He was a tad sheepish.

I wrote an introduction to my reading but didn't use it because it seemed too long and perhaps contrived. I had fun writing it though:

Good evening. Thank you all for being here. And, thank you, Salon Productions for having me. I'm Beth The HatLady, the founder and sole employee of Purple Stripe Publishing, a soon-to-be-licensed business so the DEA can't come after me for tax evasion when I start to realize profits on the sale of this book—fifty percent of which will go to an organization called W.H.E.N., Washington Hemp Education Network, because it's going to take a lot of cash, time and talent to undo sixty years of brainwashing the citizens of the United States of America have been subjected to. For those of you at the back, the book is entitled *YOUR TREE & Collected Poems for Personal Freedom* and advocates, below the lovely marijuana leaf, "LEGALIZE IT! SIGN THE PETITION, VOTE!

Legalization means different things to a lot of people and a lot of industries. Let me just say it's not about smoking pot. It's about the ideals of personal freedom that our great country was founded on. It's about *not* living in a police state, which is where we'll be if people don't pull their heads out of the sand pretty damn fast!

I want to share this Calvin & Hobbes comic with you that has been hanging on my refrigerator since 1992. You can tell by how yellowed it is it wasn't printed on hemp paper. But, it does hold a universal truth. Calvin & Hobbes are cruising through the woods, log-walking and stream-hopping. Calvin is chattering to Hobbes, "Isn't it strange that evolution would give us a sense of humor? When you think about it, it's weird that we have a physiological response to absurdity. We laugh at nonsense. We like it. We think it's funny. Don't you think it's odd that we appreciate absurdity? Why would we develop that way? How does it benefit us?"

They come to a clearing and Hobbes turns to Calvin with, "I suppose if we couldn't laugh at things that don't make sense we couldn't react to a lot of life."

Hobbes keeps walking. Calvin stops, looking bewildered. He turns to the reader and says, "I can't tell if that's funny or really scary."

What I think is scary and what doesn't make sense to me are the vast economic and ecological losses experienced in our country, and the terrible personal losses and pain caused by the prohibition of this beautiful, multi-purposeful God-given plant.

Josh's early commentary at The Globe that night was inspiration for this poem. Then I really got on a roll:

FREAK

I keep wondering
at what turn of the page in our history books
at what bend or fork in the road
was it decided
and by whom
that in order to be acceptable to society
one must be shaped by
an approved cookie cutter
and packaged with hundreds of dozens
of bland, flavor-free look-alikes?

When did the size of the cash roll in one's pocket
become more important than the size or content
of one's heart?
how is it that if one isn't wearing
the blue collar of the working class
or isn't wrapped in gray suiting
striving for the next rung up
on the corporate ladder to success
that one will not be considered
a productive contribution to society
but instead be labeled
FREAK?

I see a young woman
wearing an angelic face
poetry springing
from her warm and friendly smile
at least a dozen pink pigtails
crowning her with grace
while a cookie from the cutter of masses
labels her
FREAK

I see a glorious modern day minstrel
with unadorned fingers
cradling the neck of his guitar
while his rings are worn in lip and nose
from lobe to top of ear
a cookie from the cutter of masses deems
"He'll never go far"
and labels him
FREAK

I see two strong men strolling hand in hand
sparks of love igniting when their eyes meet
and two strong women
arms draped 'round each other's waist
no longer taking heed when told "This is your place"
and a cookie from the cutter of masses labels them all
FREAKS

285

I was a cookie shaped by the cutter of masses
but must have fallen from the spatula
on my way to the cooling rack
still, with only a small flat spot on my head
and the rest of me intact
it was decided I'd be schooled
to be like everyone else
I'd be pushed to run in the Race for More
I'd be taught the tactics of War
to shoot down the non-conforming
to bomb the camps of society's wrong
while upholding society's right
I was left to live halfheartedly that way
'til a fork was flung in my path
causing me to trip and fall
on that little flat spot on my head
now I march to the beat of my heart
on Sunday's I don't go to the Church of Right
since God lives in me every day I skate the lake instead
during the work week I compete
in cookie cutter games with flair
with kindness and love
and a majestic purple stripe in my hair
I now skip in the grass
along the edge of society's road
I can no longer
walk their walk
or talk their speak
paint me proud
to be labeled FREAK

26: Graduation

I took care of the IRS in full! Purple Stripe Publishing web-site got set-up. There are some pages still to fill in. The logo turned out cool. I hand drew it so it goes well with hand-made books. Gotta sleep!

Journal: May 4, 1998

Saturday, May 2nd, Ben and I went to a concert/festival sort of thing up at the Rexville Grange near Mount Vernon. It was a fun time and for a good cause: to benefit Hempfest. I'm supposed to be writing lists now. . .

May 10, 1998

Mother's Day

I am a faery
living in a rainbow
in another life of mine
living right next to now
I go home to my purple stripe
gliding up on a white light cord
through the middle of a star
in the middle of the black sky night
emerging into sun
on glistening wet air
I play in my rainbow
as a faery I do that well
sliding down that white light cord
into a new now
on a ferry
on the water
on my way home
Erin is a faery
at the lake
in another now
I saw her near your tree

Journal: May 12 – 13 - 14, 1998

Ben ROCKS! We burned the midnight oil and he filled in all the holes at the PSP website.

Sunday morning, before I went over to Mom's, I skated and touched base with Zoey at her tree. As I cozied into the bark a little faery strolled by. I couldn't believe it. Erin, one of the poets who frequents the Globe, had donned faery wings to go walking on Mother's Day. I love it. . .hence the poem.

Journal: May 16, 1998, Saturday

It wasn't about exercise
been busy
too windy too
haven't skated for weeks, it's okay
wasn't about that anyway
it wasn't about skating
the wind is my friend
had to connect with Earth today
walked through the trees
the lake beckoned
but I turned at each fork
taking the path less beaten
tiny white daisies dotting the grass
a sport clad gazelle bounded by
people energy on the right
to my left the road calls
I forge forward
padding of pine 'neath my feet
hill stretching my calves
till my back connects at all points
with our mother
jumping flat jack snow angels on the grass
sundog greets me, I'm humming
cartwheel clowning across the crest
somersaulting down to the earth
connecting with wind sounds on quiet
and me
I was about joy

My HatLady office had been moved out of my apartment since February when my boss, Evie, agreed that I needed an assistant. Until then the hours I'd been putting in each day were ridiculously long. My day started early, often as early as 5:30AM, for the buyers at my largest corporate client in Ohio were at their desks by then. I would finish up daily details around jobs in process and new jobs to be done with them by noon. After a quick bite for lunch, fixed in my kitchen which was adjacent to my office in the space intended to be my dining area, I'd start checking in with all my west coast skateboard manufacturing clients to give them status updates on their orders in process and to see what was new and coming up next. By 4:30 or 5PM I'd take a bong hit or two accompanied by half a beer then head out for a lap on the lake with my skate. I'd drink the other half of the beer while getting a bit of dinner made; then, settle into an evening of finishing paper work in follow-up to my day of phone.

I told Evie that it could be difficult getting an assistant willing to work in an in-home office plus getting the office out of my home would make it possible for me to stay away from my desk at night. She had been paying me a one hundred dollar stipend each month for the office use of my home so when I found an office space within a real estate office just a few blocks up the street for a mere $300 per month she signed a six month rental agreement with no argument.

I placed an ad in the University of Washington's newspaper because it would be an easy bus ride to the office for a student and part-time help was all I needed.

Late one afternoon at the top of June, after my assistant had gone for the day, I was tidying my desk getting ready to leave when the door to my office opened. I looked up to find Zoey and a couple friends walking in. I blinked in disbelief then, "Come in! Come in," and quickly moved to the foot of the few stairs giving entry to my office. I threw my arms around her when she reached the bottom and asked, "How did you find me? How'd you know where to look?"

"I saw an envelope from you in my dad's office once and remembered you live by Green Lake. We were just driving around after hanging out with some friends in the U District and I saw your car. The lady in the office up front pointed us to your door back here."

"Only you, Zoey. You're unbelievable." She introduced me to her friends. I asked the question having an obvious answer, "Are you getting excited about graduation?"

"Yeah. But I'm more excited about being emancipated." She went on to tell me that she and Crystal had not spoken for months; and, it seemed to be causing grief for her dad and her. "I had a talk with him. I told him I wanted to live my own life so he should work on holding it together with Crystal - that she'd be living with him longer than me and it would probably be easier with me out of the picture. So, he agreed to emancipate me, to sign documents stating that I am capable of managing my own affairs so I can legally move out of his house before I'm eighteen, right after graduation."

"Wow! I'm amazed he agreed to that. But, I'm glad for you. So what's your plan?"

Zoey informed me that she and a friend from school planned to get an apartment together; and, that she would start working full-time at the frame shop where she had worked after school for over a year. Then she told me she and her friends needed to get going. I gave her both my home and office phone numbers and asked her to call me as soon as she had her own phone. We got a long hard hug, exchanged "I love you" and she left me feeling a warm happiness yet overshadowed by a sense of uneasiness I couldn't explain.

June 4, 1998 - a letter from Eric

Dear Beth,

It has been a long time since we have talked about Zoey and since she is close to graduating from high school I thought that I should give you an update.

On many levels Zoey is doing great! She got first place out of fifty-nine high schools in the state for a photography contest in the area of formal portraits. She was awarded $100 and her photo is on display at the Seattle Art Museum. She has received a special award at school from the photography department. In addition, she got a 3.5 on her last report card and looks to be doing the same as she finishes up here in a few days. Since she finally got her 3.0 she started drivers' education and will be finished with that about the 16th of June.

She says that she intends to go to Shoreline Community College in the fall, and has applied and been accepted. She will need to register this summer. She has said that she wants to be a photography teacher at a high school someday. To me this sounds like a great plan!

She has only been taking four classes this last quarter as she only needed half a credit to graduate. I don't think she has made the most of high school but she is graduating. There was a time when I wasn't sure she would. She graduates June 11th and is moving out into an apartment June 12th along with a friend or two.

She has done a great job at the frame shop. This will turn into a full time job when school is out and I'm quite sure that she'll be gainfully employed as she heads out on her own. It's a very low pressure job but a good job for her and she likes it.

As a graduation present Crystal and I are going to put up one thousand dollars and Zoey is going to put up one thousand dollars and buy a car. She will need to buy the insurance. I am looking around now. I want her to have a safe car.

On a relationship level, things haven't been the best. Naturally, I'm stupid and don't know a thing about anything. Zoey feels that she has been mistreated and dealt with unfairly. I feel in many ways that she has mistreated me and dealt with me unfairly as every day has been a struggle. Trying to please me has been the last thing on her list. Hopefully in time we can look back over the years and find something good to look back on. Zoey has so many talents and good traits that it is still very hard to handle her manipulative and deceptive side. She lacks maturity but that hopefully will come in time. She can astound you with her intellect and sensitivity, then the next moment dumbfound you with her attitude and unwillingness to do the right thing – if for no other reason than to be stubborn and in control.

In my opinion Zoey spends too much time with kids with no direction. Many of them are not graduating or have dropped out all together, yet others have done real well. Zoey tends to gravitate toward real needy kids. They take advantage of each other and it goes both ways between them. I believe this stems from a void that Zoey has lived with as a result of your absence; all the treatment issues and living in a blended family (although I have never discussed this with her). Of course these are just my opinions. I think that with a car of her own, a busy work schedule, the natural transitions that occur after high school, and new friends to meet at college maybe she'll get in a circle of friends that are a little more ambitious.

Zoey and Crystal have virtually stopped dealing with each other over the last several months. Crystal tired of Zoey's nonsense, and Zoey figured she could wait it out until June 12th. It's been very hard on me as I care about both of them. As far as I can tell, she doesn't smoke, doesn't do drugs, doesn't drink, and isn't pregnant.

This next week I plan to emancipate Zoey. In as much as she refuses to follow my rules or even to confront or come up with compromises, I haven't any choice. She wants to come and go without any restriction – reasonable or otherwise. I feel that she needs to be held accountable for her actions and that she has duties around the house and to Crystal and me. I guess she'll have to go out on her own to see the "real world." If she is not going to work with me on things, I am not going to be responsible for her.

Zoey has asked a lot of questions about our relationship, how things happened etc. I have given her my perspective, but have not spent the last several years dwelling on old issues. I have tried to be the best father I could be, and have tried to be a good parent, realizing that being a good parent isn't the same as being her best friend. I've told her several times that I may not have been the perfect parent but that she hasn't been the perfect child. At her request, I have supplied her with copies of our agreements for the final parenting plan and judgment.

I'm sure that she will want to get together with you as soon as possible. She has said that she is nervous about it all. But I have assured her that she has nothing to be nervous about, that you would be anxious to see her and might be a little

nervous too, and, that there can be another opportunity for both of you.

I wish things could have been different, for
everyone's sake, especially Zoey's.

I don't expect to hear too much from Zoey in
the next few months (hope I'm wrong) while she's
exploring her new found freedom. But, as we both
know from our own experiences, her long term success and happiness is so dependent on the next
couple of years and the choices she makes. It is
my sincerest hope that all of us have learned from
our mistakes and don't make them all over again.
Lets both agree to guide Zoey towards making the
right choices, for the right reasons – if she gives
us the opportunity.

Zoey will need our help I am sure in the months
to come. I don't know in what way she will need it,
but I do know that some of the lessons she will
need to learn will come the "hard" way. It will
be very important to be supportive of her positive
choices and decisions, to help her with the choices
that may not be the best, but not to bail her out
all the time if she repeatedly gets herself in
trouble. Tough love is the hardest to give.

Zoey is very smart and capable of being very
successful. It is once again time for you to look
deep into your heart and be prepared to step up
to the challenge, emotionally and financially; to
help her make the most of her college experience
and make the sacrifices necessary and so important
for our daughter. Circumstances suggest that it
might be time for me to back away and my guess is
that you'll be needing to step forward. You knew
this day was coming.

I guess this is sounding like a lecture and
it's truly not meant to be. It is I guess a statement of my feelings, hopes, and since we don't communicate an attempt to let you know that I want the
best for all of us in the future. Hopefully we are
older and wiser. What's done is done. Zoey is her
own person and has her own personality. I love her
generosity and the spark that she carries with her.
Lets both make a real effort to keep her headed in
the right direction.

I would have never dreamed on the day Zoey was
born that her childhood would have turned out the
way that it did; or that as her parents it would

have turned out the way it has. I hope that the next passage of her life brings her happiness and success. And I hope that someday Zoey will be able to look back at her life and her parents and be proud of both.
Eric

I added a postscript at the bottom of the page:
My greatest challenge
in this life
is to find forgiveness
for you and your wife

Journal: June 6, 1998

I got the attached letter from Eric today. He blows me away, a freaking rerun! I remember once hearing how it was his obligation to not bury his head in the sand when it comes to Zoey and her doings. Either his head is buried up his ass or he is blind: "As far as I can tell, she doesn't smoke, doesn't do drugs, doesn't drink..." Hmm – this sounds just like 1995 to me; he has a clear idea of what she's up to -*how could he NOT?-* and once again this sums it up, ". . .I am not going to be responsible for her." He can't demand that I will now take custody so maybe a reminder letter will do.

He got her through high school so now it's my turn to "step forward." Only this time it's not a matter of me being the *visiting* parent who's inexperienced in dealing with my teenage daughter on a day to day basis full-time. Hell no! Now, after being banned for three and a half years, it's my time to step up and parent a legally adult teenager. What a fucking jerk!!!

June 10, 1998, the card I made for Zoey's graduation,
tucked into her 1998 bag

Arriving at the top of the hill
she found before her
hill upon hill still
beyond the valley floor
where paths converged
from all points encompassed
in a universe of choice

She turned
eyes retraced in a glance
the climb behind to find
love in every foot print
that had carried her to this point
of the plan she'd made

Origins obscured
in the mist of the mind
Freedoms clearing the way
for this day of new
Beginnings

I did not go to her graduation, of course, but Mom received an invitation. She told me she'd take lots of pictures. With an empty hollowed out feeling in the pit of my stomach it was difficult to ward off the inclination to kick myself around the block some more. And, fear still had a stronghold on my consciousness, fear for what the ramifications might be for me reconnecting with Zoey before she turned eighteen.

From Eric's letter I got that he expected me to immediately be there for her. Given I didn't trust him any further than I could throw him, for all I knew he was setting me up. If Zoey's behavior post-graduation fell out of approval I could be the fall guy, the blame.

I wondered if the terms of the Parenting Plan would become moot once she was considered a legal adult in the eyes of the law. So I asked the guys who head up Hempfest if they knew an attorney to recommend me to for counsel on the topic. Indeed they did so I called her and made an appointment.

I took my copy of the final Parenting Plan and Eric's recent letter to the appointment. The attorney looked them over then asked how the Parenting Plan had come into play. I explained the situation. She suggested to me that the only end date stated in the Plan was the date that I completed a certified treatment program and applied to the court for supervised visits. Since that had not occurred, she said I would be most wise to wait until Zoey turned eighteen and was fully, beyond a shadow of concern, a legal adult before I had blatant open contact with her.

28: H.A.T. Is Born

✦ June 1998 ✦   ✦ A newsletter for northwest hemp and marijuana activists ✦

Initiative 692 Update

by Tim Killian, Campaign Coordinator

INITIATIVE 692 — Washington State Medical use of Marijuana act

The campaign to legalize the medicinal use of marijuana is well under way here in Washington State. Initiative 692, the Washington State Medical Use of Marijuana Act, is the product of many hours of discussion, negotiation, and input from a wide variety of sources including patients, doctors, law enforcement agencies, politicians, activists, and citizens from across the State. It is based on Senate Bill 6271 sponsored by Senator Jeanne Kohl (D-36). Thanks go to those who were involved in the process, most notably to Robert Lunday, who worked hard to bring together many of the different drafts and ideas from the activist community. I-692 is truly one of the premier medical marijuana initiatives in the country.

We have entered the signature gathering stage, and are working towards collecting 179,248 valid signatures from Washington State voters prior to the deadline of July 2, 1998. We are confident that this deadline will be met, and look forward to working with many volunteers in addition to paid signature gatherers to reach the requirement. Contact us directly if you would like petitions for gathering signatures.

Our funding has again been seeded by the same individuals who funded initiative 685 last year. They told us that if 685 proved to be too much too soon, that they would be back to support us in the narrower issue of medicinal marijuana. Their commitment to this issue is strong, and those of us who support it owe them much thanks. However, we do need to raise local funds as well, and appreciate any and all contributions that can be given. Again, contact us directly if you would like to contribute. At this point of the campaign, we are busy preparing behind the scenes for the public campaign which will be waged following validation of our signatures. We are seeking endorsements from both public officials and organizations. We are already finding stronger community reception this year than was found for last year's initiative 685. The much Continued on page 3

Seattle Hempfest searches for funding

by Ben Livingston

Organizers of the Seattle Hempfest, one of the largest politically-oriented music festivals in the country, say they are flat broke.

During last year's hot summer, Hempfest fell on one of the few rainy days, said organizer Vivian McPeak in a request for contributions. "We were financially bankrupted by the unusually low turnout."

Besides last year's low turnout, McPeak cites growing production costs and monetary requirements of the City of Seattle as reasons they are broke. This year, Hempfest started $850 in debt. "We have never gone into a year without start-up capital," says McPeak.

With a medical marijuana initiative expected to make the ballot in this year, organizers feel that this is a pivotal year for the northwest marijuana movement. In such a year, they say, Hempfest could play a vital role in advancing the causes of medical marijuana.

Despite the financial woes, McPeak says they are making headway. "The official authorization for the special events permit from the City of Seattle has been granted in a record two meetings. The previous record was seven." Organizers also say they have secured 90% of the equipment required to produce the 1998 Hempfest.

Donations to Hempfest can be mailed to 916 NE 65th St. Suite 269, Seattle, WA 98115. Hempfest can be reached by telephone at (206) 781-5734, through email at hempfest@hemp.net or via the web at www.seattlehempfest.com.

Inside:

296

Letter from the publisher:

About The Activist. . .

Unless you or someone very close to you has ever been one, there is a good chance that you aren't quite sure what exactly an activist is or does or, for that matter, how they came to be one. This certainly was the case with me. The interesting thing is that the Activist Me was lying dormant for quite a long time. I saw things happening within public policy that I didn't like or that have had a detrimental effect on the environment around me but concluded there was nothing I could do about it or figured, "Someone else is taking care of it."

I now know that someone is me, you, your neighbor, the lady up the street, the student next door. These folks have full-time jobs, perhaps spouses and families, certainly a full plate of personal responsibilities. No one has been officially assigned to the task of fixing the situation. Few are paid for their efforts but they spend a good deal of their available time fighting for a cause that matters to them - learning about the politics around the issue, getting to know the political figures in their area, banding together with like-minded people and reaching out to others who might also join in to take action on the issue - rocking the boat and making waves until it rolls over, until it's resolved.

It seems that many activists have had some type of awakening or slap in the face to jolt them out of that complacent way of thinking that "It's being handled." Nothing seems to be too much of an issue until it truly touches, or more likely, *rams*, your life. And, then, it's usually on the blind side. This is certainly the case with me and with many others. This is particularly true when looking at the activists working to End Drug Prohibition. There are many people who hold the opinion that laws should be changed but they do nothing to make it happen. Again, this was me. I am making a plea to you. Don't wait for a devastating event in your life or in that of someone you love to activate - take action - become an activist.

I hope you find Hemp Activist Times interesting, enlightening and, most of all, motivating. You can hop in at any time. Whatever you have to give in the way of time and energy you will be greatly appreciated. I want to heartily thank Ben Livingston for spawning the idea for this newsletter and pulling it all together; as well as the many dedicated activists who have been working diligently for years to re-legalize hemp/marijuana. Look for us again next month!

Beth Myrle Rice

Hemp Activist Times

June 1998

PUBLISHER: Beth Myrle Rice

EDITOR: Ben Livingston

CONTRIBUTING WRITERS: Tyree Callahan, Tim Killian, Ben Livingston, Robert Lunday

SPECIAL THANKS: Eve Lentz, Seattle Gay News

HEMP ACTIVIST TIMES is published monthly by Purple Stripe Publishing. Copyright 1998.

We are always looking for story ideas, news, writers and friendly folks to distribute Hemp Activist Times in your area. If you want to help out, please contact us. We need your help!

Postal: PO Box 95227
          Seattle, WA 98145-2227
Voice: (206) 405-5862
 Web: http://www.hemp.net/hat/
Email: hat@hemp.net

ANNOUNC
RELEAS
Your Ti
& Collected P
Personal Fri

A book to benefit **The War** on **The** I

YOUR TREE is a 7 poem chronol
casualty of **The War on Drugs** - a p
the outside

Stop by any of these fine establis
pick up a book of poetry for The
Reasonable Legislation and Reg
Hemp/Marijuana

Capitol Hill: Pistil Books, 1013 Eas
The Globe Cafe, 14th @ E. Pine - .
Hemp Mercantile, top floor of Broa
Market; Fremont: Wit's End, 34th S
the Aurora Bridge; Wallingford: Op
A Poem Emporium 2414 N. 45th S

Can't get out? Visit Purple Strip
http://www.hemp.net/~purp

Washington State activist organizati

Green Cross Patient Co-op
PO Box 47347
Seattle, WA 98126
http://www.hemp.net/greencross/

The Green Cross is a patient co-op
established to provide medical marijuana
to patients.

November Coalition
795 South Cedar
Colville, WA 99114
(509) 684-1550
http://www.november.org/
moreinfo@november.org

The November Coalition is dedicated to

Washington Citizens for Hemp Reform
916 NE 65th St. Suite 269
Seattle, WA 98115
(206) 781-5734
http://www.hemp.net/wchr/
hempfest@hemp.net

WCHR undertakes the massive task of
organizing the Seattle Hempfest every
year.

Washington Citizens for Medical Rights
PO Box 2346
Seattle, WA 98111
(206) 781-7716
http://www.eventure.com/i692/
cdpr@eventure.com

Washington Hemp Educa
PO Box 1217
Olympia, WA 98507
(360) 866-6523
http://www.olywa.net/whe
when@olywa.net

WHEN's mission is to en
through educational acti
more informed choic
regulation of hemp.

Washington Media Aware
http://www.televar.co
wamap.html
thawkins@mapinc.org

Journal: June 15, 1998

Tower Books on Queen Anne has placed *Your Tree* on display right up front by the cash registers along with a

stack of Hemp Activist Times and a couple clipboards holding the petitions for Initiative 692. I go in about once a week
to pick up the filled petitions and put more empties on the
clipboards.

Journal: June 17, 1998

I made it to the final round of reading at the Poetry
Slam tonight for the first time after about two years of read-
ing/slamming. It felt so damn good. People came up to me
and told me how much they liked my reading. It felt great. I
read FREAK first, Ode to T. 2 next, and Roadtrippin' & Signs.
. . in the final round. I would actually have won the Slam
tonight except for the fact that Roadtrippin' went overtime
so my score was docked for each ten seconds over - dang.

Journal: June 20, 1998 – Haiku O' Th' Day

Faith is vitamin
E oil to the would-be scars
on my heart and soul

Journal: Friday July 3, 1998

Woohooo! Over 250,000 signatures were turned in (the
goal was 179,000) and Medical Marijuana will be on the
November ballot!!

At Pain In The Grass, Ben and I handed out four hundred
flyers with the PSP ad for *Your Tree* on one side and info for
the First Monday of Every Month Marches on the other side.
Plus, we handed out three hundred flyers for Hempfest.

Journal: Saturday July 4, 1998

Ben and I handed out about eight hundred Hempfest/
March Schedule flyers at Ivar's Fourth of July in Myrtle
Edwards Park.

Journal: Sunday July 5, 1998

I skated two laps on the lake. I paged Zoey in the morning,
noonish and night. . . nothing. . . nada. I called her apartment
and her roommate, Tom, said she hasn't been home. I am
scared shitless worried about her. He said she's hanging out
with crystal meth heads.

On Thursday June 18th she called me after getting home
to her new space, the apartment she's sharing with Tom, to
tell me that we are free. She is too busy partying though to

get together with me. Then I was out of town on business for eight days.

I paged her on Friday, Saturday, and now today. . . nothing. I haven't seen her. Once, before leaving town, she returned my page; and once she was home when I phoned over there. We've talked twice since June 18th. On one of the calls I told her about the bags I have for her. I hoped that we could get together and I could watch her go through the bags, that hopefully a light would dawn and she'd know that I had been with her every day. She asked if it'd be okay for Tom to pick them up. That request really shocked me. But I viewed the bags as a possible bridge to connect us so I said yes. It didn't feel good to let go of the bags in this way but at the same time I wanted her to have them.

On my trip I left sample books at eight stores in Ann Arbor, Michigan, home of the famous annual Hash Bash. Seven were book stores and one was an upscale hemp clothing store. In San Francisco eight book stores got sample books. The City Lights Book Store at North Beach, "home" to Ginsberg, Kerouac, Burroughs and the like, asked for a dozen books! And, another store A Different Light wants six!! Yahoody! Gotta get to bed.

Journal: July 9, 1998

I had a date with Zoey last night, our first time seeing each other. More than ever I am worried about the company she's choosing to keep, "The Party Family."

Journal: July 16, 1998

Zoey and I had our second "date." Some real communication happened!

Journal: July 21, 1998

Pearl Jam is entered into the Top Ten of my all-time favorite concerts. What an incredible show. Zoey came with me, Pat and Lonni.

Journal: July 25, 1998

To Do's: got to PSP mailbox
        talk to the Hempfest heads -
        get flyers for Pain In The Grass and general posting

Hemp Activist Times

❀ July 1998 ❀ | A newsletter for northwest hemp and marijuana activists ❀

Lieutenant Governor under investigation

by Ben Livingston

The Washington State Executive Ethics Board has determined that reasonable cause exists to believe Lieutenant Governor Brad Owen used state resources to oppose Initiative 685, the 1997 ballot measure that would have allowed doctors to prescribe schedule I drugs such as marijuana, heroin and LSD.

The Ethics Board exists to investigate violations of RCW 42.52, the chapter of Washington law dealing with ethics in public service. Section 180 of this chapter states that "No state officer or state employee may use or authorize the use of facilities of an agency, directly or indirectly, for the purpose of assisting a campaign for election of a person to an office or for the promotion of or opposition to a ballot proposition."

Two separate complaints were filed with the board regarding Owen's

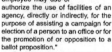

Just how ethical is Lieutenant Governor Brad Owen?

questionable campaigning, one by the board itself and the other by attorney Jeff Haley on behalf of Citizens for Drug Policy Reform, the organization behind I-685. The complaints included eight alleged violations.

On April 2, Owen responded to a request for an opinion on I-683. This initiative was reworded and later resubmitted as I-685. While public officials are allowed to respond to inquiries about their stance on an issue, Owen then forwarded the response to every legislator.

In conjunction with the April 2 letter, Owen directed Tim McGillivray, an employee of the Senate Democratic Caucus, to develop a press release announcing the letter Owen sent to all the legislators.

In response to a request for information on AIDS and marijuana, Owen allegedly directed staff member Vaughn Bunch to include a copy of the press release and the initial letter to the legislators.

On April 17 and April 24, Owen sent out letters titled "Today's Pot Shots!" in response to inquiries. The first addressed the issue of marijuana as medicine and the second touched on Arizona's proposition 200 and the

Continued on page 7

House Resolution 372
by Ben Livingston

On February 26, U.S. Representative Bill McCollum (R-Florida) and eight co-sponsors introduced House Resolution 372, which states that the House is "unequivocally opposed to legalizing marijuana for medicinal use, and urges the defeat of State initiatives which would seek to legalize marijuana for medicinal use."

The bill was scheduled for a vote on May 5, but the Republican leadership decided to postpone the vote on May 4 for reasons unknown.

Resolutions are non-binding and don't create any laws. They simply state congress's stance on an issue.

The Marijuana Policy Project (MPP), a D.C. lobbying group, has been leading the fight against H.Res. 372. On March 30, in a protest organized by the MPP, multiple sclerosis patient Cheryl Miller used medical marijuana in the D.C. office of U.S. Representative Jim Rogan (R-California). Rogan was targeted because he voted for favorable medical marijuana legislation while in the California legislature, but voted for H.Res 372 in the House Judiciary Committee, the MPP said.

Cheryl and her husband Jim were arrested and charged with possession of marijuana. On April 20, a D.C. Superior Court dropped the charges against the Millers.

It is uncertain whether H.Res. 372 will come up for a vote. In the meantime, activists can contact their Representatives and urge them to vote "no" by sending a letter to:

U.S. Rep. [name]
U.S. House of Representatives
Washington, D.C. 20515

Inside:
2 - News Briefs
4 - Democratic Convention
5 - Anti-Drug War March
6 - Marijuana Check-Up
8 - HAT Info
8 - Activist Organizations

Letter from the Publisher

Dear Readers,

I spent a lot of energy yesterday writing the letter that appears below. Or perhaps the energy was and still is being consumed by my mind dwelling on the lunacy of the DEA concerning themselves with eradicating the cannabis plant species. As a result, I'm having difficulty focusing on the topic I was going to write about, Global Days and our First Monday Of Every Month March.

The DEA is asking the USDA for an update to the 1985

and 1986 Environmental Impact Statement (EIS) on Cannabis eradication. In the Draft Supplement EIS (DSEIS), the DEA seeks to add triclopyr as an herbicide replacement for paraquat (which has been discovered to be toxic to humans since it was approved in 1985) and add amine formulations of 2, 4-D to its list of approved chemical herbicides. The DEA also seeks to implement a new technology called "aerial direct treatment of herbicides" from helicopters. The claim is that this will be SAFER than "broadcast aerial treatment." There is more but you'll need to visit their website to check it out:

http:/www.usdoj.gov/dea/programs/cannibis/pubmeet/fednoti.htm

Note: the misspelling of cannabis is the DEA's, not ours. Could this be a way to escape detection by search engines, a stealthy means to avoid the comments they say they are open to?

The letter below precisely illustrates one of the many reasons why I've become an activist for the re-legalization of the hemp/cannabis/marijuana plant. The War on Drugs is raging out of control. It is revolting. Ah! Did I hear revolt? Is it time for a revolution? Can we revolve peacefully? Can we turn it around? Yes. We must. We must speak out, folks. It *is* past time to do so. It is time to talk to everyone you know about how this War on Drugs is affecting each and every one of us. If you don't think it is, read on and prove me wrong!

June 21, 1998
Mr. Jack Edmundson, Project Leader
Environmental Analysis and Documentation, USDA/APHIS/PPD
4700 River Road, Unit 149
Riverdale, MD   20737-1238

Dear Mr. Edmundson,
It is past time to end the war on plants, the war on drugs, and the war on people. In this age of conservation and preservation the idea of attempting to eradicate ANY plant species is downright blasphemous. God created this earth and everything on it for a purpose. It is extremely arrogant of the DEA or any human being to deem it necessary or wise to tamper with God's creation, nature.
How many people will have to die before it's discovered that triclopyr, like paraquat, is toxic to humans? Aerial

broadcasting of any agent which KILLS anything will obviously be harmful to the ecosystem that sustains all life on our planet. There is no SAFE way to aerially broadcast chemicals. Even if it were possible to attain the goal of plant eradication without simultaneously taking out our earth's forests, food crops, etcetera, when it rains the chemicals will go down to our water tables and be readily available for humans, animals and other plant life to consume. Where is the wisdom in this act?

PLEASE put the chemicals away. If the United States of America policy makers would commit a fraction of the resources presently used for the War on Drugs to the GROWTH of the incredibly useful cannabis plant and offer financial incentives to those companies willing to convert to its use - i.e. the petroleum companies, the wood and paper products industries, fabric mills, pharmaceutical companies, etc. - the world would be a much better place with far less pollution, far more trees standing and plants growing to help oxygenate the planet.

Thank you for your time and consideration.

Sincerely, Beth Myrle Rice

Hemp Activist Times
July 1998

PUBLISHER: Beth Myrle Rice

EDITOR: Ben Livingston

WRITERS: Tim Crowley, Doug Fisher, Ben Livingston, Robert Lunday

PHOTOGRAPHERS: Marina Crowley

SPECIAL THANKS: Jeff Haley; Marijuana Policy Project; Media Awareness Project; Megan at Tower Books on Queen Anne; Seattle Gay News

HEMP ACTIVIST TIMES is published monthly by Purple Stripe Publishing. Copyright 1998.

We are looking for story ideas, news, writers and friendly folks to

Washington Sta activist organiz

Green Cross Patient Co-op
PO Box 47347
Seattle, WA 98126
http://www.hemp.net/greencross/

The Green Cross is a patient co-op established to provide medical marijuana to patients.

November Coalition
795 South Cedar
Colville, WA 99114
(509) 684-1550
http://www.november.org/
moreinfo@november.org

The November Coalition is dedicated to educating the public about the destructive increase in the US prison population and the erosion of our civil rights because of our drug policy.

Washington
PO Box 23
Seattle, WA
(206) 781-7
http://www.
cdpr@ever

WCMR is
Initiative 69
Medical Ma

Washington
PO Box 12
Olympia, W
(360) 866-6
http://www.
when@olyv

WHEN's n
people thro
to make mo
the regulati

Journal: August 1, 1998

Zoey and I spent Friday night at Mom's. She and I pampered Zoey and her poor feet. They look like they have walked half the streets in Seattle barefoot. She is still couch surfing but any time we have together is becoming more relaxed and real. We spent the night at Mom's so to be on the Peninsula in the morning and avoid the ferry crowds of people coming over to Kitsap Peninsula Fairgrounds for Endfest, a music festival sponsored by The End radio station.

Mom fixed us a big breakfast and we took too long getting out of there. Consequently I missed Stabbing Westward. I spent some time hanging with Zoey and her friends but ultimately went our own ways due to musical preferences. I loved Marcy Playground and Green Day rocked!

Journal: August 5, 1998

Haiku O' Th' Day: Politics exist
                        even among anarchists
                        funny little twist

The list of drop-off points for H.A.T. is expanding but I'm still the only distributor in the Greater Seattle area. Whew! It's a lot of getting around!

Capitol Hill: Pistol Books, The Comet, Red & Black Books, Godfathers Pizza, Crescent Downworks, Kincora's, Vivace

Queen Anne: Tower Books

Downtown: Left Bank Books, Crocodile Café, Sit N Spin, Off Ramp

Fremont: Wit's End Books, Rain City Video, Still Life Café, PCC

Wallingford: Nice Day Coffee Company, Honey Bear Bakery

U District: Cellophane Square, Bulldog News, Tower Music, Recollection Books

Pioneer Square: Elliott Bay Book Company, Colorbox, OK Hotel

Downtown Edmonds: Chanterelle's on Main St.

Lynnwood: Homegrown, Wherehouse @ 196th & 44th, Zumiez in Alderwood Mall

I'm stoked on working with the Hempfest. I've been

assigned to one of the two hour time slots for Master of Ceremonies on what will be the newly inaugurated Ralph Seeley stage. What an honor! In between performers and speakers I'll read poetry and promote *Your Tree...* sales.

Journal: August 13, 1998

When I talk to God these days I always ask, "Please just keep her alive, Lord, and we'll get through this." It's almost become a mantra.

28: Poisons Or Pot?

U.S. Department of Justice
Drug Enforcement Administration

DRAFT

Cannabis Eradication in the Contiguous United States and Hawaii

Supplement to the Environmental Impact Statements

DRAFT

April 1998

Hemp Activist Times, Letter from the Editor, September 1998

Dear Readers,

My letters to you and to the USDA last month, written with regard to the DEA's update to the '85/'86 Environmental Impact Statement on Cannabis Eradication, elicited two responses. The USDA sent a copy of the draft EIS which spells out the risks our Earth's fragile environment will be subjected to over the next decade of War against the Cannabis plant species.

WHO, with a lick of common sense, would support throwing large amounts of poison out of airplanes? You folks at the USDA need to delve into your archives and pull out the Hemp For Victory film that your predecessors produced in the '30's, when there was some apparent degree of common sense existing in our government and the value of hemp was touted. Would you please air this film on Prime Time TV back to back with a report from an author of the draft EIS summarizing all the risks involved in the DEA's plan and see what kind of public response you get?

The second response was from one of our readers telling us she too wrote the USDA. She ended on this note: "Hemp is going to be THE big issue of the new millennium - as Peace in Vietnam was in the 60's. I can feel the first rumblings of a real upheaval!"

I couldn't agree more! The Cannabis issue crosses many boundaries: our environment, the politics of corporate greed, and the consistent thrashing of our Bill of Rights with property seizures and the gulaging of nearly one million U.S. citizens on drug related charges.

Over $30 billion of our taxes will go to fighting the War on Drugs this year. Yes, this tremendous waste of money and senseless endangerment to our natural and human resources is a huge issue.

Peace & Purple Power,
Beth Myrle Rice

cc: Mr. Jack Edmundson, USDA

Hemp Activist Times

A newsletter for northwest hemp and marijuana activists   September 1998

Seattle Hempfest proves its worth

by Ben Livingston

By police estimates, 35,000 people attended Seattle Hempfest on August 23. Nearly one hundred vendors lined the paths of Myrtle Edwards park, hawking everything from hemp clothing to hemp lollipops. Among speakers at the event were Jack Herer, Dennis Peron, Mike Gray, Nora Callahan and Kevin Zeese. Music was provided by Second Coming,

Hempfest Director Vivian McPeak leads the crowd in a "hemp cheer."

Floater, Local 808, Bad Kitty, Herbivores, Kuli Loach, Us of All and the Lara Lavi Band, just to name a few. In addition to the Hempen Ale sponsored main stage, Hempfest dedicated the Ralph Seeley Memorial Stage this year.

Hempfest is changing the focus of its message this year, according to Director Vivian McPeak. "In the past, we've focused on the history of the hemp plant, the fact that George Washington grew it or that the U.S. Constitution was originally drafted on it. This year, we decided to move away from that and focus on the Drug War. Specifically, we wanted to highlight the prisoners of this insane war."

All day, musicians and speakers blasted the War on Drugs and encouraged people to get involved in drug policy reform.

Many activists have been discussing the overall efficacy of festivals of this sort. Concern over the image put forth by the drug policy reform movement runs high among many prominent organizations. The Washington, DC based Marijuana Policy Project won't put any pot leaves on their literature and encourages

activists to dawn suits and ties. Others see festivals as unproductive and reinforcing the tie-dyed hippy stereotype that has been lingering since the '60s.

While Hempfest did have some freakish characters walking around and even an impromptu drum circle or two, the message of the day, indeed the message being amplified from the multiple stages, was extremely political with an emphasis on individual action.

After attending Hempfest for the first time, Kevin Zeese, Director of Common Sense for Drug Policy wrote "It gave me confidence that these events can become successful political events that put out the right public image for the reform movement."

The media was suprisingly good for Hempfest. Whereas events of this nature usually garner headlines such as "Hempfest a big hit," no such nonsense graced the newspapers or the ten o'clock news. Almost every local station sent reporters to cover the event. Numerous local papers, including the Seattle P-I wrote flattering reports. Even international news outlets such as the BBC sent reporters to cover the event.

The Seattle Police Department was also rather kind this year. In all, 23 people were cited for marijuana possesion and 3 less intelligent people were arrested for selling marijuana. This is a third of the citations issued at Hempfest '97. Lieutenant Dick Schweitzer said "It was a real good crowd this year, very mellow."

Voting rights for felons

By Barbara Tomlinson

It is common knowledge that a felon, once convicted can never vote again—right? Wrong! If you thought felons had no voting rights, you've either been misled or flat out lied to.

What a political coup that would be—to arrest tens of thousands of people on drug charges, then to deprive them forever of the right to vote on any drug issues. Simply lock up your foes and lie to them!

While collecting signatures for Initiative 692, I met numerous people who wouldn't sign because they had a felony conviction in their past. Each one is a potential signature. Each one is a potential vote.

While serving a felony sentence, you lose your right to vote. After you complete your sentence, you need to obtain a "Certificate of Discharge." If you were released after July 1, 1984, you should automatically be given this document.

If you were released before 1984 or didn't receive a "Certificate of Discharge," write or call:

Indeterminate Sentence Review Board
4317 6th Ave. SE
PO Box 40907
Olympia, WA 98504-0907
(360) 493-9266

In this issue:

2 - Newsbriefs
3 - Letters
4 - High Times WHEE 2
4 - Oakland vs. Feds
5 - Hemp Voter's Guide
5 - Hemp Voter's Guide
6 - Initiatives Across the US
6 - Marijuana Class Action
7 - Bill of Rights?
7 - Activist Calendar
8 - Activist Organizations

HEMP ACTIVIST TIMES   1   SEPTEMBER 1998

We did not publish an August issue due to our involvement with Hempfest. We were excited to have our September issue professionally printed in newsprint format. Our distribution points continued to expand and we clearly had readership. When I arrived with a new issue there were few to zero copies of the prior month to remove. Unfortunately we did not delve into advertising sales early enough and I could no longer float the tab to keep the paper going.

Most importantly, I knew it was time to give my full attention to Zoey, to convince her to come live with me. Her roommate had become fed up with her behavior and told her to get out. So, she took to staying where ever she was allowed to crash. My commitment to Hempfest for 1998 was fulfilled and all were well aware of the work I had ahead of me with Zoey. They were all encouraging and wished me well on my quest to healing our relationship.

Hempfest was amazing. I was delighted to meet Jack Herer and have him sign the book I bought at his booth, a copy of the original "first edition" version of The Emperor Wears No Clothes, as the most recently updated edition had sold out. I gifted a copy of my tree-free *Your Tree & Collected Poems for Personal Freedom* chapbook to him and was honored that he asked me to sign it to him.

I am proud to have been a worker bee at the great Seattle Hempfest; and was thrilled to be among such an amazing group of friendly, hard-working, devoted, responsible potheads. All of the folks in the Core Group come from diverse backgrounds, do a vast array of work in their day jobs, and have become hemp/marijuana activists for a variety of reasons. But the one thing we all have in common is the belief that in a free country all plants should be free to grow and that responsible adults should have choice in what they put in their bodies. I am reminded of Justice Sanders' brave dissenting vote in the case of Seeley vs. State.

Journal: September 6, 1998

Haiku O' Th' Day: Rain clouds are distinct
from others but some snow clouds
which smell different

Journal: September 16, 1998

ASR was a blast. I finally have some time to write about it. I'm beginning to feel like a mini-celebrity. Nah, that's stretching it. But, I think it's safe to say that I'm becoming a recognized character in the skate zone. It was really fun to walk the trade show floor and hear "Hey HatLady!" as I neared the booths of my customers and some of those I've been working on to become my customers.

I was hanging out with Billy and some of the Abacus crew at a big table on the patio of the San Diego Convention

Center enjoying the sunshine, the view and a beer when a big, wet kiss was planted on the back of my neck. On reflex my head turned as my hand shot out and connected with the cheek of a darling yet goofily shocked looking young black guy. He and all at the table looked at me in disbelief that had just happened. The guy exclaimed something like, "Whoa, momma! Just being friendly!" and with that he walked away. Billy asked me, absolutely aghast, "Do you know who you just slapped?"

"No. Should I?"

"That was Harold Hunter!"

"Yeah?"

Billy was amazed. "You don't know who Harold Hunter is?"

"No. Why would I?"

"He rides for Zoo York and was in the movie Kids. How can you not know who he is?"

I was lost for words beyond, "I haven't seen the movie."

Later that night I was going up to my room in the Marriot—damn, that place gets crazy during the trade show, like one huge party—and who should I run into in the hall? Harold Hunter. He slid his arm around my waist with, "Hey, momma, there's a party at my place. Come hang with me." He was giving me a chance to compensate for my apparent faux pas earlier in the day so I went along.

There were a few guys and girls I didn't know lolling in his room. A couple half unpacked suitcases were laying open and clothes were all over the room. Harold introduced me to everyone but I don't remember any names because they didn't hang around long enough to talk much. They were more talking among themselves and I use the term talking loosely. They were in some lingo or jargon that I didn't grasp much of. Within a few minutes Harold and I were alone. He was sitting on one of the two queen sized beds in the room and patted the bed next to his thigh saying something I couldn't understand. I asked him to repeat. He did. I laughed and asked him what language he was using. At that, he laughed and stated in crystal diction, "Sorry, that's my lazy talk. Come sit by me. I want to be with you." The door to the room opened, a guy dashed in, grabbed a jacket off a chair, muttering as he went. He left as quickly as he appeared.

I guessed Billy had told Harold of our ventures together and figured he wanted some. I said to the effect that I'd had a long day and with another long one coming tomorrow I really needed to get to my room for some sleep. He asked me to please stay. He followed me to the door as I insisted I needed sleep. He held my arm gently enough that I slid it through his hand; but, when my hand reached his he tightened his grip and begged me not to go. I proceeded into the hall with Harold attached to my hand. He was pleading with me to stay and tears came to his eyes. That blew me away but the words, "He is an actor" wafted through my brain. I was glad no one else was in the hall as I peeled his hand from mine, turned and walked away. He softly called after me, "Please don't go." I looked back at him to see the tears had overflowed to his cheeks. I felt bad but kept walking.

The next day I asked Billy about Harold, if he knew him well. Billy laughed and told me Harold is a really good guy, that I should be nice to him. I saw Harold later in the day. When I complimented him on the cool Zoo sweater he was wearing he pulled it off over his head and handed it to me saying the day was too hot to be wearing it. Standing there in a plain white tee shirt he insisted I keep the sweater as a memento.

Billy's words have hung with me and Harold has been on my mind since ASR weekend so tonight I wrote him the following letter. I looked up Zoo York's address in the ASR guide of exhibitors and addressed the envelope to Harold in care of Zoo. I added PERSONAL & CONFIDENTIAL:

Hi Harold –

I finally got around to unpacking last night and as I put the cool sweater you gave me into the cold water wash pile (as you recommended) it occurred to me that I hadn't really thanked you properly. You've been on my mind since we parted in the hall on Saturday night. I think you can tell that I'm not an unkind person. I truly make a point to not intentionally or unthinkingly be unkind or hurtful to anyone ever. Though sometimes I miss my point, that is always a personal goal. Those tradeshow scenarios are a bit too fast and fuzzy for me these days. I'm not a "player" per se so

I don't always handle things real well. I would be lying if I said I haven't done my fair share of playing but it's not where my head and heart is anymore. So, I guess what I'm trying to say is that when we see each other again I hope things can be cool, that you don't view me as some wicked mean person.

You know, it does say on your Zoo York website that you aspire to be an actor. Since we've had no time to know each other surely you can get my viewpoint. Guys are always scamming on chicks looking to get laid = FACT. And, often chicks are looking for some fast fun. I'm no exception. But I was just into hanging out that night, not looking to squeeze in a quick one between the herds of hanger-outers coming and going in your room, ya know?

The next time you go out to L.A. take a two and a half hour jump flight up to Seattle and we'll hang out on quiet time, skate the lake, go to some clubs Seattle style and see what happens from there. I'd love to check out NYC with a native for my guide some day. If that sounds good to you give me a call or drop me a line. If that's not of interest I understand. I just hope we can be cool and friendly next time we meet up. You seem like a really good guy and I'd like to know you. Harold, I feel really bad if I hurt your feelings or insulted your integrity. I'm truly sorry.

Peace, Beth

Journal: September 26, 1998

I've been shuffling, shifting, sifting, tossing and re-shuffling STUFF since the end of August when Zoey's stuff got stuffed into my apartment. Today I took a bunch of stuff I've been hauling and storing for past long enough to a garage sale that Zoey's boss told me about. She is such a super nice boss to Zoey and helpful to both of us. At the garage sale I sold the SUNDOGZ display case, complete with sunglasses in it, to the first person who inquired about it for five dollars. Yes, five dollars. It felt so good.

October 22, 1998 – a note to Eric sent with his check

I thought things were getting better. She's taken some time to settle her stuff in at my place. But, as I told you, she has a real thing for hallucinogenics and she has been clear with me, "I like to get high."

So, I've been clear with her, "I can't trust you with a key to the apartment nor will I have you buzzing the security door after 10pm on work nights." Last night she chose to stay out. I don't believe she'll be holding it together well enough to keep her job much longer.

Journal: October 25, 1998

I skated three laps on the lake today, "D Day." We're now moving into the darkness of winter. The first lap was on my roller skates. I was riding a pair of Powell wheels that they want me to give them feed-back on. First time in over a year I've been on those skates. It was cool in that it worked a different muscle group and what not but I just don't have the love for it that I did once. I took the second and third laps on my THINK board – with Thunder trucks, China Bones, Kryptonics – and grooved on that much better. 3 laps X almost 3 miles = nearly 9 miles skated!

Last Thursday, the 22nd, Zo and I had some of the best communication so far. Things are getting more relaxed and natural.

Journal: November 4, 1998

We won!! I-692 passed and it is now legal for doctors in the great state of Washington to recommend marijuana to their patients AND it's legal for patients to grow their own medicine!

29: Clouds Of All Kinds

Journal: November 5, 1998
Haiku O' Th' Day:
You're my weathervane
some days you make so sunny
others you bring clouds

Journal: January 20, 1999, 4:50PM
HumpDay in Seattle
The sky looked promising on&off&on all day long
I finally rode my Spitfire wheels
almost
after day of too many phones
finally
almost sudden mist
out my window is
perfect training wheels
for doing slides
on my Spitfires
I am stoked
Suit up   hoody and johns
music in pouch
hit the rainy fucking sidewalk
hit a jolt stop
huffed and kicked
sidewalk into air   AND WATER
can't skate this shit GOTTA
skategottaskategotta   shit
shit   who can I call   who knows
where is there something dry
to skate? gotta skate gotta   Fuck!
fuck   it's out   over the hump   go bake

Earlier today I spoke with Tom Jenks regarding the upcoming workshop.

<u>January 27, 1999 – a letter to lay on her bed. . .</u>
My dear Zoey,

If I were to give way to all the thoughts, questions, and concerns that I have about you right now it would probably be a book in itself and I wouldn't have time to get to the main point of this letter. But I feel the need to toss out a few of them as I believe 'the point of this letter' is being voiced as a result of them.

First, I want to reiterate what you already know. I love you. I always have and I always will. Sometimes I am angry with you. Sometimes I'm frustrated by your actions. There are moments when I don't like you. There are times when I am very proud of you, times when your great sense of humor and fun are a joy to me, and times when your affection toward me makes my whole world peaceful. I know that you are a very intelligent and talented person with a wealth of beautiful gifts to share.

Zoey, you have had a tough row to hoe. Your childhood and teens have been good, bad and ugly. But, guess what? At least ninety percent of the human race has this in common with you! At some point you will recognize that you are the only one responsible for your actions and for a great deal of the 'stuff' that comes your way. The sooner you realize that everything in your life is because of you, the sooner you will begin to monitor your thoughts and actions with greater care and start bringing nicer things into your life (whatever nice is to you). This is what is known as taking responsibility for one's self. You need to take care of yourself first and foremost. If you do not, you have nothing of value to give to or share with anyone. Since giving and sharing are obviously important to you, you need to take this truth to heart.

I was glad that your boss finally let you go because she was enabling your irresponsible behavior as bad as your dad did to keep peace with Crystal and as bad as I am now. You need to come down from your dream cloud, my dear, and deal with reality. You need to learn respect and appreciation. These concepts seem to have escaped your absorption if not comprehension.

315

We made a deal when you moved in here. You were very clear with me that you didn't want to be parented and I said, "Fine we'll be roommates." You were also very clear with me that living here is not your first choice - that you want to get your own place. We worked up a budget together that would enable you to save the necessary funds to get your own place. The holidays hit and I told you we'd zoom in on the budget beginning with the new year. Well, it's here and you simply choose not to uphold your responsibility to your goal or your responsibilities as a roommate. So, I have taken to momming you. I am your mom and always will be. Because of this, because I love you, I am now giving you an ultimatum.

If you wish to continue living here you need to do the following things starting IMMEDIATELY:

• Untangle yourself from the everyday involvement in your friends' lives. They (including Johnny) need to be responsible for themselves and so do you. Seeing them once or twice during the week (IF all of the 'To Do' items on your list are handled) and on the weekends is plenty. Friends are the icing not the cake.

• You need to be starting a full-time job OR a part-time job and have your application for school TURNED IN by February 15th. You played from June through December and you have played for the two weeks you wanted since you were let go. You now have two weeks plus to take care of business. And I do mean take care of business. You will stay home on weeknights, get up by eight in the morning and be out the door looking for work. NO kids will be here at any time until I give the go ahead (probably late Feb or early March) and then it will be during the weekend only. During this time you will also:

• study up and get your drivers' license
• write to your insurance company about address change
• settle in your room & bathroom stuff tidily not half-assed less-than-pigsty
• participate in caring for the whole apartment
• do your laundry
• any and all reasonable requests I may come up with beyond the above

I am absolutely serious about this, Zoey. If you have

not accomplished the above items by February 15th I will run an ad to rent your room, pack up your belongings and put them in a storage unit, and collect your keys. DO NOT DOUBT ME FOR ONE MINUTE. I told you I will not bend my life out of shape to support your party habit or your friends and I mean it.

If your initial reaction to this is to huff out of here thinking 'fuck that' you better first ask all your friends if you can come stay with them for free and, if so, for how long. Better also develop a back-up plan (locate some shelters?) for when they tell you to move on because once I have rented your room you won't be coming back here to live and that's that.

I am doing this because I love you Zoey and I want you to be a happy, productive human being. Happiness and productivity go hand in hand. When you are accomplishing things you feel good about yourself, are happy and draw like people to you. It's hard to be happy when you're floundering around doing nothing. I recognize that you are attracted to all the drama that lurks around your present friends and that you think hanging out is better than working. But, I don't see it making you happy. And it certainly doesn't make me happy. If that is the lifestyle you choose you will need to do it under some other roof.

All my love always, Mom

January 31, 1999 - a letter to Tom Jenks

Dear Tom,

Enclosed is a part of my manuscript. It seriously needs to be edited down and tightened up but it represents the bare beginning of the third metamorphosis. You may remember I told you on the phone that I have not worked on the manuscript for over a year. After our conversation last week, when I opened up the miles of files which represent the last change of structure I became clear on two things: [a] my recent epiphany on the order in which to present the material (which differs from the Table of Contents page - that was the last plan) is absolutely right; and [b] I have a LOT of work to do!

There are about two hundred and fifty pages keyboarded so far which need to be rearranged and edited down. During

317

the crisis time in '95 I was not keeping up my journal well so I want to write some Journal Entries—as though written at the time—which will be fill between all the correspondence and other documents on file. This won't be difficult as I could nor will ever forget. When I recall and record my experience is inconsequential. It remains my truth. When finished I'm guessing the book will come in at around three hundred pages in length.

I imagine that what I have sent is more material than you might want at this time but do with it what you will. *WARNING!* It is the only section in the book which contains explicit sexual material though such activity is alluded to in other areas.

An additional note which may shed light on some things expressed within the existing text: I originally planned to include the subtitle "A decade in the life of a Middle America addict" and, with the exception of fifty to sixty pages presented in Scrap Book format (The Early Years), the book would focus on 1986 through 1996. However, after spending most of '98 as a very active activist for drug law reform and now that my daughter is back in my life I'm inclined to want to include '97 and '98. Maybe that's sequel material? Maybe I'm really silly thinking that any one might want to read this at all! I look forward to your comments.

Sincerely, Beth Rice

A note from Zoey, left on the kitchen counter

Mom – Sorry I never called back. Johnny doesn't have a phone, remember? When I got there I crashed and didn't wake up until three o'clock this afternoon, twenty-one hours on one couch. I guess I was sleepy, huh?

So we're going to go take care of business now, but I ♥ you and will talk to you later. I took two packs of your smokes and will pay you back.

Oh yeah... I took the grapes and Cheetos too!

♥ Zoey

Feb. 2, 1999 – a letter to . . .

Zoey,

I am so saddened by the choices you are making. This ad will be appearing in the UW Daily beginning next week:

318

Green Lake. Small rm in cheery 2nd story 2 bdrm apt. Sec. Bldg. Hdwd Flrs. $320/mo incl. Util/basic phone. $50 off for 8-10 hrs. lt. housecleaning/mo. Available 3/1. Call. . .

You had better revise your list of "To Do's" accordingly. I do love you and hope that you will soon wake up, slow down on your drug consumption, start caring for yourself, and start dealing with life's realities.

Love always, Mom

February 8, 1999, Monday – a note on my desk from Zoey

Mom ♥

I left with my friends, don't know exactly where we're going or when we'll be back, not too far off from now I'm sure. I feel much better but still need to rest so I'll be around, you can bet. I love you – glad you had a fun trip. Check your voicemail. It's been driving me apeshit. Page me if you want.

Outro – ♥ Zo

February 26, 1999

MOM'S RULES FOR ZOEY

Pursuant to the discussion between Zoey, Mom, and Dad on Thursday February 25, 1999, and in light of all the choices that Zoey has made from June of '98 to the present, it is agreed that if Zoey wishes to call upon either of her parents for any form of assistance she must first accept that she has no option but to perform in accordance with the RULES that either and both of them set forth in exchange for said assistance. It is further accepted that both parents will have their own set of RULES pertaining to their individual contributions and it is the option of either parent to include RULES set forth by the other.

I have read this entire three page document. I understand all terminology. I've received a copy of this document. I accept all of the following RULES must be adhered to at all times in order to continue living at 00 Green Lake Way Apt. 0 with Mom.

X_____ Date_____

ZOEY IS ON THE THREE-STRIKES-&-YOU'RE-OUT PLAN, MEANING:

ANY infraction of the following rules will constitute one strike. Should three strikes occur Zoey will be required to pack whatever of her belongings she can take with her at one time, turn in her apartment keys, and vacate the premises immediately—not after making a phone call or two, no waiting for a ride, immediately.
- Not one rule will be considered more or less important than the others
- Not one rule is to be considered negotiable at any time
- All rules must be obeyed at all times

Strike One: Date _____   _____   _____
                                  Zoey initial   Mom initial
Strike Two: Date _____   _____   _____
                                  Zoey initial   Mom initial

GENERAL RULES

1) Maintain a cheerful and positive attitude. If having a bad day or feeling unhappy do not project this onto other residents. If wanting to have discussion, ask if timing is good.

2) Maintain a peaceful household. There will be no confrontation or conflict. Do not confront Mom verbally or physically at any time. Don't slam doors, raise voice, stomp, walk heavy, or act in any similar manner.

3) Demonstrate respect and appreciation for Mom and the Rules. Do as Mom asks when she asks. If asking something of Mom, respect she may say no and accept no when first stated. If Mom complies with request, express appreciation. "Thank you" is sufficient.

4) Accept that Mom may add new rules or change existing rules at any time. In any case, no related action on Zoey's part will be considered an infraction until such addition or change is noted in writing as an addition to this document, acknowledged and initialed by Zoey and Mom.

SCHOOL, WORK, MONETARY CONTRIBUTIONS

1) One Hundred dollars will be paid to Mom each month for your maintenance in the household. When due will be determined by frequency of paychecks. You will pay for your own laundry (washer & dryer only, I'll provide detergent, etc.). You will pay for your own cigarettes, any food and/or toiletries that I do not choose to participate in. A minimum of one hundred dollars per month will go into savings.

2) Obtain a part-time job to begin no later than Monday March 8th, sooner if possible. Accept that you may have to start at minimum wage; that you may have to handle meat, that you may have to work on Saturday and Sunday. You must take any job you can get by March 8th. If you have not started (later changed to *secured* and initialed by Zoey and Mom) a part-time job by the 8th, with a start date no later than March 13th (hand-written in along with secured) this will constitute one Infraction of the Rules. Once working, you will do office-type work for Mom as requested at least two hours per day on your off hours, at the rate of six dollars per hour to be applied toward repayment of the (most recent) two hundred dollar debt at The Pawn Shop of Mom where your old camera, your lenses and tripod are presently held hostage.

3) Register for school (to begin April) in a timely manner such that you secure a class in: Photography; English, either speaking or writing skills; Keyboarding. Once in, get no lower than a "C" in any class. Each grade lower than a "C" will be considered One Infraction of the Rules.

IN ORDER TO ACCOMPLISH THE ABOVE YOU WILL:

1) Stay home on weeknights, Sunday through Thursday night. TV off and lights out by 11:30PM. You must be home by 5PM on Sundays. When working you must stay home any night prior to a work shift that begins by noon.

2) Get up by 7:30AM and be out the door by 9AM looking for work Monday through Saturday.

3) Fill out and submit applications at five businesses each day and follow up on them.

4) Until a job is secured, you will not hang out with friends at all.

5) Reserve use of intoxicants for nights that don't precede work, work search, or school.

6) No kids will be here at any time until I give the go ahead and then it will be during the weekend only. There will be NO kids sleeping over here once we have a room-mate unless I give approval at least twenty-four hours prior to the sleep-over.

In a hand-drawn text box next to the above rules I agreed to and we both initialed: Johnny may stay over on Friday and Saturday, March 5th and 6th, if Zoey has a job with a definite start date that complies with the Rules by the 5th.

If the job does not start specifically between the 5th and the 13th it will be an infraction.

HOUSEHOLD CHORES must be accomplished between the hours of 4PM and 7:30PM on weeknights or 10AM to 4PM on weekends unless otherwise noted below or with prior approval.

1) Do anything that you see needs to be done without being asked. Know that with regard to any task, if there is still dirt, dust or marks present it has not been cleaned. Going through the motions does not count.

2) When you use anything in the home -phone book, pen, remote control, et cetera - put it back precisely where you found it when you are done. Be tidy!

3) Wash any dishes you use immediately following the meal. Wash all evening dishes as requested. Wipe up peripheral areas -stove, countertops, spills on floor, top of toaster

4) Scour kitchen sink once a week.

5) Once a week pick up all throw rugs and take out back to shake them out. Every other week wash and dry them after shaking. I'll give you the quarters.

6) Scrub or mop bathroom and kitchen floor once a week and once a month damp mop wood floors by my methodology. I will demonstrate and get you started once.

7) Vacuum entire apartment once a week, moving things to get under and behind them.

8) Clean all bathroom fixtures once a week.

9) Dust living room, my office area, and kitchen window sills once a week.

10) When the kitchen or bathroom trash is full take it out and replace with new trash bag. This is to be done at least once a week. I will remind you twice before it is an infraction.

11) Never leave any of your belongings in my bedroom space. Anything that does not fit in your space in the walk-in closet must go in the main floor storage closet.

12) You must chart out chores on a calendar according to the above rules for my approval and then you must adhere to the schedule you have made. A hand-written and initialed addition: Calendar through March 14th must be given to Mom by 10PM on March 2nd.

SHARED SPACE & GENERAL APARTMENT RULES

1) "BEATS" will not be played during Mom's work hours, or after 8PM weeknights.

2) All music will be kept at a volume acceptable to Mom. This may vary from day to day and will be complied with when requested with no back-talk or confrontation. All music is to be extremely low volume by 9PM and off by 11PM weeknights. A low clock radio is acceptable.

3) Coats are to be promptly hung in the hall coat closet.

A hand-written and initialed addition dated March 1:

At Zoey's request, I will not say anything about her clothes or her boyfriend. Nor will I raise my voice or speak harshly to Zoey. If I do any of the four above stated actions and Zoey responds in a confrontational manner it will not be considered an infraction. I will no longer discuss my frustration at working hard while Zoey plays and makes adverse choices. I will not rub it in Zoey's face in a shit-rubbing face manner. March rent of one hundred dollars is paid.

After adding the last paragraph primarily quoting Zoey's words to me but then insisting on a few of my own, Zoey dated and signed the spaces provided under the first two paragraphs on the first page of this document on March 1, 1999.

March 2, 1999 – a letter from Eric via fax

Beth,

The purpose of my discussion last week was to respond to Zoey's request that we get together with her and talk. I've offered to meet anywhere, anytime (within reason) to help her find solutions to her problems. I had an agenda of my own, and made no secret about it. Despite repeated attempts to offer guidance and direction, I have failed to convince her of the value of what I have to say. It is now up to her to convince me she wants what I can offer. There is no limit to her opportunities, only the ones she sets for herself. I can and will "be there" for her, but it must be a "two-way" street from today forward. If she does or doesn't want to see me it will be her choice.

I didn't go to the meeting wanting to share MY goals and was offended that you feel Zoey threatens YOUR goals. The meeting wasn't about you. Your laying yet another guilt trip on Zoey about how she is holding you back, the sacrifices that you would have to make, the workshop you couldn't attend, and so on… simply sends the message once again that she is an impediment to you and that your goals are more important than hers. By most parents' standards, the sacrifices you have made don't add up to much at all. The goal you should be focused on is helping Zoey get her life together. I don't think you even realize you are sending the message you send.

She grew up needing you and you weren't available. When you were available you weren't willing to be or behave like a parent. Now you want to throw her out because she'll make too many demands and sacrifices on your part. You've let her down as a parent and you have let me down as a parent. Having said that, I do understand how frustrating it can be dealing with Zoey. I am frustrated too. I too am not willing to have her manipulate me. Zoey is looking to you for stability. Don't let her manipulate you!

I may have failed in some respects but I have never given up, and I'm not giving up now. I have given up many trips, events, vacations, meetings, seminars; had plans changed, stayed home at night, and HAVE been called at night by the police to come pick her up. Ask her how many times I took her WITH me (kicking and screaming sometimes) so I could do something I wanted or needed to do.

To question the relationship I may or may not have with God had nothing to do with the conversation, and was totally inappropriate in front of Zoey in any case. I would never suggest in front of Zoey that you were a Godless person.

Don't ever question my resolve on the money you owe me. To not pay will just cost you more in the long run. It's your responsibility to make the payment per our agreement. If you can't keep your agreement how can you expect Zoey to keep her agreements?

Until the last few months you haven't financially supported Zoey. I even warned you in my letter to you last June that Zoey would be looking to you in these coming months.

We can work through this. Because she (as of today) lives with you, you have the best opportunity to have a positive effect. I know you didn't ask for the duty but it is yours to perform.

She may think of me as the enemy and you may think of me as the enemy but I am not the enemy. Lack of direction, fear of rejection and abandonment, fear of failure, not having successes in work and relationships, lack of focus, drugs, misguided friends, and no skills for the future... these are the enemy and the enemy is everywhere she seems to want to be.

Can we keep you and me out of this? We each love our daughter. Can't we stay focused on her and her problems? Get her into school? Help her find a way out of the clutches of her abusive boyfriend? Help her get some self respect and pride?

He added this note in handwriting at the bottom of the page: I have not received the payment due March 1, 1999. If I have not received it by Friday March 5, 1999 I'll assume our agreement broken and pursue other remedies as may be available to me.
Eric

March 2, 1999 – my reply via fax

Eric,

I completely agree that it must be a "two-way street," as always, two of them: Zoey/Me intersecting Zoey/You. Repeatedly I have asked and suggested that Zoey call you or write to you when she said she wasn't interested in hearing what you might have to say about "get in school" or about choices she's making. I'm done with that and wonder why I concerned myself for one second in light of the time between May 1995 and June 1998 and numerous other times I can recall over the years as the eight weeks she was to spend with me during the summers dwindled down to one week "in her best interest." I'm done. How you two communicate is between you two.

I now have an idea of what you faced in your daily parenting of Zoey. But you have *no* idea what it was like getting an eighteen year old adult who refused to be parented to come live with me in my prayers and hopes of getting her off crystal meth and whatever else she was pounding down. I cannot afford to be without a paying roommate, Eric. I changed my life around, brought the office back home telling her I prefer it that way now that I know what it's like having it out of the apartment. . . blah blah blah. . . won't waste any more time. To the point, MY POINT is that I am *not* willing to make sacrifices for her to continue living here with no responsibility to the home (she has not lifted one finger to help with chores when asked as her "later" becomes never) while she spends her available cash on partying and her time hanging out with friends doing nothing.

When she's enrolled in school I'll believe it, not until then. Broken promises are a strong result of her manipulation pattern, as if you don't know. She and I talked long and hard before our three-way discussion and she and I have had much discussion since. Be as offended as you choose and think whatever pleases you. It matters not to me. She knows exactly what I meant. You have no idea what my situation is or has been. You're welcome to sit over there and judge all you wish just keep your verdicts over there.

You failed Zoey as a parent and me as a parent when you mentally and emotionally abused me to the point that I had to divorce and get away from you to keep any shred of self-belief. You can deny it all you want but your denial is just that—DENIAL! You know the term. Do you know the term ABUSE?

• Remember how you used to laugh at me when I tried to make things sexy and inviting in hopes of getting sex once in a month or two??

• Remember raising your fist to me in bed over. . . ? I only remember the clenched fist inches from my face.

• Remember the night that you repeatedly told me "YOU ARE NOTHING!" because of my addiction to cigarettes and wanting to go buy a pack?

• Remember waving your arm around my folks place one Sunday night after dinner with them saying, "One day this will all be *mine*." Did you ever love me or just what you thought you could get from my parents?

• Remember sitting with your feet on the desk reading the newspaper while I did ALL the office work and cold-calling for sales appointments? Remember how at the end of fourteen months of cold-calling, when I threw in the towel, I tallied the score in the microfiche and found that I was directly responsible for sixty-three percent of your book of business? DID I EVER SEE ONE PENNY LET ALONE A THANK YOU??

• Remember how you took over grocery shopping because I spent too much money on it according to you??

Remember telling me with a big gloat and chuckle about how you had your first wife cowering in a corner while you yelled at her for choosing to sleep with someone else? And how you laughed at the "silly" things she chose to take with her when she fled from you? You must have had a good laugh on me and the small bit I was willing to settle for just to get away from you. . .

Ah, Yes!! Our day in court! Remember the judge asking me, "You don't want the house? You don't want child support?" Remember how you glared down at me and intimidated, "We have an agreement." REMEMBER THAT?? Remember how you were thrilled to let me move to an apartment and have no available *home* for me and Zoey? (It didn't occur I could place a roommate wanted ad as a means to make the mortgage payment like how you found a roommate to share the expense.) Well, I cannot seem to forget. It has had a profound and lasting effect on Zoey, me and our lives.

DO YOU REMEMBER HOW ABUSIVE YOU WERE TO ME? Well, I DO! It has left permanent scars and it took years for the scabs to reduce to that.

Don't you DARE ever again tell me about how I failed either of you! DON'T YOU DARE! And don't you EVER AGAIN tell me how I didn't contribute monetarily to Zoey's upbringing. YOU GOT THE MANY, MANY THOUSANDS OF DOLLARS UP FRONT THE DAY WE DIVORCED!

Don't tell me about all you've done for Zoey. You chose it. You chose to cut me out whenever you could.

You have been a self-proclaimed agnostic in any of the time I've known you. Why would it be any surprise to Zoey? You sent her to a horse camp that happened to also be a Bible camp and then you and Crystal laughed at her, questioning how long her "churchy-ness" might last when she got back. Crystal voiced that to me. I heard it directly from her mouth. If you have chosen not to talk to Zoey about your spiritual beliefs or lack of them this is another of your mistakes.

Mistakes! Yes, we've both made plenty of them when it comes to parenting Zoey. Quit pointing the finger at me. If it wasn't for the War on Drugs and the irrational policy around marijuana we would definitely have had a second day in court and all your abusiveness would have been then revealed.

I know from reliable sources just how abusive you were with Zoey from 1995 to 1998 so take off your halo and shove it up your godliness.

I owe you *nothing*! I will continue to send checks (it's in the mail late because the bottom of my financial barrel is long past scratched out trying to make ends meet over here to accommodate a thankless non-participating daughter) because I owe it to Zoey—*not you!*

Maybe the day that you say you're sorry to me and apologize for being an abusive ass Zoey will follow *your* example and apologize to Crystal for her abusive behavior. You and I will work *nothing* out until that day. It's been ever so easy for you to simply tell me to get over it. You ended up with all the eggs in your basket! I'll continue to work on that humongous task, getting over it. You and Zoey work out school. Zoey and I will work out keeping a roof over her head and food in her stomach IF she starts participating (which is finally happening, beginning to show hope of happening).

I don't view you as the enemy, just a fellow human being who I have no respect or regard for. You deal with Zoey. I'll deal with Zoey. I'm done dealing with you. And, for your information, Zoey is not caught in any "clutches." She is in love with a boy who has seen his share of trouble and can't quite put it all together therefore has self-esteem problems and this manifests in treating Zoey without a proper level of regard. When his abuse outweighs all the good she sees in him (and there is) she'll be done with him. The sooner you can refer to him as a fellow human being by name and quit cutting him down the sooner she can quit defending him. I nearly choked when I heard the word "loser" fall out of my mouth that day on the phone. You really bring out the worst in me.

Don't fool yourself about anything. Zoey is going to school (I'll believe it when she has picked up the application and registered) to save herself from being homeless. With any luck she'll actually dig it, have a good experience and continue. I have TOTAL FAITH in what she can accomplish. I will keep doing what I do, in my way, to work to the end that she does learn appreciation, respect, and the value of accomplishment.

Please don't bother me again. I won't bother you. Beth

328

31: Connections

I went to Ohio to call on my favorite corporate folks. Evie met me there and it went great. They liked meeting the boss.

Journal: March 23, 1999

Haiku O' Th' Day: Keep a sense of you
                         more or a sense of humor
                         is a real good thing

Journal: March 26, 1999

I took Zoey and a bunch of her stuff over to her friend's house today. She is officially moved out. Wow

Journal: April 11, 1999, Sunday

April 9, 1999 at the Elbo Room in San Francisco—WOW HatLady Happy Hour! What a kickass time! I was planning for this gig, a party for my SF skaters, for a month. I programmed a couple of tapes of some of my favorite songs so to give them a feel for what The HatLady is about. Calvin at Superb helped me nail down the Elbo Room saying it'd be the perfect venue for such an affair. And indeed it was. Evie picked up the tab for the room, open bar from 5 to 8PM and gave me a decent budget for good munchies. I loved spending the day running around ordering and picking up food. This was our way of saying thanks for their business. I definitely had to do some talking for Evie to understand that this was far more meaningful than wining and dining the upper management exclusively, as in a more typical business model. There is not much that's typical about skaters, thank God.

Hat Lady Happy Hour
4/9/99
The Elbo Room
San Francisco
Thank you all for makin' it happen!

What? Ya wanna pose ? ok

oops! it over

May 4, 1999 - via fax from Eric
Beth - Haven't received your check this month due
May 1st. Please advise.   Thx - Eric

Hand-written afterthought:
     If it's on its way - sorry to bother you.

I hand wrote on his fax:
     You should have it today or tomorrow - #5855

and faxed it back immediately.

<u>May 5, 1999 -a letter to the Seattle Post Intelligencer</u>
(I don't know if it was published, not likely)

Dear Editor,

It's astounding that on May Day a thousand or so citizens of this area can meet in Volunteer Park on Capitol Hill, march down Broadway to Pike, with a parade permit and police escort, growing in numbers as we go, chanting things like "1-2-3-4, We don't want your Drug War!" and "Free the plants! Free the people!" and carrying such signs as "Food Fuel Fiber Medicine / Family Farms for HEMP!" with three to four thousand citizens rounding down to Westlake Plaza, passing cars honking and people waving and whistling from their porches in solidarity with the marchers, and ultimately rallying in the park to hear eloquent, educated speeches on the topic of Legalization and Regulation of the Cannabis / Hemp / Marijuana plant and Ending the War on Drugs AND THIS IS NOT NEWS IN THE SEATTLE P-I!

You were sent a Press Release regarding this global event called the Million Marijuana March. I know. Last year you covered Global Days at about this time; the first world-wide demonstration that was held in protest of the DEA's misguided call to a Special Session of the United Nations to take our Drug War global. Apparently the turn-out was not enough to draw you again. Organizers have had a year to prepare. You should have been there. It is news when thousands of people are uniting in cities around the world and peacefully demonstrating that we want the conspiratorial waste of human and natural resources called the War on Drugs to END! The reports are still coming in but check out the Million Marijuana March soon at www.cures-not-wars.org. It is past time for people to know more about the wondrously beneficial plant that has been cut out of US history in our schools' books. This issue will be to the new millennium what Viet Nam was to the '60's & '70's. Start thinking of it as news, for we are making it so.

Beth Myrle Rice, Purple Stripe Publishing - Seattle

Journal: May 5, 1999

The Million Marijuana March was amazing. What a high to march down the middle of the street in downtown Seattle with a few thousand folks who also smoke pot and believe it's time to end prohibition. Solidarity is sweet but the ultimate high for me came at the end of the march, at the rally at Westlake Center.

In between speakers I was talking with a young woman who held a skateboard under her arm. A young man near to us overheard our talk of skate and joined in the conversation. At one point he turned to me and asked, "By any chance do you know Skateress?" I asked him how he knew of Skateress. He replied, "I saw an ad in The Stranger for a really cool looking poetry book. In fact, it was the same ad that brought me to this rally! Well, any way, on pay day I went to the book store in Pike Place Market at lunch and bought it. It is awesome! I love it and my favorite poems were written by Skateress so. . . I was just wondering. . . I mean, since you skate, I thought you might know her."

I informed him he was talking to her. At that, he threw his arms out open wide and squealed, "Re-e-eally!?! Oh, my God! Will you hug me?!"

I thought I was going to melt into a pile of mush in that moment. "Of course!" and drew him to my heart in a real hug, not one of those lame pat-pat hugs. Wow. I have a fan. That is definitely among the happier moments I've known.

If you are one of the sixty or so folks who bought a copy of my *Your Tree* chapbook you know who Skateress is and Spiritress too, my poet pseudonyms. How a poem cavalcades or wafts or falls out of me tells me who is writing it. I do not credit the poet me-s, accordingly in this book. There are still a few copies of my first edition handmade tree-free chapbook available. ☺

May 5, 1999 – my prayer poem on this day

God in me
of all time   space   eternity
I pray for hearts full of love
blossoming full reaching touching growing
plants to care for us
on our path each of us
to the peaceful place
that is all of us
thank you for Zoey
friends family lovers
for choice and chance
for company in the dance
forgiveness and faith
acceptance if not understanding
for rainbows
for hope we'll each and all
find our way in
to the purple light
embrace us of all

please give guidance in the book
help me to remember my why
take me to the power of the ocean
to clear, cleanse and prepare for my journey
I see my determination and the June workshop
being a springboard to my goals
      to see an end to the war on plants and people
      to see the people rise
      to be a soldier in the peaceful revolution
thank you—let it be so

Journal: May 8, 1999

My assistant gave me her two week notice in March telling me that she needed time off to study for finals; then she'd be graduating from the U of W and returning to her home state. I didn't run an ad to replace her right away. Now, I'm glad.

I've had a couple visits with Zoey since she went to her friend's home. It seems that the girl's mom was under the impression Zoey would be staying for just a short time. It's getting uncomfortable for her there after a few weeks—no doubt for her friend and her mom as well. She told me she isn't doing crystal meth anymore and that she has been doing a lot of thinking. She apologized for being difficult and asked if we could try again.

I told her nothing could make me happier and made a deal with her. I said she could come back to live with me and she could have a part-time job as my assistant but that there would be rules and conditions. She said she needed to think about it. That was on our first visit.

On the next visit I laid out the rules. She said, "No problem; but I have a condition too." She wants Johnny to come live with us also. Maybe I'm crazy but that's what I'm doing, taking them both in so long as he is out of the apartment on his way to work before she gets to her desk after lunch time. I am praying this works out.

Journal: May 31, 1999

full moon lingers
in the southwesterly sky
light heralds a new day
of more gray

no need of warm gold
to roll the silver disk away
finding solace in celestial iron
magnet to the tide
pulse of the cycle inside
grand excuse to my why
can't I shake these blues?
yeah, blame the full moon

Journal: June 24, 1999

Thankfully Zoey has caught on quickly to her new job as, by necessity, it almost immediately changed to her having full-time responsibilities; including holding down the fort in my absence. I'm thrilled she kept everything running smoothly. She seems to be thriving with responsibility on her plate.

I haven't written about this yet and I'm not going into detail now as the flyer for the workshop is attached to this page. Last week I was in San Francisco participating in the week long intensive writers' workshop that's been on my calendar for a few months now. There was quite a lot of required reading in preparation for the workshop. And I had to excerpt two twenty page manuscripts from my book. A couple months before the workshop I mailed twenty copies of one to Tom and Carol, a copy for each participant in the workshop. So we all read and critiqued each other's manuscripts -ah poop- I said no details! The main thing I want to say is that it was truly an amazing experience and I am excited to get back to work on my book while all that I learned is fresh.

July 1, 1999 -a fax to: Evie, my boss

Re: [A] damaged hats coming to you from Bob @ Superb
  [B] the new Disk Library for my Skate Accounts
Good morning, Evie!

I am putting both these items on one fax as I am begging you to hold a quick Production Meeting on Friday so that some guidelines are set before you leave for vacation.

[A] I have told Bob that we can't credit Superb for the hats he's returning to us as they all come from different runs and are under the three percent damage allowance that is our policy and an industry standard. He accepts this but is not real happy as the damages are *not* embroidery damages. He wants you to see them. Evie, you must get it

335

through to the guys who are hooping hats:

1. Do not hoop hats that are pulling apart at the seams

2. If a hat pulls apart at the seams while they're hooping it, DO NOT EMBROIDER IT!

3. Return the blank damaged hats to the customer so they can get credit from their vendor!

4. And, whoever is clipping the stitch on the label (so a back logo can go down low) USE CARE! I have heard complaints from both Superb and Mind that it looks like it was just yanked apart, not *clipped*.

[B] Today, you will receive two boxes of my floppy disks. (The balance will be done today—labeled appropriately and sent down. But, I wanted the Superb disks to be there before you left for vacation so that Sonia can load logos onto them as she gets the current Superb PO's out for production.)

• Please make ALL production people (shop & office) aware that these disks are absolutely NOT TO BE RE-USED. They are to be used *only* by Beth's Production Coordinator!

• Make Sonia aware that as new orders come in from my skate customers she is to load the approved logo(s) onto the respective disk(s). Zoey and I will remind her.

• Once the correct logos are loaded onto each disk they're to stay on the disk!

Thanks, Evie! Have a great day!   Beth

July 28, 1999 – Email from a cousin

Hi Beth!

Just wanted to say hi and let you know I got your email. It's interesting that you have Zoey and her boyfriend living with you. You are such a good sport. But, my dear, learn from me. The sooner you quit enabling your children the better off you and the children will be. I know, you think you are helping them for just a short time, and I hope that is true. You deserve to have your life now, exactly the way you want it to be. So, there's my "not asked for" advice. I know it is really hard. We will have to talk soon. I will let you know when I get back from Wenatchee. I may be there for a week or so. Between us three sisters, Mom and Dad will be well cared for.   Love, Cuz Joanie

July 29, 1999 – my reply to. . .

Joanie - I hope you got my voice mail to say hi to everybody and give them all hugs! I hope it all goes well for my Aunty D. Surgery seems so extreme for a lady her age. Why is she having surgery? What part has given out? I look forward to hearing from you when you get back.

I read back over my note to you; had no idea I sounded so frustrated when I wrote it! Ha! It's funny how writing often lets out so much more than you know. I totally hear what you're saying. It is a big concern for me. Over the last year it first took eons to get Zoey to come live with me. Then I had to throw her out because I wouldn't enable bad drug (powders) behavior. She got clean and came back but then was irresponsible to her job and lost it. And, she was using and abusing me so I had to throw her out again. (It just about killed me after waiting so long to be with her and, knowing she had no job or income. But, I looked forward to being with her, not enabling a powder head who is someone else).

After six weeks or so we negotiated terms under which she could come back. Things have been getting so much better, wonderful, actually. However, now it's becoming a bit too relaxed and I have to keep cracking the whip a bit; but both she and Johnny are cool about it. They step up to the call when I put it to 'em but SHIT it takes so much energy! Here I go sounding all frustrated again when it really isn't bad. I love this time of having them here. I love Johnny too. My biggest concern is will it all fall apart when I pull out the rug and move or will they step up to the plate and get REAL about what they need to do? Hard to say but they are both intelligent people with lots of good stuff going for them if they'd just know that, trust it, and apply it! The thing I have to hold on to is that it is up to them, not me. They will make their choices and have to live and deal with them. Okay, there's my thought for the day. Talk to you soon.   Love, Beth

August 4, 1999 – email from Cousin Katy, Joanie's sister

Hi Beth

Great to hear from you! Yes, Mom had her surgery Friday and she's doing very well. She's up and walking today. It was great to have Joanie and Betsy here. We did our best to keep dad cheered up! Mom will probably be in the hospital a week.

The rules for being human are some of my favorites. Did you read the book they're from: *If Life Is a Game, These Are the Rules by Dr. Cherie Carter-Scott?*

Good to get your e mail. I'll be able to chat with you from time to time now that I have your address. Thanks for writing. I'll tell Mom.   Love, Katy

August 5, 1999 – my reply to. . .
Good Morning, Katy!

Wow! It's Thursday already and raining again. Yuk! I'm so glad Aunty D. is pulling through the surgery well. Give her and my dear uncle Hugh both a big hug from me. Joanie called and talked to Zoey a couple days ago, to let me know Aunty D. is doing fine and that she'll be home in a few days.

The Rules for Being Human heavily harkens to the writings of Seth, a spirit entity channeled by the medium Jane Roberts, who is now deceased. Have you read *Seth Speaks* or any of the books by Jane Roberts? The Rules and Seth gave me assurance and helped me keep sane through some pretty tough times. I have not read *"If Life Is a Game. . ."* but will now. I had no knowledge of where The Rules came from as I found them typed up and placed in a notebook (I hand copied them verbatim) in the waiting room at Teresa Carol's office, the psychic self-empowerment counselor Victoria and Denny referred me to back in '92. I've consulted with Teresa a number of times but haven't had a reading in a couple of years now. She is such a marvelous woman. Have you ever had her do a reading? She's amazing. I've been wanting to lately as there are big changes coming up on my horizon soon and it'd be nice to have insights to it all.

I can't take another winter here in Seattle. I need a break badly so am planning to move to Santa Cruz, California come January. It's just an hour or so over the hill from San Francisco, a sleepy yet spunky little bohemian beach town with a population of 55,000 or so, right on the Pacific coast. Yessss! I don't know if Joanie has mentioned it to you or not but in June I was in San Fran for a seven day intensive writers' workshop taught by a couple (married) of very accomplished writer/editors with a combined list of credits a long as your arm, Tom Jenks and Carol Edgarian. It was an amazing experience. There were only eighteen participants, admitted by application/audition, each of us working on a manuscript in process.

Well enough about me. I want to say congratulations

to you in all your accomplishments: going back to school for your counseling certification and starting your own practice. Wow! That's some guts and determination! And double YAY! to you for simply removing yourself from a failing, faulty system where health and the caring for our Human Earth-suits and the souls inside has become a big money-making enterprise for the pockets of the few at the top, like most everything else in the world around us. I've read many of your newsletters at Mom's and would love to be on your mailing list. Can I get a subscription? :-)

YIKES! I gotta get to work! Hope to hear from you again when you have a minute.   Love, Beth

It felt good to reconnect with my cousins. It was nice to be reminded they also had some difficult times and dysfunction with their teenagers, that I wasn't all alone floating adrift at sea. For more than four years that is how I had felt, not daring to talk to family members about my situation. Partly, that was due to not wanting to be an embarrassment for Dad and Mom. But, mostly, I had not wanted to be judged—to be caught standing under my Bad Mom banner.

I wish to extend special thanks to Dr. Chérie Carter-Scott for allowing me to present *"Ten Rules For Being Human"* in the unofficially excerpted format shown in Chapter 7, as I was first introduced to her words.

The full context of her teachings can be found in her book *If Life Is A Game, Here Are The Rules,* Broadway Books, 1998; which is readily available for purchase at her website:

www.drcherie.com

32: Pulling Out The Rug

Zoey flourished in her new responsibilities and was abiding by the rules and conditions I'd set forth prior to she and Johnny moving in. I then made the mistake of lightening up a bit. Just like in 1995, unfavorable momentum started to build. Some of her and Johnny's friends started coming by more frequently when our work day was done. They'd go sit in their room and hang out. I suspected they were doing more than smoking weed, which was bad enough considering I knew what the law was and had no idea how old all these kids were. I hated to do it but on a couple of occasions I knocked on their door so to see what they were up to.

Each time it was obvious they were doing drugs of some sort, from "huffing" nitrous oxide (commonly referred to as laughing gas) to smoking pot to God only knows. I told them straight out, "You cannot do that here. If you need to get high you need to go somewhere else. I want your paraphernalia to leave with you."

I had a talk with Zoey and explained that as I am now an outspoken activist for ending the war on drugs I gather I'm a blip on a radar screen somewhere and she, Johnny, nor their friends could get high in my place, that I was not going down this road again. Nonetheless, they persisted so I got ready to make the necessary changes.

As stated to cousin Katy, I was sick of Seattle's gloom. My main office was in L.A. as well as some of my skate customers. A number of my skate companies were in San Francisco, and two were in Santa Cruz. I decided to move south.

I told Johnny and Zoey of my plan to move to Santa Cruz, adding that they would need to find a new place to live and pack up their stuff—unless, of course, Zoey wished to keep her job and move with me. She was not to be pulled away from Johnny.

I told them I planned to give notice, to vacate the Green Lake apartment October 1st; after my commitment to Hempfest was fulfilled and after the September ASR trade show—so for them to plan accordingly. I added, "If you or your friends get high in my apartment again I will have you all leave and the locks will be changed."

I told Zoey her first responsibility was to her job; and that she needed to stay home on work nights. On weekends I saw very little of her, Johnny or their friends.

I talked with my mom about this proposed change and asked if I could come live with her for the months of October thru December. It would help create some distance between me and Zoey's actions while remaining close enough to retain contact and be there if she needed me. I'd put my household in storage for those months, bring my office to Mom's large home on the Olympic Peninsula. When I felt assured Zoey was alright I would then head to Santa Cruz, with the goal of January in mind. Mom said she thought this all sounded like a good idea.

Journal: August 12, 1999

I've volunteered to be in charge of the donation buckets at Hempfest this year. Someone has twenty or so five gallon white plastic paint buckets. It's my job to turn them into donation stations and build a crew to employ them day of 'Fest.

I wrangled Zoey to the bucket decorating party at Burt's house. Burt is the nice guy in Ballard who answered my call to the number on the Initiative 685 poster about donating poetry book proceeds. He's the one that introduced me to Hempfest as a volunteer. But Zoey would come only if Johnny also came. They must have been really high on something or maybe they were coming down from a big one. I don't know; but the bottom line is they were not functioning well. They carelessly slapped the labels I'd made onto the buckets such that wrinkles wrecked some of them; on others labels were crooked. I was embarrassed but, thankfully, I was in a crowd of empathetic understanders. Good or bad, it gave way for me to focus on being scared shitless for the safety of Zoey and Johnny.

Journal: August 27, 1999

Hempfest was incredible! Paramedics estimated from eighty to ninety thousand people came through the park between 10AM and 8PM. Wow! From about 5 to 7PM I was at the front gate relieving the poor kid who had been at the Donation Station for too long. This was the most amazing two hours of the day for me because I graphically saw the diverse cross section of people who came—all ages, races, and economic sectors.

The People were well represented. I saw yuppie types pushing baby strollers, preppy looking student types, some mainstream couples in their fifties. There were punk-rockers, Goth garbed kids and, as one would expect, a sizable dose of hippies—both young and old. I watched one conservatively dressed man who I'd say was in his late sixties fold up a one hundred dollar bill and stuff it into the donation bin. So cool!

It takes better than forty-five thousand dollars to execute this free-to-the-public event. My donation bucket crew closed the gap between monies in from vendors and business sponsors and the balance due on bills so I'm damn proud of 'em! Zoey and Johnny were much better at collecting donations than they were at decorating the buckets, thank God. A few of their friends came to help too. All did an awesome job.

Since I was working all day I didn't get to see much of the 'Fest but I found one of the booths interesting in that it had a display on how used cooking oils can be made into biodiesel that cars can run on. I found it weird that at Hempfest this individual did not present the fact that hemp seed oil is the original biodiesel—that Mr. Diesel designed his engine to run on seed oils such as hemp and flax. It was quite a coup for the petroleum industry to rapidly change the course of history and for the US government to bury this fact.

Journal: August 30, 1999

I took Zoey and Johnny out to dinner early this evening as they had plans for later on. It was the first time in many years that I have been with Zoey on her birthday. In route to their restaurant of choice we had quite a cosmic visual experience that started falling out in a poem at the restaurant on a napkin. I just now finished it. . .

Better than any god picture I've ever seen
she said
we said
it's 3D
words cannot show or feel
the vision of soul
we said
wondering how many people saw
our windows down
we saw not a walker not a driver not a bus waiter
not another person in our range looking up
we gawked spewing upness and amazement
at our good fortune in looking up
our eyes fingered through gold dusted neon
sun in on through clouds artfully splayed
at over under azure canvas
strokes of genius we said
did anyone else see the cave?
did anyone but us see the light?
we agreed it was for only we three
in another three it was down
Seattle gray resumes
consumes what's left of the day
what a gift in that moment we looked up
happy birthday baby
19 in 1999
for Zoey with all my love

September 2, 1999, email to the Hempfest Core Group
Hello to all High Hempy's!!

I wanted to be at debrief but am battling a gnarly sinus/bronchial infection and listening to my body for a change. It's saying rest (so does the Doc).

I must say I am gratified to see the recognition given to the awesome Bucket Brigade. Thank you. Had I been at debrief I'd have mentioned that there were more folks who gave to the effort than those holding the buckets day-of-event. Thanks to Burt for being the bucket painting place (and putting up with the smell) and to all those folks who were out with buckets on the big day that hadn't planned for it.

The last thing I want to say about Buckets is that the performance of my kids—Zoey, Johnny, and the others—is true testimony to what happens when a pack of lovable but unruly kids is empowered by having a valuable task entrusted to them. Thanks for welcoming them to the crew. It was an awesome experience for all of us.

I am majorly bummed that I'll be out of town on business for the Recognition Picnic on 9/11 as I think the kids will be too shy to come if I don't tow them in. I'm taking the sinuses to bed now.

Peace, Love & Purrrple Power to you all!   Beth

September 6, 1999

Crystal Fear

My fear was found among tater-tots
perfectly spaced and squared golden brown
on a cookie sheet atop the stove
she said I don't want to talk
tension tersely tossed
I SAID I DON'T WANT TO TALK
I thought to say
That's crystal clear!
and did in a way of accuse
I won't excuse your say
she said in a way
and slammed the door harder than ever before
I guess her too fast-n-hard
was afflicted by osmosis
hanging with those moving too fast
to care too-quick needs to quit
caring too much about those who won't care enough
to slow down
TAKE CARE OF YOURSELF
Nothing could frighten me more
than you racing
where you went before

yet I must now choose
to no longer be affected
by your choice to be affected
by those who choose
to make bad choices
I can only hope
you change your choice
along with free
is responsibility
to account
to choice

Calendar:

Leave for LA and San Diego Tues. 9/7 thru Sat nite 9/11
returning to Seattle at 8:30AM on Sun 9/12 from LAX

Journal: September 14, 1999

Wow. ASR is just getting better and better, both for biz
and for Beth. Saturday I was hanging out on the patio with
Billy drinking a beer when Steve-O came to join us. He is such
a goofy guy. Billy introduced me to him at the February trade
show and it became clear he must have told him about us
or maybe just that I'm good in bed. Or, who knows, maybe
Steve-O thinks I'm hot or maybe he was just horny BUT, in
any case, he came on to me pretty hard right after being
introduced. He is a cutey in his own goofy way and sweet as
could be but I shut him down. Just like I told Harold in that
letter I sent him last September, I told Steve-O, "Sorry, I'm
just not much into playing anymore."

Okay, so, right after Steve-O showed up, Billy finished his
beer, said he had to get back to his booth and left. Steve-O
said, "Hey HatLady, if you buy me a beer I'll show you my
latest trick. You'll be the first person to see it." How could
I resist? I went and got him a beer, which is served in a tall
plastic cup at ASR, and handed it to him. Instead of drinking
it he bit down on the crimped edge at the top of the cup and
extended his arms into the air at shoulder height. With the
cup in his mouth he managed to say, "Okay, watch this."
He proceeded to do some sort of super slow motion back
flip with a twist, returned to a standing position with the
full glass of beer still clenched in his teeth and threw his

345

arms out into the air again. He then tipped his head back, drained the entire beer into his mouth in one huge gulp, grabbed the cup out of his mouth, turned to me with a wide grin and proclaimed, "Didn't spill a drop!"

I clapped hard and realized, at the sound of many hands clapping in unison, that quite a crowd had gathered around us. I'd been so engrossed in what Steve-O was doing I hadn't noticed all the other people enjoying the spectacle, including Harold who had apparently been standing behind me. After I told Steve-O what an amazing trick that was, as he was walking away with a guy who'd offered to buy him another beer, there was a hand on my arm and I turned to find myself eye to eye with Harold.

His first words were, "I liked your letter." We sat down and talked a long time. He was being so sweet in playing Get To Know You, but after a while I told him I had to get to work, that ASR wasn't just fun time for me. There was little over an hour left for me to walk the trade show floor to see if I could drum up some new business. He asked if we could meet up later. I told him he could find me in the lobby bar at my hotel at the end of the day. He did and, after a beer and hanging out with a bunch of people at the bar, we went up to my room. We hooked up – boy, did we! Wow. It was amazing. After resting a bit, we headed into the night to get some dinner and do a little partying in the ASR reverie we could hear from my room. Of all the many young guys I have played with in private, Harold is the only one who ever wanted to hold my hand or have his arm around me in public. Unlike the others, he was proud to be with me regardless of our age difference. We had such a good time hanging out.

September 12, 1999
Haiku o' the Day

the sun fell down fast
behind blue silhouette peaks
gold rimming the ridge

September 14, 1999 – a letter to. . .

Hi Harold

I'm sending you the poem about kissing that I wouldn't recite because I knew I'd screw it up. (next page) And, below is a ramble of poetic inspiration. I wouldn't call it a

346

poem but it fell into my cowbook (journal) when I got home
and, since it's about you, I want to share it:

It feels good to feel good
I recall you said
I confirmed
4:40AM Sunday: I-5 North on my way to L.A.
had a bowl for breakfast
turned in the ride
and shuttling to LAX
panoramic mind movies kept rolling
while I imagined all on the bus
whose eyes came my way
were watching my replay
in a cartoon bubble next to my head
the rerun of me feeling how good you feel
I felt so exposed
Have you seen this movie yet?
quiet, time, space
feel good when feeling good
when there's a carnival outside the window
with you
yes, that was fun

Hope you made it home safe and sound. What's the
name of the trick you're doing at the Zoo website? I am so
clueless in this department but equally curious.

Aaah
kissing
the yin yang dance
the chance for both
lead and follow
both in fervid tango
tongues
gliding and dipping in
the yin yang fuck
of mouth
you can both be both
nibbling   embracing   playing
tongues both   in   out
touch   tease   tickle   tag

you're it
spin the bottle
kiss me
kissing
mmmm
    Beth

~ * ~ * ~   printed on tree-free paper   ~ * ~ * ~

I mailed my note and poems to Harold at his home address in New York City. He'd given it to me in case I wanted to write him again.

Zoey did a great job of holding the office together in my absence. She continued working her afternoons in my office. But outside of work time I didn't see much of her and Johnny. In the evenings I was busy packing up my household.

Journal - September 14, 1999

We're one week away from being moved out of my Green Lake apartment. It's going to be tight but it's starting to come together. Zoey and Johnny are going into a shared house deal. They get the whole basement for their room.

I'm going to Mom's with a skeleton HatLady office in tow for October, November and December. On December 26th I will leave for Santa Cruz.

Haiku o' the Day   nostalgia skated
                        your tree beckoned to my heart
                        tree bark in my hand

By the time my household was all packed, not a thing of theirs was and I couldn't foresee it happening so I did it myself. When the day came the rental moving truck was loaded with my household I packed my car with Zoey and Johnny's stuff. It was like they were in complete denial that this was happening. I told them they needed to show me where we're taking their stuff; including those items of mine I'd boxed up to give them: some pots and pans, dishes, glasses, silverware, and my TV.

We wound through the University District on narrow residential streets. They told me to pull to the curb in front of an old ramshackle house. I wanted to crawl in a hole and shrivel up. This looked like a serious party house. As far as I know, I've never been to a crack house but it seemed to me that this is what one would look like. Zoey, Johnny, and I unloaded their belongings onto the patio nearest the entry to their room. Then they toured me through the house. We hugged hard, I got the phone number at the house, and I left. It was terrible.

It's hard to say which has been the worst day of my life: the day in 1995 when I got the call from Zoey's dad about taking her to rehab, the day in Dick Carville's office that I signed out of motherhood, or this day.

For a week or better I'd been working with Mom's local phone company to have a second phone line brought to her home for my office. I'd manage to get by with just one line for the three months I'd be there. I could plug in the fax as needed. I had already sent an email to all of my customers to explain that I'd be without an internet connection until January.

Not long after dropping the kids off at their new place of residence I landed at Mom's and soon learned that the new phone line had not been set up. I immediately gave the phone company a call and was told there would be no second line in the near future; that the present capacity for the neighborhood was topped.

I called Evie to apprise her of the situation. We agreed the sensible thing to do was to head to Santa Cruz. I needed a phone, a fax, internet. . . and my household was in a moving truck.

I called the house I'd left earlier in the day and luckily got to talk to Zoey. I told her of the scenario and that I'd be heading south the next day. She sounded detached in response, like it was no big deal. She'd see me when she sees me. "Have a safe trip, Mom."

"You be safe, Zoey. I'll see you soon, when I fly up to get my car. I love you more than you can know." I stayed the one night at Mom's, grieving for what the day had brought.

Afterword

On November 14, 2009, just after finishing the first draft of this book, I travelled cross state with my daughter and a friend to attend a memorial. On November 8th the first true love of Zoey's life, Johnny, passed away in a heroin overdose. It was sad circumstances in which I met his parents for the first time.

Johnny and Zoey had not been boyfriend and girlfriend for nearly ten years but they remained large in each other's hearts and were in contact by phone frequently. In the course of those ten years Johnny struggled with drug addiction. He would get clean and remain so for various lengths of time, and then relapse. Johnny was a beautiful soul—intelligent, playful, artistic, kind, loving and restless. Unfortunately he could not love himself enough.

The War on Drugs has had zero affect in curtailing drug consumption. Humankind has been attracted to altered consciousness throughout all of recorded history. Nothing is likely to change this going into the future. If there was a survey of all parents who have lost children to drugs would they say the trillions of taxpayer dollars dropped into the War on Drugs has been a good investment?

It is time to end the war and divert these dollars to offer academic tutoring as needed and broaden after-school programs in sports, music and the arts such that every student can partake. Preemptive counseling should be made available to those who seek help regarding drug usage; and treatment should be made accessible to those who want to heal. All would be tax dollars better spent.

Regarding war and anger, the two seem to go hand in hand but one does not justify the other. Love is the only path to peace. At the time of writing some of the documents included in this book, I was so enraged by the laws that gave way to my former spouse manipulating my "*agreement*" in the signing of those horrific documents that I did become a warrior.

A

Now, I am not proud of my choice to add the words "Proceeds to benefit *the War* on the War on Pot" to the front of my *Your Tree* chapbook. Nor am I proud of the tone I took in some of my letters; particularly to the USDA and to the Seattle PI. I considered editing those documents to fit how I would write them today but decided against it. I don't believe in changing history. I hope to help shape a more peaceful future. Pursuant to that end I sent the following letter February 2009:

Dear President Obama,

I write to you with hope that the anticipated appointment of Seattle Police Chief Gil Kerlikowske to the position of Director of the ONDCP (Office of National Drug Control Policy) is an indication we can see reform of the failed "War on Drugs" policies—particularly the laws prohibiting the growth of hemp and marijuana, or the Cannabis Cousins Coup as I think of it—as might thousands of Seattleites. Last August approximately one hundred eighty thousand people attended Seattle Hempfest, the world's largest annual "Protestival" seeking reform to laws prohibiting hemp farming and the responsible, regulated and taxed personal use of marijuana. Reference: www.seattlehempfest.com

Where there's much to be said on the marijuana debate, I wish to focus on hemp, the key reason why marijuana has been so demonized. It is past time to shut down the lobbying efforts of the petroleum, forestry, cotton growing and textile industries—to name just a few—who seek to keep hemp out of the competitive marketplace. Where I realize the pharmaceutical industry is one of the most powerful lobbying forces against cannabis, that would bring us back to marijuana. Accordingly, I choose to leave medicinal value out of this discourse.

Hemp is fuel (the seed oil), fiber (for paper, textiles and building materials), and food (high in essential omega fatty acids). No chemical pesticides or fertilizers are necessary to grow thriving hemp crops. Once harvested, when the remaining hemp plant is tilled back under, it refurbishes the soil so to be ready for replanting in the following season. While growing, many thousands of acres of lush green plants would aid oxygenation of our fragile environment.

Hemp farming could play a key role in the economic recovery of our nation via the creation of truly green jobs, as well as play a vital role in slowing the deterioration of the ozone and the results of the human contribution to global warming. I wonder if you, President Obama, are one of the millions of Americans who are unaware Mr. Diesel designed his popular engine to run on seed oils such as hemp and flax seed; that the development of diesel fuel was the petroleum industry's way of putting a stop to such ecologically sensible competition. No doubt, you are aware that the first American flag was made of hemp fabric; that the founders of our great nation—Washington, Jefferson, et al—farmed hemp; that it was at one time federally mandated for farmers to rotate in a crop of hemp each season in support of the war effort: for parachute fabric, ropes for Naval ships, etc.

Is it not curious that the institution of the Cannabis Stamp Act in the 1930's, causing hemp farming to be unprofitable, coincided with both the end of alcohol prohibition and DuPont's discovery of petroleum based nylon? Mr. Harry Anslinger, Assistant Prohibition Commissioner in the Bureau of Prohibition (before being appointed as the first Commissioner of the Treasury Department's Federal Bureau of Narcotics) would perhaps have been distraught at the prospect of laying off all of his still-busting agents, thus seek a new "outlaw." And surely, as all companies seek a means to outsell their competition, DuPont would as well. Is it not curious indeed that the 1936 propaganda film, *"Reefer Madness"* (originally titled *"Tell Your Children"*) was released to plant fear in U.S. citizens such that the idea of illegalizing cannabis altogether was fully supported and now Mr. Anslinger's agents had a new product to hunt down and prosecute? That DuPont could now readily slash a huge gouge out of the farmed textiles market?

Mr. President, I beseech you to appoint an unbiased commission to delve into our federal archives, which are rich with data drawn from previous scientific studies showing the tremendous value of hemp, and allow the publication of these reports such that the American people are given the truth for consideration, so that decisions around legislation can be formulated on FACT over fictional propaganda.

Please release this vital information to the public so that our farmers can be paid to farm hemp and farm subsidies can be reduced if not ended altogether; so that the billions of dollars wasted on propaganda against what is truly a miracle plant, and the share of those dollars spent on the DEA's absurd strategy of dropping poisons out of airplanes with the intent of eradicating the cannabis species can be spent more effectively. Reference: April 1998 *"Cannabis Eradication in the Contiguous United States and Hawaii: Supplement to the Environmental Impact Statements"* prepared for the U.S. Department of Justice, Drug Enforcement Administration, by the U.S. Department of Agriculture, Animal and Plant Health Inspection Service. I have this near 300 page document/book in my possession. It was mailed to me in response to a letter I wrote to Mr. Jack Edmundson, USDA in 1998 in follow-up to a call for public comment.

Thank you for your consideration. I hope very much to see the restoration of common sense on this topic, for the good of our nation.

Sincerely, thanks for your time and consideration,
Beth Myrle Rice

Dear Reader, I must confess to improving some of the phrasing in this letter for clarity prior to publication. It was originally penned in haste at President Obama's website when he was asking citizens to voice their priorities for an economic recovery plan.

Bringing this book to fruition, to print, has been quite a journey. In the while since I penned the *Afterword,* above, nothing has changed in public policy but I'd like to share the most current statistics available with you. In an effort to get information straight from the horse's mouth, as they say, I sent the following letter on February 7, 2011 via Priority Mail with Delivery Confirmation requested. The letter was received:

Dear Drug Enforcement Administration,

In early November 2010 I sent a query to you via the "Comments" window at the "Contact Us" page of your website. As I have not received a reply, I am writing to you again via USPS in hopes that my letter will land on the desk of someone who will give me the courtesy of a reply.

In 1998, I became aware of the DEA's practice of dropping herbicides from airplanes and helicopters for the purpose of eradicating cannabis plants. I responded to the USDA's call for public opinion regarding the DEA's requested update to the 1985 and 1986 Environmental Impact Statement (EIS) on Cannabis eradication. In response to my letter, Mr. Jack Edmundson at the USDA mailed me a copy of the Draft Supplement EIS.

I would like to know, please, what herbicide and method of aerial distribution is presently in use and what other means of eradication are being applied.

Lastly, can you please tell me what the annual budget is for cannabis eradication efforts and/or direct me to an area

at your website where this information is available to the tax-paying public? I'd like to know how much was spent on eradication efforts in 2010 and how much you have budgeted for 2011.

Citizens hear quite a lot about the budget or expenditures for various activities within the U.S. government so I assume any area of the federal budget is or should be publically available.

Your attention to this matter and a reply sent to my address as noted at the top of this letter will be greatly appreciated.

Thank you, in advance.   Sincerely, Beth Rice

Yes, I included the small graphic of the big book that Mr. Edmundson of the USDA landed in my mailbox within one month of mailing the letter I sent to him in 1998. As of May 1, 2011— three months after sending the letter above—I have received no reply from the DEA.

Feeling disgruntled at this lack of response, my brain was churning while listening to President Obama's address to the nation in late April of 2011. As he spoke of the national debt and the needed budget reductions that will enable America to recover, I wasn't surprised but was very disappointed in his choice of cuts. My response was to send the following letter which I now share with you and refer to as:

A4

AN OPEN LETTER TO PRESIDENT OBAMA

May 1, 2011

Dear President Obama,

You promised change and I voted for you with good faith in your promise. A change in your point of view as you consider the following facts and philosophies could result in a near $2.8 billion annual budget reduction, a figure representing the approximate cost of incarcerating the 95,205 citizens who have committed non-violent drug related crimes according to Bureau of Justice Statistics Bulletin: Prisoners in 2009; December 2010 NCJ 231675 [1].

As the BOJ Statistics Bulletin reports no costs, my calculation is based on the states' reported average expenditures as presented by the PEW Center On The States in their March 2009 report entitled *One in 31: The Long Reach of American Corrections* [2] which says our fifty states spend an average $29,000 per annum to house one inmate. With a total of 251,400 drug offenders reportedly in the custody of all state prisons as of yearend 2008 our states would share in an aggregate annual budget savings of nearly $7.3 billion by bringing an end to the imprisonment of nonviolent citizens. Many of these people are serving time for minor possession of, the farming of, or the sale of marijuana.

For untold additional savings, end the Drug Enforcement Administration's budget for cannabis eradication which includes funds for bombarding our earth with toxic herbicides dispensed from airplanes and helicopters. I'd quote the actual dollar amount if the DEA had given the courtesy of a reply to my inquiries sent in November 2010 and again in February 2011. But they did not. End the War On Drugs for all the associated costs noted above are but a fraction of the total bill presently burdening our tax-payers in the continued enforcement of these failed policies.

The War On Drugs rhetoric calling marijuana a "gateway drug" is simply untrue. It is not addictive and is no more a stepping stone to heroin than alcohol is — or, as caffeine and nicotine are gateways to methamphetamine. The tax dollars wasted on the War On Drugs would be better spent reducing the national debt, our states' debt, and by also diverting a portion of these funds to schools for expanding both curricular and after school programs in academic tutoring, in sports, and in the arts; programs that teach positive self-development and embracing diversity; and, to no-charge addiction counseling and/or drug treatment for those wanting to heal from the effects of truly dangerous addictive drugs such as heroin and meth. Please re-legalize marijuana.

Marijuana is a viable medicine for many—particularly patients undergoing chemotherapy and patients experiencing the wasting syndrome associated with AIDS or any terminal illness. Stop imprisoning patients and their providers.

Further, as citizens of the Land Of The Free, it should be a matter of choice whether to ingest marijuana or a martini at day's end. Yes, just as alcohol can be abused so can marijuana. But, as alcohol prohibition was ended in the 1930's so should marijuana prohibition end now. It is the responsibility of every human being to learn what works for them or against them and to act accordingly. To legislate against lessons of this nature negates free will. God gave humanity both free will and cannabis. How is it the privilege of the federal government to take away either or both?

Tax revenues generated for federal, state, and municipal budgets by the legalization and regulation of marijuana would make a tremendous difference in the debt laden condition of our nation. In February 2009 I sent my suggestion for growing a green economy in response to a request for citizen input at your website, Mr. President. I suggested that hemp farming be re-legalized for all the benefits hemp offers: bio-fuel, nutritious foods, and fiber for a multitude of uses. The tax base created by reviving hemp farming in our country would be a boost for our economy via growth in industry as well as through personal income taxes in the re-employment of many of our out-of-work citizens, while saving the tax dollars now being distributed as Unemployment Benefits.

Please hear my words this time, President Obama. End the war on cannabis and the war on drugs now. For the good of our nation, please legalize. Just say, "Yes, we cannabis!"

Sincerely hoping for change I can believe in,

Beth Myrle Rice
4616 25th Ave NE #45
Seattle, WA 98105

CC: The Honorable Maria Cantwell, U.S. Senate
    The Honorable Patty Murray, House of Representatives

[1]Found at http://bjs.ojp.usdoj.gov/content/pub/pdf/p09.pdf

[2]Found at http://www.pewcenteronthestates.org/uploadedFiles/
SPP_1in31_report_FINAL_WEB_3-26-09.pdf

Both of the footnoted documents above present a wealth of information regarding what is, in my opinion, a matter of national shame. The United States of America, Land of the Free, has incarcerated more citizens per capita than any other nation on earth. We are the world's largest jailer and a high percentage of the inmates are serving time for nonviolent drug related charges at tax-payers expense. Why? We must ask why and ask for change.

What the *One in 31* report illustrates is that when offenders on probation and parole are included the corrections picture, one in every thirty-one US citizens is under correctional supervision. All of this is at tremendous cost to tax-payers. Another point illustrated in the *One in 31* report is the racist nature of the War On Drugs.

I am making a plea to you to help put a stop to this. Please write letters. We can make a difference. The more voices expressing the same or like sentiment the more likely we will be heard and heeded. Let us manifest change. Know that it's not just me making this plea. Please investigate who else is:

Additional Notes and Noteworthy Information Resources

Law Enforcement Against Prohibition, both active and retired police officers, federal agents, judges and prosecutors in the United States and other countries around the world. http://leap.cc/cms/index.php

Common Sense for Drug Policy: The medical community, among others. This is one of the most comprehensive sites on the web for current US news and from around the world regarding the War on Drugs. http://www.csdp.org

The November Coalition, a prisoner advocacy group: http://www.novembercoalition.org

Marijuana Policy Project, lobbying for change in Washington, DC: http://www.mpp.org/

Cannabis Defense Coalition, based in Seattle but far reaching in their efforts: http://cdc.coop

Learn about hemp seed oil, an original biodiesel, and what it can do for our country and the world: http://hempcar.org/biofacts.shtml

The Seattle Hempfest: http://hempfest.org/drupal/node

Grammas For Ganja: www.grammasforganja.org

Are you an avid fan of travel? Are you familiar with PBS's travel guru, Rick Steves? For Rick's informative essay, *Europe: Not "Hard on Drugs" or "Soft on Drugs" ...but Smart on Drugs,* please visit: http://www.travelasapoliticalact.com/excerpts/drugchapter.html

Numerous books have been written on the tremendous value and varied uses of hemp. I recommend one book above all as it will not only answer any possible question you might have regarding hemp and marijuana but will teach you infinitely more than you likely know to ask. Much of the information presented is taken directly from our federal archives. Please invest in a copy of *"The Emperor Wears No Clothes"* by Jack Herer. It is available at www.jackherer.com or www.amazon.com. Or, Jack made much of his book available to read for free at his website.

Do you smoke pot? Are you ready to come out of the

closet? If so, visit: http://cannabisconsumers.org. If not, look to see who has come out of the closet—perhaps a neighbor, a coworker, or a relative. If you have never smoked pot and wonder what it's like to get high or just wonder what the attraction is please visit: http://cannabisconsumers.org/reports/gettinghigh.php for a detailed and accurate essay on the getting high experience.

Across these sites you'll find a vast amount of information regarding hemp, marijuana, and the failed yet continuing war on drugs. Plus, they offer enough links to like-minded sites to keep you surfing for hours acquiring knowledge and, hopefully, motivation to join in and take action.

Perhaps you're asking, "Take action? What can I do to change anything?" Something we all can and should do is easy, use our voices and our votes. Write letters to Senators, Representatives, Governors and, yes, even to President Obama. They care about the opinion of their constituents.

If you feel you don't have time to write letters, do you have time to make a photocopy? Please feel free to copy either or both of the letters I wrote to President Obama in February 2009 or May 2011 (just turn back a couple pages in this book), sign your name, add your voter registration mailing address below your signature, and address an envelope to:

> President Obama
> The White House
> 1600 Pennsylvania Avenue NW
> Washington, DC 20500

Perhaps you could run a few copies of my letter[s] to mail to your Senators and Representatives. Simply visit:

http://www.senate.gov/ and http://www.house.gov/

where you can easily locate mailing addresses for the folks representing you and your state. The cost to our economy, to our environment on earth, and to our fellow citizens for doing nothing is huge. Please take action.

Visit: www.purplestripepublishing.com for a special offer in appreciation of your effort to help end the war.

Many of the resources cited above are live links at the

Purple Stripe Publishing website. Additionally, the graphics found within the pages of this book are available to view in full color and enlarged.

"Never doubt that a small group of thoughtful committed citizens can change the world; indeed, it's the only thing that ever has." Margaret Mead

It is my hope that we can join together to become a voice too large to be ignored. Let's flood the White House with letters saying it is indeed time for a change.

Thank you!

Beth Myrle Rice

You might wonder where things flow for Zoey and me. The answer is coming along.

Pigs, Polar Bears, and Porn picks up where *Clips and Consequences* leaves off. . .

Poetry Index

Listed in alphabetical order by title and/-or- by first line.

Pigs, Polar Bears, and Porn

1: Santa Cruz

Journal: October 9, 1999

My God, how quickly everything can change. The phone company determined there was not enough cable available or space on the trunk line—or something to that affect—to hook up my business phones at Mom's; and, there was no telling when it might happen. So, the only thing that made sense was to get a loaded truck rolling south and make the move to Santa Cruz as planned—albeit three months ahead of schedule. I did it and everything has fallen into place incredibly well—office space in Aptos, very decent condo in Santa Cruz, with cool roommate who is fifty going on twenty.

Evie leased a company car for me, a shiny new Toyota Corolla. I guess she doesn't want me to be an embarrassment to the company calling on accounts in my granny car.

Yesterday, at the end of a first week of phones being connected in my new office, I drove up Highway One to San Francisco to call on Superb and Mind. Wow, it is *so* beautiful here. Thank you, God. Yes, all things happen for a reason. I spoke with one of my favorite advertising specialty customers and heard about gray skies in Seattle. I nearly burst with joy to be looking out my office window at golden sun on trees before a backdrop of luscious blue sky. Yes!

October 8 as told on October 9, 1999

I feel to be on a trip
driving in a rental car
I said to Steve
it's slowly sinking in
that this is home
and this is my car
cruising south on Highway 1
with ocean calling me
to step in

so I did
and remembered the warm feeling
of his welcome kiss on my mouth
and his words welcoming a place to ground
I'm so happy to be home
thank you
and another life begins
with me in my right place
pumpkin fields for ever
palms, broadleaf, evergreens
thrive in union
with the last sliver of sun sliding down
behind the ocean

October 31, 1999

Haiku o' the day:
a gaggle of geese
stopped north and south cars for blocks
crossing Green Lake Way

Journal: November 1, 1999

I flew up to Seattle to touch base with Zoey and to give her the keys to the Pontiac. She didn't have much time for me but was happy to get wheels. I am so afraid for her choices. Attached is a copy of the letter I put in the mail to her today. . .

My dear sweet Zoey,

I hoped we'd have had more time to hang out and talk but we both had plenty to do so that's the way it goes. In the time we had, I feel I dropped a lot out to you—the thoughts that have been weighing on my mind and feelings that have lain heavy in my heart. For both of us I need to recap my message to you. And, I need to add a couple thoughts that there wasn't time for but feel important for me to make you aware of.

First and foremost, as ever, I love you. This fact is, of course, the reason for all that follows.

Secondly, I love you because you are a beautiful, big hearted loving soul. I hope you will soon start loving and caring for yourself at least as much as you do for Johnny and others—that you'll take care with your karma.

Because I know that you are a strong and capable person I hope you'll begin to apply practise to your artistic talents. Drug usage will inhibit—if not prohibit—all of my hopes for you, but worse, your dreams and hopes for yourself. I know you know this. Listen to yourself. Trust your heart and gut.

As I clearly stated, I will not in any way, shape, or form support what you are doing right now. I perceive this to be both using and dealing. I pray you quit both before you find yourself paying a very high price for either or both.

When you take positive action toward changing your lifestyle I will help you in any way I can. To me this translates as get a job in an arena somehow related to the arts or an area of true interest to you. The work can or may be a grunt job but it's a way to get started and placed to move up into something more to your liking. It also means move out of that house, attend school, drop Johnny if he can't do the same—if he insists on continuing on his present path. When you have taken these steps I will support you as I'm able financially. Always and ever I support you emotionally but you also know what I'm willing and not willing to listen to. Complaints and excuses for the results of your bad choices are pointless. Show me you're changing paths and I am there for you.

Twice daily I will give you all my focus, send you purple light, love and positivity. The rest of the days I will focus on my own needs and dreams. This is my survival mechanism. I must remove myself from the choices you are making. There is no sense in two of us going down. When you choose to rise above your present path with positive change I am here strong and healthy, to help. Show me.

Thanks so much for my beautiful new polar bear. You can be so thoughtful and sweet. I love you Zoey and hope for you to be healthy and happy. Talk to you soon.

always & *ever*Mom

P.S.—Thanks a bunch for the yummy treat this morning too! I forgot to say so.

Journal: November 12, 1999

I went kookoo on a customer for the second time now. Thank God it wasn't the same guy that shared the onset of my first ever anxiety attack. This second buddy/customer on the phone with me was not the only witness. My newish assistant was at her desk right behind me. I felt the fullness of my chest, like the first time, and started to do the laugh/cry thing again. I got off the phone quicker this time, only to dial out again to the nearest urgent care center. I told them, "I know you don't know me but I can feel the symptoms that accompanied my first ever anxiety attack and I'm calling to beg you to please call in a prescription for four Xanax pills for me to Safeway and I'll come see you immediately so you'll understand that I cannot sit at the Safeway prescription counter alone waiting because I just might *really* lose it. . ."

He interrupted with, "I'm sorry but I can't do that. Are you alright to drive to the clinic?" I told him I was and went. After telling him what a horrible mom I am and I cut lose on all my worries for Zoey, I then described my first anxiety attack. He called in my prescription for four Xanax pills as requested and told me to hang in the waiting room a bit to assure it'd be ready on my arrival at Safeway.

I feel better now. Recognizing the symptoms and handling it quickly made this an easier bout than the first time, thank God. It hit me that this was like an anniversary bout; or, was it two years ago? An uncomfortable outcome is the shift in my assistant's attitude toward me. It hit me that maybe the lesson in this is to not write to friends or family projecting being strong and healthy or at a higher level of inner peace. The base truth is I am a wreck attempting to hold it together by beaming positivity and at the moments of elevated anxiety it all collides and I break. And. . . the solution?

Journal: December 23, 1999

I decided to drive my nice new car up to Seattle for Christmas. I saw a sign to turn off the highway to go to Fenton Glass in northern California. Mom used to carry their goods in her shop and is collecting a few pieces so I thought it'd be cool to buy her Christmas gift there. Well, everybody on my list is getting glass for Christmas. I got Zoey a beautiful blown glass dragon which became inspiration for my second tattoo.

When I unpacked the lovely purple dragon Zoey made

for me, the one that's been protecting my sense of humor these last few years, one of his little eyeballs rolled off into my hand. I glued it back on and he looks none the worse for wear. Nevertheless, I became concerned to preserve him in a way I know he will always be with me. A tattoo.

Zoey's Christmas dragon was dancing around in my head along with the little purple guy as I continued my northbound drive. As soon as I arrived in Seattle yesterday I went to Mind's Eye looking for Viki, thinking it only fitting that she do this tattoo. A guy there told me she moved to a shop on Capitol Hill and gave me directions. Fortunately, she was there when I arrived and she had an open slot for me today. I entrusted the two dragons to her so she could work up a drawing based on the sugar dragon plums dancing in my head as I drove. I told her I saw them both upright, dancing, with their tails entwined in such a way that their bodies created a heart in the space between them.

She had the drawing ready when I arrived. Interestingly, the heart she envisioned as I spoke, and incorporated in her art, created a heart in the space between their heads and front paws, leaving the little purple guy's body drifting afar from his partner. I looked at her with, "Wow! You found a second heart but missed the one I was talking about. Look, if you bring the purple guy in closer and tuck his hind legs in like this," as I gestured over the drawing, "there is a second heart. Can you make those changes, please?" She seemed reluctant but asked me to wait and left the room. I waited longer than I'd have preferred and was just about to go out for a smoke when she returned.

She held up her revised art, "Like this?"

"Almost perfect! Just pull them in a little closer for a nicer heart shape in the lower half and you've nailed it! Let's go."

I was on my way into the new millennium well protected, with gifted dragons dancing in hearts on my right arm. This tattoo application was like a picnic compared to my stomach tat. Zoey was totally blown away when she saw it but seemed to like my explanation, that I want to keep my little purple guy safe forever. She wondered where I'd found the second dragon so I crossed my fingers behind my back and said I got him out of a book. The next day, Christmas Eve at Mom's house, Zoey opened her dragon gift, got it and liked my tat all the more.

December 27, 1999

Me and Zo leave Crescent City
head north by mistake in fog
turn back
drive into sun on huge redwoods
through the end of the rainbow
surrounded by majestic trees
we rise above the ceiling of clouds
I feel like I'm on an airplane, she said
rapid decent through trees of mystery
into the clouds to the beach
hummin' through Humboldt
down the Avenue of Giants
trippin' on the immortal tree
nearing a millennium under its roots
crossing into the city over the gate of gold
City Lites showed books sold
Little Italy at North Beach had pasta in hold
but we just said no
Humboldt high found us at Travelodge
and smoke benevolence
rolled over us like fog
12/28 - sun breaks on a beautiful morning
we snake down Lombard
into the city by the bay
making our way to Haight
where shops and clothes and shops and clothes
are our fate through three full meters of coins
we're westbound to the 1
where Pacifica waits in the sun
for Zoey to dabble toes in the sea
and pluck a sack of sand
for friends back in the land of gray
we make our way down the coast
cruisin' to Santa Cruz

Haiku 'o the' day: final sunset bloop
cosmic canoe glowing low
stays long on water

12/29 - touring and trolling for more clothes
touch down at the ramp
tramp over the hill on Highway 17
hard hard **HARD** to say goodbye to my baby
it went so way too fast
away you fly and
I miss you already

January 7, 2000 - letter to a friend

So Hey! Happy New Year! I had such a good time with you at Christmas. When I e-'d saying "watch your mail" I expected to have a little box with a couple cool things out to you the same day. But, I still have it all at the office. Dang it. So, I imagine this note and the photos will land first.

Zoey and I had a blast on our li'l trip. We left Seattle at about 9AM Sunday. Met up with Zo's friend, Femme Beetle, in downtown Portland for some lunch and shopping. We continued south at about 3:30PM; gassed up in Grants Pass (way south Oregon) and headed west to the coast. Spent the night in Crescent City, California.

In the morning we headed south along the coast through Humboldt and the Redwood Forest. That was awesome. We smoked out all along the way, took turns DJing and played a game, "IF." She got this book from her Grandma Loo that poses all sorts of IF questions. It was a great way of finding out each others' views on a wide variety of topics and really made us both think. We crossed into San Francisco on the Golden Gate Bridge at about eight in the evening on Monday. Spent the night up at the top of the town, ate dinner at a cool little Italian place in North Beach, walked two blocks to City Lites and there was *Your Tree* in the Small Press Poetry section. Some have sold and I need to go back to talk to my contact. I was very proud knowing Zoey was proud of me.

Thank you again for my beautiful gift. When I showed it to Zoey I told her what a great friend you have been to me through my BAD MOM trials and my fears around her crystal meth spree etc. etc. And, that your gift tells me you think I'm an awesome mom which is very nice coming from a peer. I asked,

"So, what do you think? Awesome mom?" She looked me straight in the eyes and nodded.

Next day, Tuesday, I took her to Haight Street as she wanted to shop. We went via the switchbacks on Lombard. That was cool. I finally said, "This is the last time I'm feeding the meter!" She knew I was adamant about being on Highway 1 by three thirty so to catch the sun go down. Which we did. Pacifica was beautiful in the golden glow as we headed south to Santa Cruz. We stopped at the beach so she could dabble her toes in the water and get a bag of sand to take home. Funny, huh?

Wednesday, we went down to my office; next, to Consolidated Skateboards to say Hi! and see if anyone was skating the ramp. Then we visited NHS where my buddy/client gave us a full tour of the place. Wow. Every Santa Cruz skateboard deck ever printed is hanging out in their shop. We scrambled through the seconds cage and emerged with about four hundred dollars worth of stuff, if buying first quality at retail, for only eighty-six bucks. That was a BIG help in rebuilding Zoey's wardrobe. I told you about what Johnny did to all her stuff, right?

. . . January 8, 2000 - CONTINUED FROM LETTER WITH PHOTOS BUT CONNECTED TO GOODIES IN BOX

Hi again! While driving through the redwoods in Humboldt we stumbled on this glass blowing studio/shop. Had to stop as it was kind of funny how glass started my trip, heading north. Souvenirs of Humboldt seemed very appropriate. I bought one of these for Zoey and thought you should have one too. Mine is purple, of course.

I hope you enjoy the tape. No doubt the trivia questions will be easy for you. But, you have to prove it. I want to hear your answers. I made two but, as far as I can tell, you'll be the sole recipient. Such is life. It's always so easy to tell what others should do and to philosophize regarding the situations of others—i.e., me telling you to quit worrying about CONNECTING and to just go with the flow. Ha! Let's see if I can quit desiring connection at least long enough to focus on finishing my book! Gotta go! XO B.